9781348241867

D1743679

In Mem

VILLAGE SERMONS

VILLAGE SERMONS

Preached at Whatley

BY THE LATE

R. W. CHURCH, M.A., D.C.L.

SOME TIME DEAN OF ST. PAUL'S, RECTOR OF WHATLEY,
FELLOW OF ORIEL COLLEGE

FIRST SERIES

London

MACMILLAN AND CO., Limited

NEW YORK: THE MACMILLAN COMPANY

1899

First Edition printed January 1892
Reprinted February and October 1892, 1894, 1895, 1897, 1899

CONTENTS

SERMON I

THE BIBLE A GIFT OF GOD

Preached Second Sunday in Advent.

SERMON II

THE DISCLOSING OF SECRETS

Preached Third Sunday in Advent.

SERMON III

THE MYSTERY OF THE INCARNATION

Preached Christmas Day.

" Seek ye the Lord while He may be found, call ye upon Him while He is near : let the wicked forsake his way, and the

SERMON XV

TO KNOW GOD IS LIFE ETERNAL

Preached Trinity Sunday.

SERMON XVI

THE DANGER OF THE WORLD

SERMON XVII

THE NEVER-FAILING PROVIDENCE OF GOD

SERMON XVIII

TRUST IN THE LORD

SERMON XIX

THE CONSEQUENCES OF UNBELIEF

I

THE BIBLE A GIFT OF GOD

"Whatsoever things were written aforetime were written for our learning, that we through patience and comfort of the scriptures might have hope."—ROMANS xv. 4.

TO-DAY'S collect [1] reminds us of one of the greatest and most important things given us by God, to prepare for the coming back of Christ. When we are led to dwell on the thought of the second Advent, it is natural to turn to that Holy Book of which the second Advent is the burden, and promise, and last object. It is from the Bible we learn that Christ will come back ; and when we consider all that we have in the Bible to help us to think and feel as we ought about His coming, it is a plain and wise lesson of the Church to say as it does in the collect, " Now go with increased interest and hope to your Bible ; now that you are thinking of the return of Jesus Christ, think also of what you possess in the Bible to instruct and comfort you against that certain but most awful time, that time of greatest hope and greatest fear, and pray that God will give you grace to make the right use of your Bible."

[1] The Collect for the Second Sunday in Advent.

S   C.   B

One of the uses of Advent ought to be to make us examine ourselves about our Bible reading, and to stir us up to be more earnest, and careful, and hearty in studying it ; because it is the one book in the world which is the visible sign and consequence of Christ's having been here, and the continual token and pledge that He is coming back. " The Scriptures," as St. Paul says, " were written for our learning," our learning about what has been done ; that, by the comfort and encouragement given in them, we might have hope.

There are two things worth dwelling upon about the Scriptures, when we read them with the thoughts and feelings which Advent brings ; that is, with the thoughts and feelings called up by the belief that Jesus Christ has really been with us, and is as really coming again.

1. Think of the Bible then, first, in this way. It is all that now remains to us of the actual teaching of those by whom the world received the word and the hope of God. When we read the Bible, we read the very words of those who were by when God's mighty works were done ; with whom God spoke when they were wrought ; who were present, and sharers, in all the great beginnings of religion among men. In the Old Testament we have the very words of God's prophets and messengers, Moses, David, Isaiah,—men who had God's secret, and by whom He prepared the way for the coming of His only Son. In the New Testament we have the very words of those who were with His only Son when He came, or who were directly sent and charged by Him to set up His Faith, and His

Church; the words in which they tell what they
heard Him say, and saw Him do; the words in
which they tell us what they understood Him to
mean, what they learnt from Him, what His Spirit
made them think, and feel, and do.   Here, in the
Bible, we have what they have left of their reports,
and records, and ways of teaching; and besides these
remains of their actual teaching, we have no other.

We have a great deal besides to help us to the
truth and knowledge which God meant us to have.
God filled His Church with light, and doctrine, and
wisdom; and much of it has come down to us, and
we enjoy it now, and every day.   But it has come
in another shape, and not in the very words of those
who were the ministers and eye-witnesses of the
Word at first—the Prophets, and Evangelists, and
Apostles, whose very words we have in the Bible.
Christian truth has been preserved in remembrance
by preaching, by teaching, by writing, by worship,
by psalms and hymns, by the life and spirit of holy
men.   To be used, to be profitable, it must be spread
abroad, and turned to account, by men thinking
about it, and applying it, and drawing lessons from
it.   And so, as I say, the Bible is not the only means
by which Christian truth is preserved and taught in
the world.   But the Bible is all that remains of the
actual, very teaching of the first teachers.

There is Christian truth of the most precious
and certain kind in the Catechism : no one can doubt
its being Christian truth; no one can doubt its
value ; and it would be hard to put so much truth
in shorter and plainer words.   A man who is not
scholar enough to read the Bible, may learn all saving

truth in simpler words in the Catechism which he was taught to say by heart when he was a child. Truth is truth, wherever it is, and by whatever means it is taught ; and the Catechism is the record and monument of Christian truth, which is in its safe keeping. But there is this difference between the Bible and everything else, however true, however much to be trusted and valued, that the Bible contains the actual words, at first hand, of those who saw and heard Jesus Christ ; and of no other book in the world, however precious, can this be said. In the Bible we seem to reach back to the very days of the Son of man : we hear what His own companions heard Him say : we know what they saw Him do, how He appeared to them, what they learnt from Him. We come straight into His presence ; we follow about with His Apostles, as they taught, and preached, and wrote their letters.

Of course we cannot doubt that they said a great deal more than we know of now. How many words of Jesus Christ are lost to us ! How many things must He have done, how many lessons must He have given, how many acts of mercy, and tenderness, and love, must He have shown, which we would give anything to know, but which are lost to the world ; known to Him, known to the Saints in Glory, but which will never be known on earth now !

And so with His Apostles. We have heard who, and how many they were. We know what labour they went through, what work, daily and hourly, of explaining and teaching, and writing, and building up the truth. But of all this, so important and fruitful at the time, how much has been completely

lost to us! Of all St. Paul's labours and preaching
what a comparatively small portion must his epistles,
as we have them, be ; how much must he have said
that we can never know!

Well then, what does remain, how unspeakably
valuable and weighty and dear to us ought it to
be. And, as I say, what we have in the Bible is
all that is left us of St. Paul's preaching, and of his
Master's. It is their very words, and it is all that
we have of them. Surely, if we remembered this
when we read or hear the Bible, we should read it
and hear it with more care, more humbleness of
mind, more reverence, and more hope and comfort.

2. And this brings me to the second point on
which I wish you to think.

The one great feature observable in the Bible
is the way in which it throws us forward on things
to come. It is the one everlasting, permanent,
perpetual prophecy in the world. The Bible is
essentially a forward-looking book, a book which,
from first to last, prophesies, and turns our thoughts
onwards to the future. In this it is different from
all other books, and in this it is meant to be our
strong encouragement and comfort.

I don't mean, merely, what is quite true, that the
Bible has a great many prophecies in it ; that it is
half made up of prophetic writings. It is this, and
it is also very much made up of historical writings,
—writings about what is past, and has been done,
and is over. But besides all this, the Bible, as a
whole, has no meaning except we think of that time
to come, to which it keeps pointing us, to which
it is throughout bidding us look for the fulfil-

ment of our hopes, to which it is continually urging us to press forward, waiting, watching, preparing. All that is now, it declares, must pass away ; not only man's life, not only kingdoms and states, not only all the glory and power of man ; but the very heavens and earth around us are to make way for something greater and better. All that has been done, has been done only for the sake of that which is to come ; not only the long history of God's dealings with the world, His discipline of mankind, His wonders and judgments, and all that He has done in the glorious days of old, but that mighty and inconceivable act, the Word made flesh : the everlasting Son of God crucified, and raised from the dead. And all that He has ever done, all that His grace and love has accomplished for the world, and even now accomplishes, is but imperfect and unfinished : nothing is to be finished, no hope is to be satisfied, here. Men's minds and hopes, their treasure and their perfection, are all carried forward to the life to come. The Bible, every time we look at it, is the witness and protest to us, that our business is to look forward : that what man is here for, in this life, is that he may prepare for something, beyond measure and imagination greater, which lies in the future, in eternity. It is the perpetual witness of that which is in such strange contrast to everything here : it is the witness of our immortality.

Christ is indeed to come. He is come. Wonderful and awful thought. God has been made man. God, made man, lived, and died, and rose again for us. But even this is, if we may dare say so, little in comparison with what is to be. How indeed can we doubt that something infinitely greater *must* be, when we have seen so much done. This is what we believe, this is what we are now recalling to mind, and trying to fasten and deepen in our minds.

Now let us remember. In our Bibles we have all that remains to us of the actual words and writings of those who saw Him when He was last here. We have their very words ; and we have them only in the Bible.

And next, let us remember what the Bible, in its complete shape as one book, is specially meant to remind us of. There it is on our shelves, on our tables, in our hands, ever pointing onwards from the time present to that which is to come. From all its many and various sounds the voice is heard as one : —You are made for the future, for that which is not yet, but shall be hereafter. So let us read it, as if we heard the words of those who had seen and heard Christ. So let us read it, as discerning in every word the promise and the prophecy, which never ceases, either in open declaration or still more solemn undertone. " For yet a little while, and He that shall come will come, and will not tarry." And so may God give us patience and comfort of the Scriptures, so may He help us to embrace in them, and hold fast by them, the blessed hope of ever-lasting life ; so may our hearts learn to echo the last prayer of the Bible—" Behold I come quickly : even so come, Lord Jesus."

THE DISCLOSING OF SECRETS

"Therefore judge nothing before the time, until the Lord come, who both will bring to light the hidden things of darkness, and will make manifest the counsels of the hearts."—I CORINTHIANS iv. 5.

THE Bible teaches us that there is to be, not only a day of judgment, but a day of making known all secrets, and bringing to light all hidden things. When our Lord comes back it will be, not only to reckon with His servants, not only to pass the everlasting sentence on all that we have done, but to show what has been in all hearts and thoughts, and to take away the veil of darkness, which covers so many things in our lives from the knowledge of all the world. We all of us have our secrets: and we must be prepared one day to give them up. "For there is nothing covered, that shall not be revealed; neither hid, that shall not be known. Therefore whatsoever ye have spoken in darkness shall be heard in the light; and that which ye have spoken in the ear in closets shall be proclaimed upon the housetops." These are the words of Christ, and they are repeated over and over again. And St. Paul is constantly reminding us of the same thing. It is not only that every one of us "shall give account of himself to God." It is not only that "we shall all

stand before the judgment seat of Christ." It is not
only that "God will render to every man according
to his deeds." But it is also that "God, in that
day, shall judge the secrets of men by Jesus Christ,
according to my Gospel." "Some men's sins," he
says, "are open beforehand, going *before* to judgment,
and some men they follow after. Likewise also the
good works of some are manifest beforehand ; and
they that are otherwise cannot be hid." That is,
not only, nothing, good or bad, but is to come under
God's judgment ; but nothing, whether open or
hidden, notorious or unknown, but, in that day, is to
be published.

Now it is impossible for us, at present, to understand or imagine what all this making known of
secrets will be like, and how it will be done. And
it is no use trying to fancy anything about it. All
we can be sure of is, that it will be something very
different from what we can conceive of now. But
the thing itself is certain ; the thing itself is plain
enough. There is no difficulty in understanding
what is meant by bringing to light the hidden things
of darkness, and drawing away the veil from all secrets
of men.—We know what it is when something which
we wish to hide is found out. We know what it is
when something which we have wished to keep in the
deepest darkness gets abroad, and is in every one's
mouth. Now this is what the Bible tells us is to
happen with all secrets in the day when the Lord comes
to judgment. Secrets may be kept for a long time,
but they cannot be kept for ever. The day must
come at last when they shall be known : we cannot
tell by whom ; but, at any rate, by those from whom

people wished to hide them. Who are to be the
witnesses of that great exposure,—before whom all
our secrets are to be dragged into light and our souls
laid bare, it is useless to guess. All we know is the
awful fact,—the awfulness of which we can partly
imagine by what we feel *now,*—that we shall have
to give up everything that lies hid in our hearts and
knowledge ; that it will be impossible to hide anything, or keep it secret any longer ; that if there is
anything which we should be ashamed should be
known, we shall no longer be able to help its being
discovered and disclosed ; that then every man will
be seen as he is ; the truth about everything will be
made clear, the light will have poured in, brighter
than the sun at noonday, on all dark places, and all
dark things and words.

One part of this great revealing of secrets will be
the discovery of men's real character, the making
known what each man really is. *Now,* this is only
half known. We think that we are something or
other ; and other people think of us according to
their views. But all the time *we are* what we *are* in
the eyes of God ; that which God sees us to be, *that*
we *are*, whatever different thing we may fancy of
ourselves, or others may fancy of us. *Now,* we
mistake about ourselves ; and do not know what
our neighbours have found out about us. We think
ourselves one thing ; they, with their sharper eyes,
or more impartial judgment, see that we are another.
We, perhaps, think ourselves humble ; they see that
we are vain. We think, perhaps, that religion is the
main thing in all we do ; they see that, behind all
our religion, our actions are worldly and selfish.

They see that we are cowardly, and we fancy ourselves manly and brave. We never doubt that we
are true : they see that we are slippery and insincere.
They see that we are ill-natured and ill-tempered,
while we never imagine that such a charge can be
made against us. We dream that we are full of
zeal for something altogether out of ourselves, while
they see clearly that we are all the while following
our own spirit, and seeking our own ends. We do
not half know ourselves ; but in some things, perhaps,
we know ourselves only too well. We know, perhaps,
that we seem better than we really are. There are
ways of thinking and feeling in our hearts which we
keep in the background, which we know will not
bear the light, which we do our best to make a
secret of :—ways and feelings which we indulge in,
and which yet we know are unchristian and wrong :—
ways and feelings with which if any one were to
charge us, we should be very angry, but yet which
we cannot make up our minds to struggle against
and conquer and give up ; which we hope and try
that men shall know as little as possible about, but
which, between God and our conscience, we know
are too deeply part of ourselves.

Now, to all this the day of the Lord shall put an
end. Then, all mistakes, all disguises, will be at an
end. We shall be forced to know and see what we
really are. If we are conceited, and selfish, and self-
indulgent, and untrue, we shall be made to know it.
We shall see ourselves as we have looked to other
eyes. And all those secret faults and sins which we
have, perhaps, taken so much trouble to wrap up
and hide, which we have known of ourselves, but

hoped that no one else suspected,—these, too, must be shown in their true light.   We must for once— we must at last—be seen as we are.   We shall feel that wilful blindness to ourselves, that all shows and pretendings, are at an end.   Our real character will be made clear.   The truth about us will have to come out.   As Almighty God knows us, so we shall, at last, know ourselves, and so we shall be known by all who then see us.

This must be one part of that great revealing of secrets : the " making manifest the counsels of the hearts."   But the Bible speaks more distinctly and pointedly of another—the bringing to light not merely the general character of men, but particularly certain secrets which especially avoid the light, the " hidden things of darkness."

What does the Bible mean by that ?   Can it mean anything less than this, that the veil which now rests on so many secret sins of men, the veil which in this world it is possible to keep drawn over them, even to the grave, that veil will then be torn asunder, and all those secret sins will then be as manifestly displayed as the most public sins that were ever committed—the sin of Pharaoh, of Saul, or of Judas Iscariot ?

Think what this means.   We know what it is to stand convicted of some public sin which a man cannot deny.   We know, in the case of others, what is the horror, the confusion, the miserable shame of such a sinner, when his sin is brought home to him. But the righteous sentence of God makes no differ- ence in the end between public and secret sins.   The difference between public and secret sins is a very

real difference now.   But the Bible warns us that it
is merely a difference for the few years of our life, and
that as soon as life here is over, it comes at once to
an end.   There are no secret sins to God.   There
will be no secret sins in the day of judgment.   All
sins then will be so far on a level, that all will be
known just as they were done.   All will be made
known.   All will be made manifest in the brightness
of that day.

Is this so?   Is it indeed true that the most
hidden things of darkness must at last be made
plain, the darkest secrets of men's sins be made
known?   Could any one reasonably expect that
it would be otherwise, if God is all-seeing and
righteous?   Why should sin, because it is secret for
a time, be spared the shame and punishment of being
brought to light?   But we are not left to guess.
The words of the Bible which tell us of the coming
of our Lord to judgment, tell us as plainly that
He comes "to bring to light the hidden things of
darkness, and to make manifest the counsels of the
hearts."

And if it must be so, if all secrets must at last
be known, the prospect is a serious one, for all who
have a witness within them, that among the secrets
to be revealed in that day will be found some of
their own.   I am not speaking now of innocent
secrets ; of the many numberless things which we
naturally and rightly wish to keep to ourselves—
and, from no wrong feeling, would be ashamed and
distressed that others should know.   It is not of
these that the Bible speaks, when it speaks of the
" hidden things of darkness."   It speaks of *sin*, of

what has been done wrong : it speaks of what men keep secret, and blush at, because they know that they have done wrong. If we have any secrets of this kind,—sins which we have been able to keep from being known ; sins which we, in a sort of way, triumph in, as being certain that they can never come to light in this world ; sins into whose mystery we need fear no one ever breaking ; sins which we need never talk about, or fear any one asking of ;—if we have any of these secrets, these are the secrets of which the Bible speaks, as doomed to be made known ; these are the secrets which we must one day meet again before an eye which none can avoid.

For these secrets are those hidden works of darkness of which it is said that Christ is to come back to bring them to light. There can be but one way to escape this terrible revealing of our secrets. There can be but one ground of hope that they may at last be buried, and brought against us no more. If they are repented of *here* ; if here, where we have done them, we in truth forsake them ; if here, where we have dared God's eye and God's judgment, and trusted that what man did not know of, *no one* would ever know of ; if here, where we have triumphed in our secrets, we confess them with all our hearts to God ; if here, where we have flattered ourselves that we are safe, and masters of our secret, we feel and own the wickedness and shame of our secret sins ;— we may hope that they may be forgiven and taken away ; and we may hope that what Christ has forgiven, He will not bring up against us to our confusion in the day of judgment. But, till we have repented of them,—as long as they are a secret between us and our conscience, and we feel comfortable only because they are not known to man,—so long we must lay our account to meet them once more, where there is no hiding them.

And how should this thought of the discovery of all hidden things of darkness restrain our thoughts and actions? Oh, let us not make to ourselves any of these dreadful secrets of sin, which we would almost rather die than man should find out, but which, after all, must be found out, and laid bare at last. When we are tempted, and are doubtful, let us say to ourselves, This must all come to light at last: am I prepared to face the disclosure? dare I do it, with the certainty of all being one day known?

Oh, let us have no secrets with God. Let us live with our life and conscience all day long open before him. Let the secret sins of our past days be no forgotten or dissembled matters between us and God. Let us be sure that, if there is anything of which we feel that we dare not think of it and God together, dare not think of it and of its one day being made known,—this is a warning that we had best have nothing to do with it. Let us live with the most certain law of God's kingdom ever before our thoughts : " There is nothing covered, that shall not be revealed "; " nothing is secret, that shall not be made manifest ; neither anything hid, that shall not be known and come abroad."

THE MYSTERY OF THE INCARNATION

> 'Seek ye the Lord while He may be found, call ye upon Him while He is near : let the wicked forsake his way, and the unrighteous man his thoughts : and let him return unto the Lord, and He will have mercy upon him ; and to our God, for He will abundantly pardon. For My thoughts are not your thoughts, neither are your ways My ways, saith the Lord. For as the heavens are higher than the earth, so are My ways higher than your ways, and My thoughts than your thoughts."—ISAIAH lv. 6-9.

GOD'S ways are indeed higher than our ways, and His thoughts are above ours. We cannot search them out, we cannot come near them. We do not need the Bible to teach us this. The world we live in, the things we see and know around us here, are enough to make us confess that His ways are wonderful, above our understanding, and His thoughts beyond our reach. All round us we see the works of His hands, great and small, in the depth and in the height ; and, in the smallest as in the greatest, we see ways and thoughts, power and wisdom, which the thoughts of man try in vain to comprehend. He made the sun, and the stars, and the light, and no understanding of man can conceive the power by which they were made, and are kept safe. And He made the grass under our feet, and the millions of living beings in the air and in the water ; but how and why He made them all, the mind of man cannot understand. Men are continually searching into His wonderful works, and thinking to find out something more of the ways and thoughts by which God has ordered the things which He has made ; and yet what they do find out only shows how far off they are from coming to the end of the wisdom and power of God.

And if we are taught this every time that we open our eyes on the world round us, and think of what we see, much more is it forced upon us in matters higher than this wonderful and beautiful world in which we live, by that which the present season brings before our minds. The ways and thoughts of God in the worlds of the sky, or in the doings of nature, are indeed wonderful ; but what are their wonders compared with the wonder of " God manifest in the flesh " ; God coming down to take on Him the nature of man, that He might be with men in their life, and share with them in their death, and win them to love Him, and to become one with Him for evermore ? What wonder of the sky or of the deep can equal the wonder of Him, who made all these things,—whose are the paths of the stars, and the might of the lightning and the life of every living thing,—becoming for us incarnate of the Virgin Mary, and being made man ? What ways are those, what thoughts are those, which counted the salvation of human souls so precious, that the Maker of those souls saw no other way of saving the creatures which He had made, and which had sinned against Him, but sharing their weakness and their sorrows, being born a child like them, that like them He might also die ? Who

C.   C

among men could have conceived of such a way of
saving men ?

Wonders, indeed, had been done for man ever
since he first sinned against God, and God's love
was exercised in recovering him. Wonders too,
greater than any that had yet been seen, had
been promised by God's messengers, the prophets.
Words had been heard of old, such as we repeat
to-day : " A Virgin shall conceive, and bear a Son,
and shall call His name Immanuel ; " " God with us."
" Unto us a Child is born, unto us a Son is given :
and the government shall be upon His shoulder : and
His name shall be called Wonderful, Counsellor, the
mighty God, the everlasting Father, the Prince of
Peace." Words, indeed, to raise men's hopes, and
make them look out for some great thing. But
I do not suppose that these words were the same
to those who first heard them as they are to us.
To them they were a glorious, but still a dark
promise ; to us they are no longer dark but light ;
—light in all the glory of an unhoped-for deliverance, found to be true indeed. However much
the prophets understood of them, we know that
their eyes were not allowed to see the things
which we see. They knew, indeed, that God
would do wonders to save mankind, but they
little thought of the wonder that He was going
to do, in sending His own Son, God of God, and
Light of Light, to become man, to be born as we
are born, to live as we live on this earth.

What, indeed, are all the wonders that God had
done before for His people, compared with this one,
that God was made man, and dwelt among us ? We

sometimes speak as if the wonderful thing was, that
He should come in such lowly guise, not as a great
king and conqueror, but as a mere teacher of the
people ; that He should be so humble and without
show, content with a poor man's lot and with the
form of a servant, instead of appearing in the glory
of the Messias, or with the greatness of a prophet
like Moses.   We dwell on the humble lot of His
mother, and on the manger, and the inn, and the
swaddling clothes at Bethlehem, and on the carpenter's shop at Nazareth.   It is very well to do
so, if we thus make our hearts feel more really
what our Lord and Master was when among us.
But the wonder of all is the great fact itself, that He
did become man at all.   It is not so wonderful really
that when He became man He also took with manhood poverty and obscurity and contempt and shame.
For what is all that man thinks most about, all that
he values most highly,—riches, and honour, and comfort, and pleasure,—in the sight of God most high ?
If He became man at all what would He care about
such things as these ?   That He renounced all this,
that He was poor, and despised, and humble, is but
a light thing compared with the overwhelming marvel
and mystery that God became man, and was made
flesh for us.   Who can imagine of this rightly ?
Who can fully take into his mind all that is meant
and said in those few words, God became man ?

Look at the world around you, and all that is in
it,—all the countless millions of living souls that are
in it, that have lived and died in it since it was first
made : look up at the sky, and count the stars, and
remember that each star is a world, and think who

it is who made and upholds all these, and knows
what is going on in every corner of them ; and then
imagine that Being, clothed in flesh, standing a man
at your side. And think of Him, drawing human
breath, fed by human food, speaking human words
like yourself, being Him who at the very same
moment keeps all these worlds in being, and who was
in existence, perfect, all-wise, all-good, in an eternity
without beginning, long before those worlds were
made. Take in that thought, fix your mind on
it, try to get hold of something of its surpassing
wonderfulness ; and, after it, all other wonders will
seem hardly worth naming ; even the wonder of His
lowliness and humiliation will seem but small compared with the wonder of His having been born man
at all.

Surely God's thoughts are not our thoughts, nor
are our ways His ways. Surely it was no mere way
of speaking, when it was said that, as the heavens
are higher than the earth, so are His ways higher
than our ways, and His thoughts than our thoughts.
To-day, at least, we ought to feel it to be so indeed ;
to-day, which shows us how much God cares for
our salvation ; to-day, which reminds us what His
thoughts were for accomplishing it, what way He
took to bring us to Himself. To-day, sounds once
more God's promise of pardon to man, and the
pledge that that promise will be kept. To-day,
once more, by the marvellous grace and honour
done to our race by the Incarnation of His Son,
God calls on us to come to Him and be saved.
" Seek ye the Lord while He may be found, call
ye upon Him while He is near : let the wicked

forsake his way, and the unrighteous man his thoughts: and let him return unto the Lord, and He will have mercy upon him; and to our God, for He will abundantly pardon."

If we doubt whether He means what He says to the full,—if we doubt whether He is in earnest in calling such as we are to come to Him, whether He can pardon as abundantly as man has sinned,—here is the answer to our unbelief: He does not work by the rules and manners of men. His ways are not our ways, nor His thoughts our thoughts. He shows His desire for our salvation, and His readiness to accept us, in doing what none could have imagined possible, in sending His Son to take our nature upon Him, and to become man for our sakes. Here is the pledge of His faithfulness. Here is the assurance that none can doubt, that He loves the souls of men with the love with which He loves His only-begotten Son. When we will not come to Him, He comes to us. When we refuse to seek Him, He comes Himself to seek and to save us. He does not send, He does not call merely. He comes down from heaven, and lays aside His glory, and speaks to us face to face, with the words of man, with the fellow-feeling of man, with the affectionate love and tender earnestness of man. He who made the light, and rules beyond the stars, comes and calls on us, and speaks to us with the simple plainness with which a father speaks to his little children, or a little child appeals to grown men.

Once more Christmas is come, to show us how inconceivably God has loved us; loved us with a reality and earnestness that even, in the contemplation of His love, makes us tremble to think of it. What, think you, must be the glory destined for those for whom the Maker of the world became a man on earth? What must be the certainty and the depth of ruin to those who, when such an offer has been made, such a step taken for their salvation, yet refuse it? How can we estimate the greatness of that blessedness which God keeps in store for His servants, when we see what He was willing to do in order that we might attain to it? His ways, indeed, are not our ways; and He, whose way was so far beyond man's imagination to bring us this blessedness, must have ways far beyond our thoughts too, to make His promise good in the kingdom of heaven. And how can we suppose that human thought can penetrate and measure the awful completeness of that overthrow of happiness and hope, which awaits the impenitent and the ungodly, when we see what their Creator and Judge was willing to submit to, in order to turn their hearts to Himself, and bring them to repentance and peace with God? What can be imagined of the fate of those who have been so loved, so sought after, and yet could not be found?

O seek Him while He may be found; call upon Him while He is near. By all the mysteriousness of His inconceivable love, by all the strange marvels of His way of redemption, seek *Him*, whose ways are so wonderful, and whose thoughts so unfathomable. Now you know that He has done all this to win your love, to bind your hearts for ever to His sacred name. Seek him while His arm is stretched forth to shield and guide and bless you. It will not always be so. The wondrous ways and gracious thoughts which

God has towards you now, must, if you are *not* won and touched, and made better by them, give place to ways and thoughts, equally wonderful, but wonderful in the judgment and vengeance to which they will prepare the way. If you are delaying your repentance, if you are putting it off to a more convenient season, measure your danger and guilt by those wondrous doings which we are celebrating to-day. By those ways that are so much higher than our ways, by those thoughts which are so much higher than our thoughts, listen to the call which invites the wicked to forsake his way, and the unrighteous man his thoughts, and which promises that the Lord will have mercy on him, and that our God, who came Himself to save, will abundantly pardon him. Let none of us turn away from this gracious call. Let none of us think that we do not need it ; that our heart is already right, that we have sought and found God, and need not listen to words which call on us to seek Him still. Surely we, all of us, need Him. Surely none of us have found Him, as He might be found by those who seek Him earnestly. Surely none of us have yet found to the full the extent of that pardoning and healing grace which we need so much, and which He has in such abundance to bestow. Think how little our lives have been like the lives of Christ's disciples. Think of all the burdens and troubles which have grown on our consciences during the busy or the idle days which have passed over us since last Christmas. Do not we want pardon for them, and an ease from their weariness and vexations ? And to whom shall we go for it except to Him, who took our flesh that He might share its burdens, and feel for its temptations, and heal its wounds? To whom should we go but to Him who came down and lived among us, to show us how He loved us, and to win us to love Him? This day reminds us how near He is to us, even our brother, bone of our bone, flesh of our flesh. This day reminds us how easily He may be found. This day we rejoice that the world has such a Creator and mankind such a Saviour. Oh, let us show that our rejoicing is not a vain rejoicing, by answering His call of love, by coming to Him, that He may make our hearts and lives His own.

THE THREE CHRISTMAS-TIDE FESTIVALS

" These are they which follow the Lamb whithersoever He goeth. These were redeemed from among men, being the firstfruits unto God and to the Lamb."—REVELATION xiv. 4.

CHRISTMAS DAY is followed, as you know, by three other holidays. The three days that follow it are kept in remembrance, first of St. Stephen, next of St. John, and then of the Innocents. St. Stephen, the first Deacon, was the first martyr also, the first who laid down his life for Christ's sake. St. John was the beloved disciple who leaned on Jesus' breast at the Last Supper, who outlived all his companions, and died at last, not as most of them died, by the sword or the cross, but quietly in his bed in a good old age ; who wrote the last of the four Gospels, to whom was shown the Revelation of things to come, and the vision of the New Jerusalem ; the favoured servant of his ascended Master, the preacher of love. The Innocents were those young children whom King Herod slew in Bethlehem, when he was seeking to take the life of the young child Jesus; little children who had done no actual sin, who were not old enough to know evil from good, but who yet were old enough to do Christ service, to be made of His household and family, and to glorify Him by their deaths.

Now, why is this ? Why is Christmas thus followed by these three holidays? Why are they put close together, one after another, as a sort of carrying on the thoughts and feelings of Christmas Day? Why, out of all the other saints of the New Testament, should St. Stephen, St. John, and the Innocents be specially chosen to be, as it were, the train of companions and followers appointed to wait on the Saviour of the world at His birth in Bethlehem?

I suppose that these days are kept along with Christmas Day, and immediately after it, to show us instances and examples of the fruits among mankind of the coming down of Christ to take our nature on Him. By being born man, like ourselves, He hallowed and consecrated our nature. By coming among us, and joining us in fellowship with Himself, He raised men to heights of holiness and grace to which they had never reached before. He came to exalt the sons of earth. He came to purify them, to strengthen them, to show them a new way of love unknown before, to lift their thoughts and hopes above this life, to fill them with the spirit of power, and with a heavenly mind; to make men—sinners and degraded—like in heart and spirit, like in deeds and suffering, to Himself. This He began to do when He was born for us. So with the remembrance of His birth follows also the remembrance of the great things He wrought in changing so wonderfully the sinful nature of men.

With Christ, the Restorer of mankind, are shown us at Christmas examples of His work, instances of what He has indeed done among men by coming in the flesh, instances of the restoration which He came down to bring about in the world. Stephen was a man like ourselves, yet Christ's coming in the flesh raised him so high above himself that he gladly shed his blood for the truth, and with his last breath prayed for those who killed him.   John was a common man like one of us, but Christ's coming in the flesh so raised and purified and sanctified him that he was able to speak of the love of God as no other man did, as only the Lord Himself spoke of it. The Innocents were but children like other children, yet Christ's coming in the flesh brought a blessing on that death which seems the saddest fate that can happen to a child, and turned Adam's curse and the penalty of Adam's sin into a crown of glory, even for speechless infants, unable yet to know their Saviour.

These three days show us instances and examples of Christ's restoring and cleansing and refining that nature which in Adam had been ruined and lost ; instances of what His coming down among us in the flesh could do to make men like Himself, and fit for His glory.   They were joined on to Christmas Day as the marks and trophies of His Christmas victory.

Further, they were joined to it to show us that Christ's blessing is not confined to one way of serving Him, to one sort of people, but is meant for all sorts and conditions and ages ; that He has saved and sanctified all ; that He has place in His kingdom for young and old, for small and great.   He came not to call the old only, but the young and strong, in their prime of health and hope ; not the grown-up only, but also the children and infants at the breast. His band of saints, His army of martyrs, His household and Church, is not a human company or army where only a particular sort of men is wanted and picked out ; He takes all sorts in who need salvation, all souls which His Father created to be happy and holy for ever. The fruits of His Incarnation and Redemption will be seen, not in one class or division of mankind, in one form of human nature, but mani-fold and varied as the differences of men. This is one reason why these three days follow Christmas. His saints will be young men cut off in their prime, yet having in a few days fulfilled the work of many, like St. Stephen ; yet not all like him. Others will be like St. John, filling the whole of a long life with the glory and love of God. Yet not all like these even, men of the highest stature and noblest mould that man can attain to ; but others also, among those whom the world despises as weak and poor natures,— children in age and children in understanding, too feeble or too unknowing to fight for Christ, but gentle and sanctified enough to be His witnesses, and to suffer for Him in quietness and silence.

Further, these three days follow Christmas for another reason : to remind us that there are many different ways of serving Christ appointed to us, many different gifts, many different ways of glorify-ing Him ; yet all are of God, all belong to His one great purpose of sanctifying and saving man, all help on towards His kingdom. St. Stephen's glorious death does not make St. John's long life and peaceful end less Christian, less acceptable, less becoming to the beloved disciple of a crucified Master. What St. John did and St. Stephen endured, with full knowledge of the reason why, with hearts and feel-ings drinking to the full the cup of suffering given them to drink, did not make the death of the Inno-

cents less precious in God's sight, though they knew
not why they suffered, and felt nothing but the last
momentary stroke of the murderer's sword.   After
such a life and such a death as Jesus Christ's, after
those awful words of His about taking up the Cross,
about him who loves his life losing it, and him who
hates it gaining it, it might have seemed that no
death but that of St. Stephen could be fit for a
follower of Christ, could duly glorify God.   But
there were others also as Christian and as holy.   St.
Stephen's zeal, St. Stephen's boldness, St. Stephen's
swift and early death, like that of a soldier in the
beginning of a great battle, gladly endured to show his
companions the way to fight and conquer, was indeed
following his Lord's steps, and doing what his Lord
had taught him.   It was one high and excellent way,
but not the only one.   It was as much following in
Christ's steps, and doing what Christ had taught,
patiently to tarry through a long and weary life,
seeing friends drop off by death year after year,
ready to suffer, yet still left ; left the last of all whom
he had known, with new faces and new ways all
round him,—and to die alone.   And that was St.
John's quiet, noiseless, monotonous (as many would
call it), dull way of doing Christ service.   Yet he
was of all others the disciple whom his Master loved.
Early to die, or long to live, are both ways which
lead to glory.   To die in public, to live unknown, to
die a death with which the world shall ring for ever,
to live a life by which no one seems the better, and
in which no one is interested but the one or two
friends near us, equally may turn out at last to have
been that path of the righteous which shines more

and more unto the perfect day. Nay, not only that. To be cut off in childhood, without even the opportunity of knowing God, without having yet named His holy name, or bent the knee before Him, sorrowful as such a death, useless as such a life seems to man, it is not so to God. It is the life and death of His own little child, of one whom He has taken into His family, and sealed as His soldier and servant at baptism. Even such a one dies, though we cannot see how, to his Father's glory; even such a one is a fit follower in the great company of faithful souls of the Lamb who died for young and old; even such a one, like the Innocents of old, is fitly named as a companion of Him who was born for us at Bethlehem.

Again there is another reason why these three days should have been chosen out of all other saints' days to be joined so closely to Christmas. They not only show us that Christ came to bless, and to make use of all sorts of persons; that persons of very different gifts are equally useful, and equally able to do Him service and glorify His Name; but they also put before us, in human examples, those special graces which He came down on earth to show the perfect pattern of, and which were all joined together and united in His person. What was it that marks that life of Jesus Christ which began at Bethlehem? Was it not, in the first place, His readiness to die, to give His life an offering and sacrifice to God? Was it not, in the next place, His unfathomable and overflowing love? Was it not, in the third place, His purity and innocence, and with that His lowliness and humility, as of a little child? And did He come merely to show us

an instance and image of these things, which we
were only to look at and admire, but not to follow?
Or did He come, that what He was, *that* His servants
also should be ; that as He was in the world, man
should also try, and in time learn to be?   Surely
He came, He showed us all this vision of holiness
and love, that we might be like Him.   And He did
not come in vain.   Men—sinners like ourselves—
have been like their Saviour, God-like, Christ-like
men.   It has been found possible for man to fulfil
the purpose for which He came on earth and took
our flesh on Him.   By being with Him, by following
His steps, men have become indeed like Him ; have
become saints.   That is what these days remind us of.
They show us reflections,—faint reflections indeed, yet
real ones,—in human souls like our own, of the glories
of the Sun of righteousness.   They show us that man
can, like Christ, gladly lay down his life for the sake of
God and his brethren.   They show us that man can love,
after the example of Christ, and in the way in which
Christ loved.   They show us the type among men of
that perfect innocence and humility which was in Him.
They show us, one by one, the chief parts which
together make up in a human soul that likeness of
Christ which He was born to re-create among us.
If we want to be like Christ, we must be like St.
Stephen, like St. John, like the Innocents, in those
special graces for which we have them in remembrance.

There can be no true Christian character without
that readiness to deny ourselves, that readiness to
take anything disagreeable, anything dangerous, for
the sake of doing our duty, which we see in St.
Stephen.   Self-denial, self-forgetfulness, was the foun-

dation on which his service rested ; it was at the
bottom of all the great things he did for Christ. He
counted nothing, not even his life, dear to himself,
so that he might do what his Master had given him
to do. What Christ had given him to do was to
rebuke the sin of the Jews, and to bear witness of
Christ before those who hated Him. Stephen knew
that he was rebuking the very people who had crucified his Master ; but, for all that, he went on and
was not afraid, whatever they might do to him.
And so he was the first to follow Christ in His
death. He died, as Christ had died, praying for his
murderers. Here is the very beginning of Christian
service. Without this readiness to deny ourselves
we cannot be the servants of the crucified ; we cannot in any way do as He did, or be like Him.
" Whosoever will come after Me, let him take up his
cross daily and follow Me." " He that loveth his
life shall lose it, and he that hateth his life shall find
it." " Greater love hath no man than this, that a man
lay down his life for his friends. Ye are My friends
if ye do whatsoever I command you." Therefore, I
say, is the example of St. Stephen shown us after
Christmas Day that we may be reminded that to
live as Christ lived, to be like Christ, we must
begin with the readiness to deny ourselves, to die
for Christ.

There can be no true Christian character without
love,—that love of which St. John was the great
teacher and example. To be a Christian, and yet
to be without that which was the very life of Christ,
His endless love, is a contradiction and an impossi-
bility. Love is the life of souls. Without it they

are dead, and a dead soul has nothing to do with
that which Christ was born on Christmas Day to do
for us. So if you care about Christmas, if you care
about Him who came among us in the flesh to make
us His brethren, see whether you have love,—I do
not say like His,—but anything after that human
pattern which is shown us in the disciple whom
Christ loved for his fulness of love. How much
have you of the spirit of St. John? He it is who
taught to the utmost his Master's love. He it is
who has told us most of Christ's outpourings of love.
He it is who has told us that Christ said, " This is
My commandment, That ye love one another, as I
have loved you." " A new commandment I give
unto you, That ye love one another." He it is who
has told us that Christ said, " As the Father hath
loved Me, so have I loved you." He it is who has left
the blessed record, " God so loved the world, that He
gave His only begotten Son, that whosoever believeth
on Him should not perish, but have everlasting life."
He it is whose own words are so full, so burning with
his Master's love. " My little children, let us not
love in word, neither in tongue ; but in deed and in
truth." " He that loveth not knoweth not God ; for
God is love." " He that dwelleth in love dwelleth in
God, and God in him." "We know that we have passed
from death unto life, because we love the brethren."

Before we pass away from the thoughts of Christmas, St. John, the chief pattern in Christ's Church of
Christian love, is set before us that we may be reminded
how men ought to receive the love of God shown to
them in Christ's birth ; and how by God's grace they
may—sinners as they are—be enabled to receive it.

C.   D

And the day of the Innocents reminds us that, as there can be no Christian character without self-denial and without love, so there can be none without the lowliness and purity of which they were examples. "Whosoever shall not receive the kingdom of God as a little child, he shall not enter therein." "This then is the message which we have heard of Him, and declare unto you, that God is light, and in Him is no darkness at all. If we say that we have fellowship with Him, and walk in darkness, we lie, and do not the truth." "He that saith, I know Him, and keepeth not His commandments, is a liar, and the truth is not in him." He that hath hope in Christ "purifieth himself, even as He is pure." There can be no mistake about this. Christ was pure and holy, and the impure, the sensual, the unholy, are none of His. Let a man's professions, his zeal, his confidence, be what they may, if he is a follower of the lusts of the flesh he can be none of Christ's. He can have no part in that new creation which began when Christ was born at Bethlehem. He who is not trying to be like the little children who suffered for Christ at Bethlehem, and like the children whom Christ took up in His arms, and set forth as examples to His disciples, is as yet no follower of Him who was born of a pure Virgin, and without spot of sin ; and at His entrance into the world which He came to save was laid in the manger of the inn.

These then are the reasons why these three days follow Christmas Day ; why these special examples are joined with the remembrance of Him who came to restore and save mankind. Together they show us what was all in one in Jesus Christ. They show

feelings. Our /
Our ~~farthis~~

us what, if we are to be like Christ, must be all in one in us.   St. Stephen, though he is the pattern of self-denial, had the love of St. John.   St. John, because he had the copy of his Lord's love, was just as ready as St. Stephen to lay down his life for his brethren, if Christ had bidden him do so.   Remember, it is not one grace alone that makes the Christian like Christ or His saints.   We may have St. Stephen's zeal without St. John's love, and it avails us little. We may think that we have St. John's love because we are kind and tender-hearted, and ready to do a good turn to our brethren, or because we often have on our lips that great watchword of our religion, *love* ; but if we are but talkers about love, if we use it only because it is a fine and beautiful word to use, if while we talk about love we are practically pleasers of ourselves—disobedient, unfaithful in our duties to others ; if while we are kind and good-natured we indulge in fleshly lusts, and give way to impure and sinful thoughts,—we must not deceive ourselves,—it is no use thinking we have love like that of St. John. There is no love, no Christian love, without St. Stephen's self-denial and hatred of evil, and without the purity, the lowliness, the freedom from pride and self-conceit of the little children whom Herod slew for Christ.

Such as our Master was, such must His servants be ; what He was born to be, they must grow to be. May He, of His mercy, make us more and more like Himself, that we may be fit to see His face in glory. May He " sanctify us wholly, that our whole spirit and soul and body may be preserved blameless unto the coming of our Lord Jesus Christ."

CHRIST'S NEVER-FAILING SYMPATHY

"And the third day there was a marriage in Cana of Galilee ; and the mother of Jesus was there : and both Jesus was called, and his disciples, to the marriage."—ST. JOHN ii. 1, 2.

THE miracles of our Lord were of different sorts. Some were to show His power ; others were to show His goodness ; others were a kind of type or sign of His office as the Redeemer and Saviour of souls. Others were, in like manner, a type or sign of His office as the Judge and Punisher of the impenitent. Most of them were miracles of mercy in some shape or other. A few were miracles to warn men and startle them ; but almost all had a spiritual meaning and significance, over and above the wonderful display of tenderness, or wisdom, or heavenly justice in the miracle itself.

When He fed the five thousand with the few loaves and fishes in the desert place, besides the gracious act of love and care for the poor hungry wanderers, He gave a token of how He, all day long, prepares a table before His people in the wilderness, and feeds them with the bread of heaven ; how He strengthens their heart with food which is more divine than man could provide, and supplies the wants of their souls when they are fainting and ready to perish.

When He healed the sick, and opened the eyes of the blind, and made the dumb to speak, and the lame to walk, and stanched the issue of blood, and cleansed the leper, and gave strength to the sick of the palsy, and drove out the devils, what are all these precious miracles but tokens of the way in which He deals with the diseases of the soul ; making the drunkard sober, and the liar true, and the proud humble, driving out the devil of lust and uncleanness, of hatred and malice ; teaching the careless to be watchful and earnest, the idle waster of his time to dedicate it to God's service, the lover of this world and of money to open his eyes and see the better things which God has to give.

When He walked on the water, and bade Peter come to Him, and held him up when he was sinking, what was it for but first to teach His disciples that He had good reason to tell them to put their faith in Him, and that without Him they could hope for no deliverance ; and next, to teach us too that in the troubles and storms of life He is greater than the power of the storm, full of grace and love in the thick of trouble ; that He is with us in it all ; that with Him in company we may boldly venture to cast ourselves into it ; but that also it is only too likely that we shall " begin to sink," and that there is only one arm in all the world which can hold us up, and that is His ?

When He raised the dead, He showed us the image and type of that Almighty power, which can raise the soul, dead in trespasses and sins, to the life of righteousness. When, under His curse, the fig-tree withered away, He showed us what must become of those who promise and profess, but bring forth no

fruit ; who honour Him with their lips but their heart
is far from Him.

And so, in all His miracles, we may look for
some likeness to things spiritual, some figure of
spiritual goodness, some type of the supply of
spiritual needs, some lesson of spiritual truth, which
belongs to *us* as much as to those for whom the
miracles were first done.   They were done for our
sakes, as truly as for the sick whom Christ healed, or
the disciples whose faith He wished to strengthen, or
the multitudes who looked on, and whom He tried to
draw to Him.

What shall we learn of this miracle of turning the
water into wine at the marriage feast in Cana ?   We
must all feel it to be a very wonderful and a very
beautiful miracle.   Very wonderful as a display of
power, creating with a word one thing from another
so entirely different,—wine, that is made by the art
of man, from simple water,—giving in a moment to
the water the new properties and nature of wine ; as
wonderful as that other miracle, when at His word
the five loaves grew and multiplied, no one saw how,
into the abundant banquet of five thousand men,
besides women and children.

Very beautiful too ; — done so quietly, done so
humbly and without display, caring for no thanks
or honour from it ; simply taking thought for the
pleasure, and enjoyment, and merry-making of the
company He was in, without letting them know how
He had contributed to it.   Very wonderful and very
beautiful, I say ; but what is it to us ?   What may
we learn from it ?

1. We learn from it, first, that Christ is willing to

be with us, not merely in places and times of religious service, but in all the times also of our pleasure and enjoyment, in our marriage feasts and days of rejoicing and happiness, and daily at our table, and meals, and fireside, when we talk freely, and open ourselves, and laugh and are merry with our friends ; and that as He is willing to be with us there, and to bless our enjoyment, so we ought by faith to see Him there ; to see Him by faith, not to make us gloomy, or restrain our mirth, but to make us thankful for our enjoyments, and to keep them innocent.

We are apt to think that nothing could be worthy of such a person as Jesus Christ was, nothing could be worth His thought, nothing worth His speaking or caring about, but what was plainly and visibly a matter of salvation. We fancy Him busy only with what we call important and serious things,—preaching, teaching, explaining the things of the kingdom of God ; healing, rebuking, calling to repentance. We have a kind of feeling that anything lower than this would have been not high and heavenly enough for Him ; that it would hardly have become Him, that it would have been a waste of His time. We can hardly fancy Him having anything to do with the round of every-day conversation, or enjoyment, which fills up our time, or taking any interest in it. In our thoughts we set Him apart from it all, only speaking of religion and God, only doing the things which we call religious, praying and exhorting, and trying to convert the sinners round Him. And, perhaps, while we think of Jesus Christ as entirely separate from all the common affairs and pleasures of this life, we draw the same line between religion and our daily life for ourselves, and follow the business, and enjoy the pleasures which come in our daily life, without thinking that religion has anything whatever to do with them. While we cannot fancy Jesus Christ taking part with men in the eating, and drinking, and making merry, as if it was something too low for Him, we go on day after day eating and drinking, talking to one another and making merry, and thinking it the most natural thing in the world to do all this, without ever letting the remembrance of Jesus Christ into our minds; as if anywhere, but in church and at our prayers, the thought of Jesus Christ was too high and exalted to be joined with matters of common life. We think of Jesus Christ as being too much devoted to religion, too much belonging to heaven, to have anything in common with the ordinary work and pleasures of men; we take for *our* portion this ordinary work and pleasure, not caring that Christ should bless them, only afraid lest Christ should hinder and spoil them.

How unlike to all this is the history of the miracle at Cana. How unlike to what we fancy of Jesus Christ, and His keeping aloof from the common ways of men, and being busy only with what is directly and professedly religious, according to that notion of religion which makes church and Sunday the only place and time when we are bound to be religious. Jesus Christ came to the marriage at Cana, not to preach, not to talk about the great business He was in the world for, but merely to be there; to give pleasure to those who had invited Him, to show His kind feeling and interest in those by whom the feast

was prepared.   He went no otherwise than as one
of us might go to a friend's wedding, simply to give
pleasure, to do honour, to be one of the guests.
The feast went on, and the house was full of company, and people's hearts were full of the joyful
occasion, and the guests talked and made merry ;
and with them, and as one of them, was the Saviour
of the world, not checking their joy, not stopping
them *then* to make them hear of more serious matters,
but letting them go on, and take their fill of the
happiness which God had sent them, without reproof
or hindrance.

And more than this.   He helped their gladness ;
He was not content with gracing and sanctioning the
feast with His presence, He contributed to the feast
Himself: more than this, He condescended to put
forth His Divine power, as the Creator and Ruler of
nature, to supply what had run short at this occasion,
as we should call it, of mere earthly merry-making :
He condescended even to take care that the wine,
which He provided, should be better to their taste
than what they had had of their own.   And at the
time He provided for their enjoyment without letting
them know at whose hands they received it.   He
would do nothing openly.   He stopped His mother,
when she seemed to interfere ; He would not be
brought into public, as a worker of miracles.   Only
" the servants which drew the water knew " at the
time whose gift the wine was.   The ruler of the feast
wondered at the good wine which was come to gladden
the heart of the company ; but Christ added no word
to the benefit which He had done, and left the miracle
to work its effect.   After the feast was over, men

remembered the Holy Presence, and the gracious
mark of divine blessing and favour, which they had
seen or heard of.

And so Christ will be with us. He will be with
us not only in church and in prayer ; not only in
times of trouble and visitation, when we need Him
to help us, but in times of rejoicing and holiday, to
make our joy greater and our holiday brighter. He
is ready to be with us on those great days, which
are the white days of our life, and which we keep
in remembrance all our days after : a marriage, a
christening, a first sight and visit in some new place,
which fills us with wonder and gladness, a meeting
with an old friend long out of sight, a pleasant company, a happy day of pleasuring, an unexpected
piece of good fortune. Christ is willing to be with
us in these familiar things, which make up the course
of our day, and which to many are so full of happiness, and to few without much that they find enjoyment in : our morning and evening meal, our visit to
a friend, our social talk with a neighbour about our
common interests, the pleasure we receive from a
walk, an interesting book, the sight of a beautiful
country, the sound of music. He will be with us to
bless our table, to sanctify our hearts and feelings in
conversation, to warm our love to our friend, to give
fresh delight to the beautiful view, or the sweet
music, to throw a fresh charm over the pleasant talk,
to give a new meaning to the interesting book.

In all these delights and employments of our
common life He will be with us if we will " call
Him," as He was called to the marriage at Cana.
He does not despise them. He does not tell us to

give them up, as not belonging to the life of a Christian.   He does not come to change their nature or diminish their enjoyment.   He does not disturb, or frighten, or chill us in them.   He will be there as He was at Cana, only to increase them.

But what we have to take care of is, lest we refuse to have Him.   Our way is to think that it is enough to have Him at church ; that we do not want Him, that He has no business, at the pleasuring, by the fireside, at the daily meal, in the friendly talk, or the marriage feast.   And church takes up but a small part of our time, and these things, together with the works and cares of life, take up the rest ; so that it is little indeed that we have Christ with us. He is not wanted when we are busy ; and when we turn from our business to refresh and enjoy ourselves, He is not wanted either.

And yet He ought to be there.   He must be there if we are to work, and to enjoy ourselves as Christians, and not as mere worldlings.   He does not refuse to be with us : He does not think it beneath Him to join us.   It is because *we* have no faith ; because *we* do not believe or care about His love for us and His promises to us, if we say that it will spoil our pleasure, or hinder our business, to think of Him as being with us and blessing us.

See Him with you, by faith, and your conversation will not be less unrestrained nor your laugh less hearty, but with Him present you will shun all that is unholy, all that is wrong to say or to laugh at, all that is false, and proud, and ill-natured, and uncharitable.   Remember that He is with you, and your rejoicing will not be merely a rejoicing of this world, which is without thankfulness, and without kindness ; which puts out of your head the thought of eternal things, and makes you indisposed and cold towards them, and, at last, goes out like a candle when it is burnt out, and leaves only sorrow and bitterness behind.

Set Him before your face, and He will show you how far to go in your free and familiar talk, and where to stop. He will make you feel and see the bounds within which your mirth and enjoyment ought to be kept, and will also make it all the more cheerful and hearty within those bounds. Set Him before your face, and be thankful for His making your life so easy, and conversation so pleasant to you, for the daily meal that He spreads before you, and for the feast at which, from time to time, He collects you and your friends ; and your thankfulness will separate and sanctify your enjoyment from that feasting which forgets God and despises man, and your joy will come to you with the blessing of Him whose mercy is over all His works, and who has appointed a time for all things ;—a time to laugh, as well as a time to weep ; a time to dance, as well as a time to mourn ; a time to rejoice over His gifts in this world, and to use them without abusing them, as well as a time to give them up and to do without them.

2. Nor is this miracle without its peculiar lesson of encouragement and comfort. It was a miracle of turning the weaker into the stronger, the common into the precious, the despised into the excellent, the tasteless into that which gladdens the heart of man. It was not merely the increase and multiplication of

something already made, like the feeding of the five thousand with the five loaves. It was taking so common and cheap a thing as water, and raising it to the higher uses and excellences of wine ; changing and exalting it, and giving it new strength and new pleasantness. And is not this the type of the wonderful way in which Christ deals with the souls of those who put themselves into His hands? *He makes the water wine.*

A sinner turns in weakness and fear from his sins, hardly hoping that he can ever become fit for heaven ; hardly hoping that his infirmity will ever be healed ; hardly hoping that the will within him, which has so often yielded to temptation, can ever become strengthened to will what is good, and pure, and holy ; but he goes on, humbly trusting in Christ's mercy and faithfulness and love, striving with pain against his old sins, and their after entanglement, but striving in faith ; and in time, according to such an one's faith and earnestness, the old man begins to be destroyed and the new man to be formed in him. *The water is made wine.*

Or God puts on us some duty above our strength. We seem as if we should be crushed to the ground by what God requires of us, by the confusion and misery which must come on us in doing what He has called us to. But, if the person so called goes on in Christ's strength, he finds in time that what once seemed hard, comes by degrees to be easier and lighter ; he finds that he can do, by Christ's help, what he thought he never should do ; his fear is turned into boldness, his hanging back into forwardness. *The water is made wine.*

Or some grievous dispensation visits him : one
that he has long made up his mind he never could
bear ; some sickness, some separation, some downfall.
It comes, and Christ strengthens him to bear it ; it
comes, and, with it, new experience of Christ's tenderness and love ; it comes, and he finds it a visitation
of comfort, and the secret communication of peace
that he never knew before.   It comes, and what
threatened to be so terrible, opens to him the
windows of heaven, and draws aside the veil from
the mercy-seat of God.   The earthly sorrow has
been glorified with light and grace from heaven.
The water has been made wine.

And Christ is ready to do this for all who will
trust Him ; to take them by surprise, as it were, as
He did the guests at Cana, and make the water wine
when they least expect it.   Only let us attend to
what was said then : " His mother saith to the servants, Whatsoever he saith unto you, do it."   He
must not be pressed to work before His time.
Only let us do whatever He saith unto us, and be
sure that in His own way He will do the rest, in a
more wonderful way than we could either have done
or imagined it.

Call Him to be with you, in the house and by
the way ; when you are glad as well as when you
are driven to remember Him by sorrow.   And so
shall you find Him ever ready to prepare a table for
you, and to crown your cup with joy, till He brings
you to that marriage supper of the Lamb, and calls
you to eat bread in the kingdom of God.

VI

THE DANGER OF DELAY

" What must I do to be saved ? "—ACTS xvi. 30.

THE man who first asked this question was an
ignorant heathen, who had never heard of Jesus
Christ, except, perhaps, to blaspheme Him, or mock
at His name and gospel.   It was, as you remember,
the gaoler at Philippi, who was frightened when the
earthquake shook the prison, where St. Paul had
been shut up, and brought before this poor untaught
man the terrors of his own sins and conscience, and
the prospect of death and the wrath of God, without
any means of saving himself.   He knew no better.
All he knew was, that sin is sure to be found out,
and punished at last.   But he rushed to his prisoners,
St. Paul and Silas, and cried out to them, " Sirs,
what must I do to be saved ? "   He knew nothing
of the Gospel news which they brought.   He only
knew his own danger and sin, without being certain
that they could deliver him from it.

Very different indeed are we : we, who have been
baptized into Christ's Name, and been taken into
covenant with Him, and have heard of Him all our
lives.   Very different are we, even those among us who
know least.   For the most ignorant and neglected

among us has had advantages and blessings, and opportunities of knowing, which the poor heathen gaoler never had. Those of us who know least, know more than he did ; and might,. but for their own fault, have known much more. Yet in a Christian land, and among those who know the name of Christ, it is still very necessary to ask the question which the heathen gaoler first asked.

The return of this season of Lent reminds us once more, as it has done so often before, how necessary it is to ask it. These solemn days of humiliation and repentance which began on Ash Wednesday call to us all to ask ourselves the question, " What must I do to be saved ? " For the days of Lent are a call once more, from Almighty God to His people, to consider, each man for himself, what is going to become of him. They are the solemn declaring to the whole world of God's terrible and most certain judgment on all kinds of sin, and on sinners of every sort, high and low, if they still go on sinning, in spite of God's long-suffering and mercy. These days of Lent are the public warning forced upon us once more, that sin will be our ruin, if it is not put away and pardoned before we die ; and that there is one way open, and *only one* way, for our escape from death and hell ; the way of true repentance, and turning to God, with a steadfast, and true, and obedient faith in Jesus Christ. The evil of sin is set before us, on the one hand ; its deceitfulness, its obstinacy, cleaving to our souls, like some dreadful and deadly disease, which it is difficult to cure ; its manifold shapes and sorts ; the way in which it keeps hold on, and surprises, even good men ; its hatefulness in God's sight; the certainty that, unless it is healed and taken away, it must bring our souls to ruin, just as a consumption or a fever, if not stopped, must kill our bodies. And, on the other hand, we have set before us all that God has done and spoken, to save us from this destruction. Over and over again we are warned to repent, we are promised that He will spare those who *do* repent; we are shown all the marvellous means which His grace has provided, to save us from our sins,—not only to pardon and wash them out, but also to cleanse us from their power, to change our sinful hearts and to make us new creatures; to strengthen us against the enemies of our salvation, and to help us to walk worthy of our calling as His servants and children.

These are the thoughts which are *forced* on us at this time. If we go to Church at all, we cannot help feeling that we are in the midst of a time of repentance, when a great deal is said about sin,—its certain dangers, and our own share in the sins of the world. We cannot put any of these thoughts from us, even if we harden ourselves against them, or make a mock of them. God is indeed calling us loudly to repentance, as the only way of escaping from the wrath to come; as loudly and as solemnly as John the Baptist called the Jews, when he went forth preaching in the wilderness, and showing them their sins.

"What must I do—what am I doing—to be saved?" that is the broad, simple, and most awful question which this season sets before us. In what road am I walking—where am I going to—where shall I end? with God, or with the devil?

C.   E

There are many important questions to be attended to in this world, for all of us; many important businesses to be looked after, and to take up our time and thoughts. God does not forbid our thinking about them. He gives us plenty of time to employ ourselves about them. But after all said and done, there is one question, one simple question which is above all others; one important business, in comparison with which, if it is not attended to, all others are like chaff and smoke;—the salvation of our souls. The question is, Are we in the way to be saved, or in the way to be lost? That business God lays before us now: that question He calls on us to attend to, and answer, now: and in God's name, and by His authority, I put that question before each of your consciences, and require you, as you will answer for it before the Great Judge at the last day, to see what you can say to it. Are you trying to walk in the way of salvation? If not, where are you going to? And what is your hope against the threatenings and the power of God?

" What must I do to be saved ? " It is a question for us all : a question which means that we have, all of us, need to look into our souls and consciences, and to see whether we are using this short life of ours on earth to any good purpose, or whether we are throwing it away, letting it slip, without any fruit ; alas ! even worse than that, whether we are laying up for ourselves at last a heavy load of con- demnation and misery that never will end.

" What must I do to be saved ? " It is not only a question for those who have not yet thought on religion at all,—for those who have yet to begin the

Christian life, the life of the new creature. It is a question also for those who have lived the longest as Christ's professed and earnest servants, for those who have begun, perhaps long ago, to repent and fight against their sins, and to try and please God in their daily life. It is a question even for those to whom faith in Jesus Christ is no new thing ; who have already put their trust in Him, and are really walking according to their faith. Yes, my brethren, it is a question even for you who may have a comfortable hope that you have believed in Christ with your whole heart, and who remember Him in your ways. For sin is a subtle and deceitful thing, and sin will most surely deceive and entrap you, in spite of your earnestness, unless you are on the watch against it. You know what the condition of your warfare is. There is no standing still in it. There is no peace or compromise with your mortal enemy, your enemy who will hate you till your death, and, till the very last breath you draw, will try to tempt you away from God. There is no truce in that war. There is no standing still in that race. If you are not going forward in the way of God, you *must* be going backward. If you are not improving in the fruits of the Spirit, you must be worse than you were some time back ; if you are not getting stronger you must be getting weaker ; if you are not conquering your besetting sins, they are conquering you ; if you are not pleasing God more and more, you are pleasing Him —oh ! dreadful thought !—less and less. Is not this then a question even for you who have already begun to feel anxiety about your souls? Have not you, too, to ask, " What must I do, what am I doing, to be saved?" None of us can trust to his beginnings, however good and promising. We must see from time to time where we are going, or we shall drift out of the right path, like a ship sailing without a pilot: however fair the wind may have been when we started, we shall fall among the rocks and quicksands, unless we look to see what course we are following.

And who knows more surely the terrible power of sin than he who has truly and earnestly tried to repent of it, to root it out of his heart, to fight against it? And shall any of us, however far we may be advanced in religion, turn a deaf ear to the question, "What must I do to be saved?" and think it no concern of ours when the forty days of Lent remind us both of the evil of sin generally, and of our own particular sins, and their guilt besides; and warn us to take care, lest while we are self-confident, and think ourselves safe, and in the right way, some secret sin may be entrapping us, and leading us unawares, to lose all our labour and hopes,—leading us, it may be, to destruction?

"What must I do to be saved?" It is a question for those to ask themselves who think that they shall be saved by leading a quiet, orderly, and respectable life in the eyes of men; by keeping out of gross and shameful sins; by bearing a good character in the world. *Will* such a life save us? That is the question; a question, indeed, of the deepest importance to many, because so many take it for granted that it will, and go on trusting to the chance that they are right. *Will* such a life save us? a respectable life, in which we do not actually go against God, but

merely forget Him, merely never think of Him?
My brethren, if there be any here who are trusting in
such a life, there is only one way in which you can
find out about it, in which you can get an answer to be
depended on.   Look to the Bible—see what it says
about your question.   I read in the Bible that God,
though the God of love, is a jealous God; that He
requires us not only *not* to forget Him, but to love
Him, and to love Him best; to love Him with all our
hearts; that He will not have lip-service; that we
cannot serve God and Mammon; that without holiness,—and holiness means a good deal more than
being respectable and doing no harm,—no man can
see the Lord; that God searches the hearts and
reins; that He looks not on the outward appearance,
as man does, but on the heart; that we may commit
murder and adultery in our hearts, by angry and by
unclean thoughts, though we outwardly do nothing
that men can see or find fault with; and that at
last God will bring not only our outward deeds, but
every idle word and every secret thing into judgment;
and that even the servant who hid his lord's talent
will be cast out into outer darkness.   I read that it
is only by the grace of Jesus Christ that any one can
be saved; only by repenting, and believing, and
loving, and serving Jesus Christ that there is hope
for any of us.   That is what seems to me the answer
which the Bible gives to the question, "Will a
respectable character and a quiet life save a man?"
Do you think that you can find a different one?   No,
my brethren, you do not, as soon as you come to think
of it; but the thing is, you do your best not to think
of it,—not to frighten and tease yourselves by asking

the question. You put away the thought, you try to escape the question by shutting your eyes to it, by burying your fears when they arise in the multitude of your earthly cares and business. For that very reason I call on you now,—now that the curse of God on unrepented sin is again solemnly proclaimed in our ears,—to ask that question. I beseech you, in the name of Christ, think, what are you doing to escape that wrath? how do you hope to avoid that curse?

The curse of sin made Jesus Christ fast forty days in the wilderness,—made Him suffer and die on the cross; and do you think that a good character, and not hurting any one, and doing as much of religious duty as will make men speak well of you,—and, for the rest, taking the world easy, and getting what good you can out of it,—that this is enough to save your souls, and bring you to be with Jesus Christ for ever?

But what are *you* going to do to be saved who have not even the miserable cloke and shelter of an outwardly fair and decent life to screen you from the wrath of God against sin? What are *you* going to do to be saved who openly break God's laws by gross and presumptuous sin? You, who sin with a high hand in the face of heaven,—you, to whom all the world, all who know you, bear witness week after week that you are sinners, even in the eyes of men? What are you going to do to be saved who have all your life long despised God's commandments, and rebelled against Him? Who have set your heart on sinning, in spite of His having sworn that He would punish you; and in spite of His having promised that, if you would leave your sin and turn to Him, He would pardon and bless you? What are you going to do who are getting on in life, who are drawing near to the edge of the grave, with all your sins on your head, unforgiven, crying out for vengeance?

God has said, " Though your sins be as scarlet, they shall be as white as snow ; though they be red like crimson, they shall be as wool." He has offered you His Holy Spirit to change and cleanse your hearts. He has said, " Turn yourselves from all your transgressions; so iniquity shall not be your ruin." This is His way of salvation. But you would have none of it. You would not do what God bids you do, and offers to help you in doing, to be saved. Then, what *are* you going to do to be saved? " Now also the axe is laid unto the root of the trees : every tree therefore which bringeth not forth good fruit is hewn down, and cast into the fire." " It is a fearful thing to fall into the hands of the living God." " On the ungodly He shall rain snares, fire and brimstone, storm and tempest; this shall be their portion to drink." You do not choose God's way of mercy : what are you going to do to escape from His power and wrath? What do you mean to do to be saved? Day after day you add sin to sin. The devil, your tempter now, and your accuser afterwards at God's judgment seat, is marking them down, one by one,—every oath you swear, every lust that you give way to, every drunken riot that you fall into, every lie that you tell, every act of spite and revenge that you commit, every tale of slander that you carry, every theft, or dishonesty, or unfair dealing you are guilty of—all are marked

down against you ; and at the end the devil is ready
to meet you with the black list and number of your
sins.　What do you expect to do or say against
him when, with that dreadful accusation, he claims
you for his own ; as one who did him service on
earth, as one to whom *he* did service too, by giving
you the pleasures for which you have sold yourself
to him,—as one who was always his on earth, and
whom, therefore, he may take for his servant in hell.
What will you say against him ?　Will you plead
against him then the precious blood of Christ ?
Alas ! you despised it on earth.　You were made a
member of Christ once, but you broke away, and fell
from Him : you crucified Christ by your sins, and
trod Him under your feet.　Will you cry to God for
His mercy ?　Alas ! when it was the time of grace
you hardened yourself ; " then shall it be too late to
knock when the door shall be shut : and too late to
cry for mercy when it is the time of justice."

Oh, my brethren, in that day, when the day of
salvation is over, what will you do ? unless you are
stronger than the devil, to whom you have sold
yourself, and who will then be able to have you in
his power ; or than God, whom you have forgotten,
mocked, blasphemed, and rejected ?

If there are any here who are going on doing what
they know to be wrong, following unrepented sin,
and who have never yet said to themselves, " What
must I do to be saved ? " let them ask themselves that
question now.　If they have put away the question from
their minds, and shut their eyes to it, it is put before
them now.　Unless they stop their ears, they cannot
help hearing it now.　" What are you going to do to

be saved ? "   It is God's question, though He sends it
by man's voice.   It comes to them now ; they must
try to answer it, or despise it, and pass on.   They
are, as it were, come to where two roads divide.
They must take one of them.   This very day, this
very hour, this very sermon, may be the turning-
point of their lives for the time to come.   God is
calling them now.   He is calling them to make up
their minds whether they will choose Him, or take
their chance of everlasting damnation.   He is calling
them to repentance now ; it may be the last time.
If they listen now, it may be the beginning of their
salvation ; if they turn away now, God may never
again give them the opportunity, or the grace, to hear
and understand the warning He has sent us, to flee
from the wrath to come.   Their hardening in sin,
their final impenitence, their ruin at last, may depend
on to-day and its issues.   To-day the way of salvation
is open to them ; to-morrow it may be shut for ever,
as it was to Judas, and to Pharaoh, even though they
were not at once cut off.

What will you do to be saved ?   One thing I
pray you, do not say in your heart, " I will wait till
I am sick, and near my end ; and then the clergyman
will come to me, and read to me, and say some
prayers, and I shall hear about the mercy of God,
and I shall trust in that mercy."   This is what many
do say, if not openly, yet in their hearts.   They live
as long as they can in sin and disobedience, impenitent and unconverted, and comfort themselves
that somehow or other it will be well with them at
the last.

It is quite true that it is never too late for true

repentance—*true* repentance, mind—not *any* repentance, but repentance to which God gives grace to be true. But a *late* repentance is very seldom a *true* repentance, in those who have had warning of the danger of leaving repentance to the last Such persons know that they ought to repent sooner ; they have known it all along ; they have made it a reason for sinning without fear that they should be able to make up at the last moment. Now to such persons the Gospel has a plain word ; " To him who knoweth to do good, and doeth it not, to him it is sin."

May God give us all grace to return into our own hearts. May His great and heavy judgments awaken us from our dream of safety and selfish ease, to see how we are getting ready for that judgment seat to which so many are called with short warning. " The day of the Lord so cometh as a thief in the night." Merciful Lord, give us grace to prepare, while there is yet time, to be called before Thy face.

VII

THE COMFORT OF REPENTANCE

" For while I held my tongue : my bones consumed away through my
daily complaining. For Thy hand is heavy upon me day and
night : and my moisture is like the drought in summer."—PSALM
xxxii. 3, 4.

WE all of us know that repentance of our sins is
necessary for us if we hope to be saved in the next
world. We all of us know how much true repentance
does for us in preparing us to receive the mercy and
blessing of God. True repentance is the path, the
only path, of forgiveness, of restoration to God's
favour, of becoming good and holy. And therefore,
in the solemn words in which God's pardon is
declared to " all them that truly repent and
unfeignedly believe His holy Gospel," we are
exhorted to " beseech Him to grant us true repentance, and His Holy Spirit, that those things may
please Him which we do at this present ; and that
the rest of our life hereafter may be pure and holy;
so that at the last we may come to His eternal
joy." But I am not going at present to speak
of the benefit of repentance ; nor of the necessity of
it to all who have sinned and done wrong, if they
would hope to shake off the burden of their sins.
I wish to speak of another way of looking at it.

I wish to say a few words about the *comfort* of repentance.

By repentance I mean breaking off with our sins altogether. I do not mean merely being sorry for them. I do not mean merely looking them fairly in the face, fairly giving way to our conscience, and admitting the truth when our conscience tries to convince us that we have done wrong. I do not mean merely the honest, manly, owning against ourselves that " we have done those things which we ought not to have done, and have left undone those things which we ought to have done." All this is very necessary, very important ; without it there can be no true repentance. But it is short of repentance.

Confession and acknowledgment of sin is part of repentance ; it is the beginning and foundation of repentance ; but it is the beginning, and not the whole. Sorrow and self-reproach, the broken and humbled heart, is part of repentance ; but by itself it is not repentance. It may stop short of repentance. There is no true and real repentance until, after seeing our sins, after acknowledging our sins, after lamenting and being sorry about them, after being ashamed of them, after asking mercy for them, we break off from what we know to be wrong and sinful. Then, at last, is repentance fulfilled in earnest. Then, at last, we can begin to speak no longer merely of pain of conscience, of confession, of regret and self-accusation, but of what is in truth repentance.

Now, besides all the other good things that there are in repentance, there is great and solid *comfort*. There is comfort in much that is short of true repentance. There is a kind of comfort, not a very real and trustworthy one, but for the time a kind of shadow of comfort when we feel sorry for our misdoings. There is very likely pain and bitterness of heart. According as our souls are awakened to the truth, according as our hearts are quick to feel, according as our consciences are tender and honest, there may be very deep and sharp pain, yet there will be a comfort even in feeling this pain. There will be the comfort that there always is in seeing the truth, in feeling ourselves awake out of deceit and falsehood, in knowing that we are alive to what we ought to be alive to. But it is a comfort which, *if it is all*, will not stay long with us, will not profit us much.

There is a better and more true comfort in being able, fairly and honestly, to own and confess our sins. It is a comfort spoken of in the thirty-second Psalm. As long as the Psalmist tried to hide from himself that he was doing wrong, he was miserable. As long as he tried to shelter himself under vain excuses, which his conscience told him were false and hollow,—as long as he was too proud and too much ashamed to own his sin, there was a load and a grief on his heart. " For while I held my tongue, my bones consumed away through my daily complaining. For Thy hand is heavy upon me day and night, and my moisture is like the drought in summer." Then he resolved to be bold and honest to his own sin : " I will acknowledge my sin unto Thee, and mine unrighteousness have I not hid. I said, I will confess my sins unto the Lord." And then came comfort,—the comfort of the sense of

being at peace with the Father who forgives the
sins of His children when they own their sin,—" And
so Thou forgavest the wickedness of my sin :"—the
comfort of feeling that there was no longer a war
between him and the mercy and righteousness of
God ; that, having confessed all, he had nothing
more to hide, nothing more to make him ashamed.
He could venture to think of God's nearness and
God's power : " For this shall every one that is
godly make his prayer unto Thee in a time when
Thou mayest be found ; but in the great water-
floods they shall not come nigh him." Then did
comfort come to the sinner, who, without flinching
and making excuses, dared to look his sins in the
face ; gave up hiding them, and laid them before the
eyes of God and the light of his own conscience.

But this comfort is not to be depended upon, and
will not last unless something more follows. It is a
strange thing, yet it is a very certain one, that people
can confess and acknowledge their wrong-doings, and
yet make no real attempt to put an end to them
and change them. There is, as I said, a comfort
when we have done wrong in manfully owning that
we did wrong. But it is possible to rest on that
comfort, to stay in it, and get no farther. And then,
whatever comfort our acknowledgment of our sins
may have given us either goes away or turns into a
very dangerous delusion and self-deceit.—This is not
yet what I mean by the comfort of repentance.

When we do wrong there are two ways in which
our sins are made bitter and troublesome to us.
Either we go on doing wrong, knowing that it is
wrong, with our conscience ever convicting, reproach-

ing, condemning, burdening us; and that is a very
wretched, miserable way to live.   Or else there is a
struggle between what is good and what is bad in us;
a daily wrestling within our souls, between our wish to
obey and please God, and our wish to do something
which He will not give us leave to do; a battle,
sometimes swinging to one side, sometimes to the
other, between the powers of grace and righteousness and the powers of death and evil.   And in the
struggle our heart is, perhaps, torn to pieces.   We
cannot make up our minds which service we will
take.   Now we resolve to follow what is right; then
comes something which tempts us grievously, and
we cannot resist it, and we give up our resolutions
and go after what is wrong.   To-day the good
influence seems to have gained the victory; we feel
how pleasant, how easy, how good it is, to choose
the right way and to walk in it.   To-morrow all
may be changed.   Temptation meets us; the pleasure
of some forbidden thing seems beyond our power to
resist.   We give way, and find ourselves clean opposite
to what we were yesterday,—clean opposite in our
feelings and hearts; liking what we hated, hating
what then we liked, following what then we shrank
from, turning away from what then seemed so true
and beautiful and good.

Is not this a miserable state?   Is it not miserable, if we are living boldly and openly in sin and
wrong, to have our conscience continually telling us
in our secret hearts that we *are* wrong, that we *know*
we are wrong?   Is it not miserable to have this
conscience, which we cannot get rid of, cannot help
hearing when it speaks, which we cannot put down

by a rude and scornful answer? Is it not miserable to have our own heart telling us that *it* judges us, that *it* condemns us?

Or, again, is it not miserable not to be able to make up our minds between what is right and what is sinful? Is it not miserable to be tossed about from one to the other; to be torn to pieces within our souls by going first after one and then after the other; by not being able to give ourselves to either heartily and perfectly; by having one part of our life always coming in to disturb and quarrel with the other? Is not this wretchedness?

And yet, unless a man has utterly sold himself to evil, unless a man's conscience is dead and perfectly destroyed within him, one of these two must be the state of every one who knowingly and willingly follows what is wrong. Either he does wrong with his conscience always accusing and vexing him; or he is divided between right and wrong, sometimes follows one side and sometimes the other, and is torn in pieces by the vain attempt to serve two masters, and join together things which the eternal laws of God will not allow to be joined together in peace.

Seeing, feeling, owning, confessing all this will not of itself mend or relieve it. There is only one way,—breaking off for good what is wrong. And this is repentance. Repentance is, *after* we have seen and felt and confessed and bewailed our misdeeds and wrong-doings, really breaking off from them, really giving them up. And this will not only bring us safety, forgiveness, the favour of God, the hope of everlasting rest; it will bring us, besides this, comfort.

Because it will set us at peace with ourselves ; it will put an end to that fierce strife and storm within us by driving out for good one of the two powers which are fighting to gain our soul. Let us only choose one side. Let us only make up our mind what to follow, and half the trouble and difficulty of what we have to do is at once cut off. Our path may be rugged, but it is plain, straightforward, simple. We know that our steps are in the right direction. We do not lose ground by trying to go two ways, and by going first one way and then the opposite. The work may be hard and trying, but our heart within us is one with us ; our conscience is on our side to cheer us in our work. So is it when we have once made our choice by true repentance. There will be a wrench perhaps. We may have to give up what we can hardly part with. We may have to tear ourselves away with pain and tears. We may have to make a heavy sacrifice. This is what Christ means when He talks of cutting off the right hand and plucking out the right eye to save the soul. But when once the resolution is taken, when once the wrong thing, the evil tempta-tion is finally given up and parted from for ever, then comes peace,—then comes the feeling, which swallows up all others, of having done the right thing. And then, at last, our life moves on with that perpetual and unfailing comfort which nothing can take away, of having, for good, separated ourselves from what we knew to be bad and forbidden,—of having given up for ever what we knew to be the wrong path,—of having finally broken off with the things which disturbed us even while they tempted

C.   F

us, and which, however sweet they might be in the
first taste, turned bitter in the mouth afterwards.

This is repentance, and this is the comfort which
repentance brings with it.   With its trials, with its
sacrifices, with its self-denials (and repentance has all
this), let us not forget that it has also comfort which
outweighs them all—the comfort of being at peace
not only with God but with our own hearts.

We can bear much when we are at peace within.
That which makes trouble so dreadful, so hard to
endure, is our own secret knowledge that we are
unfaithful to our duty, unfaithful to Christ and our
Father.   That which gives the sting to our difficulties is the conscience which tells us of our own sin ;
which tells us that we have not yet made our honest
choice between what is right and what is wrong ;
which tells us that, while we are trying to think
ourselves followers of what is good, we are, under-
hand, trying to see if we cannot have dealings with
sin.

But let us break the yoke.   Let us not only be
sorry for what we have done wrong, but honestly
seek the grace and help of God to have done with it
for ever.   Let us turn our backs on it, not looking
behind, but with undivided heart giving it up for
ever.   The wrench, painful as it may be, will soon
be forgotten.   The sacrifice, whatever it may be,
will soon be made up for an hundredfold.   But the
rest, the consolation, the peace which will come at
the very first, will go on increasing for ever to the
end.   Daily we shall find our path more clear.
Daily we shall find how many troubles, how many
difficulties, we have saved ourselves by having taken

our side, by having for good separated ourselves from what is wrong.

The beginning of repentance may be with clouds and storms, with perplexity and distress and anguish of heart. But let it be repentance in earnest,—the earnest and honest breaking off from what is evil and sinful ; and the clouds will soon give way to calm and sunshine, and it will be to us the path leading us through peace and contentment, and the rest of a good conscience here, to the rest of glory, without regret and without stain, in God's kingdom in heaven.

VIII

STRIVING AFTER PERFECTION

" Be ye therefore perfect, even as your Father which is in heaven is perfect."—St. Matthew v. 48.

" PERFECT," of course, does not mean anything impossible or inconceivable, as that man should, even if a saint, be without sin and faultiness, or that he should really be absolutely like his Father in heaven. Our Lord spoke to reasonable men, and did not expect His words to be understood unreasonably. By "perfect" He meant something which men might be if they would,—something which, by the help of God's grace, they might become, without ceasing to be men, before they die. He meant that they should not be willingly, and by their own fault, less good than they might be. He meant that they should not willingly, and by their own fault, stop short of what they saw to be right, and saw that they ought to try to become. He meant that, as God is not good at some times and not at others,—as He is always good,—so men should feel it their duty to try always to be like their Father in heaven. He meant that men should not pick and choose among God's commandments ; that they should not keep them as much as they liked, and no further ; that they should not think they had done their duty by an outward observance of the letter, without any care for observing them in their own hearts, and according to their spirit and meaning. He meant, not that every Christian was to do everything that was spoken of as good and holy in the Bible, or that other Christians might be called to, but that, in doing his duty, every Christian was to feel that he was bound to do his best in his own calling.

It must strike us, when we read the New Testament, that for men to do their best *then* meant something very different from what we believe ourselves called to now. There is nothing wonderful in this. Differences of times and circumstances make differences of duties. We live in quiet times ; but suppose we lived in rough and troubled times, plainly our worldly duties, the things we should all be called upon to do, would be very different. In war, or if a country is filled with enemies, it is plain that people must feel called on for many things for which they are not called on in peace ; they must make up their minds to trials, hardships, sacrifices,— as a matter of course, which they would not think of under other circumstances. So it is plain that in the days of the New Testament men were called to do their best in a different way from what they are now.

There was a time when it was said, " If thou wilt be perfect "—that is, if thou wilt do thy best— " sell all, and give to the poor, and take up thy cross, and come and follow Me." When this was but what the Master did, what wonder if the disciples were called to do the same. There was a time when it was said, " Take no thought for your life, or for your raiment : " " for after all these things do the Gentiles seek ; for your heavenly Father knoweth that ye have need of these things." " Take therefore no thought for the morrow ; for the morrow shall take thought for the things of itself." There was a time when for a man to pull down his barns and build greater was mere laying up treasure on the earth, for which he received the reproof of his Lord and Judge : " Thou fool, this night thy soul shall be required of thee." There was a time when it was said, " Unless a man hate father and mother, and brother and sister, and wife and children, yea, and his own life also, he cannot be My disciple."

There was a time when Christians had to take, for their regular, natural lot, trouble, persecution, abuse, hatred, sorrow and suffering of every kind ; when their blessing was mourning, and their promise was tribulation ; when their great Apostle could describe their condition in these words, " If in this life only we have hope in Christ, we are of all men most miserable."

The call everywhere was, to deny themselves ; their continual lesson and example, the cross of Christ ; their unceasing warning against the world, against riches, against being full, and rejoicing now. To do their best then, to accomplish the conversion of the world, Christians had, as a regular thing, to take up the lot and live the life of missionaries or of soldiers ; a life of hardship and danger ; a life which gave up the ordinary works and thoughts of this world ; a life in which everything of the dearest and the most natural had to be utterly sacrificed and surrendered to the great call of duty ; a life with violent and painful death waiting at every step, and sure to come at last.

So had Christ used life to work out the salvation of the world. Those who were with Christ, and followed Him, were called to the same thing : " the disciple is not above his Master." The Gospel began in the hardest self-denial and suffering ; and its first words and first days answered to this beginning.

This is what we most certainly find when we read the New Testament ; and it is equally certain that it is a very different state of things from any-thing we have ever known. Our call, our trial, comes in a different shape. We are still called to deny ourselves, but it is not by leaving all. We are still called to take up and bear the cross, but it is not by persecution and the martyr's death. God still chastises those whom He loves, but not by appoint-ing to them a life like St. Paul's.

We believe that God's providence, which has ordered the course of the world, has given us peace, and means us to labour and be industrious, and gives us, with His blessing, the fruits of our labour. He makes us households, and bids us rejoice in them ; He bids us use the world, and yet not abuse it ; He keeps far from us His scourges and great plagues ; He calls upon us, and gives us the opportunity to " lead a quiet and peaceable life in all godliness and honesty." This is our condition. Our trial is not in war, but in peace. Trials we may be sure we have ; the trial goes on in our inmost hearts just as truly, and, if we only knew it, just as sharply, as it did when men were called to leave all for Christ. But it certainly is not the same thing to be tried by being called to leave all, and to be tried by having to serve God faithfully, to keep ourselves pure, to be unselfish, true-hearted, unworldly, in our quiet pleasant home. We need not be afraid that God leaves us without trials,—severe, searching, refining trials,—in spite of all the changes which have come upon the world, and the altered life and discipline which Christians have now to go through.

It is true that times are changed. But for this very reason that times are so changed and so soft-ened to us, there is the more need for marking our Lord's words, and thinking what they meant, what they still mean. They may have become, in a literal sense, inapplicable. But they were the words of life and truth, meant for all ages ; and for all ages they must have their eternal lesson. And if they sound stern and hard and severe, the more reason is it that we should remember that they were once *really spoken* and *really obeyed*; and that we should see in them a warning against the dangers our own easier life is likely to run into.

"Take no thought for the morrow" meant some-thing different to those to whom it was first said from what it means to us, whose business it is to work for our livelihood, and to provide for our own. But surely to us it preaches as solemn and earnest a lesson as it did at first. For if it is our duty to work, it is our danger lest our hearts should be entangled in our work ; if it is our duty to look forward, it is our danger to trust our own right hand, or wealth, and to forget that we are every moment in the hands of God. If it is our duty to use the means and talents His Providence gives us, it is our danger to forget the Giver in the gifts,—the end in the means,—the real power behind, in the outward instruments, the bread, the raiment, the money, by which God supports us. If it is our duty to work hard, as if all depended on ourselves, it is our danger to forget that all depends still more on God. If it is our duty to value what He gives, it is our danger to give our whole heart to it, to care and be anxious only for what this world is to give us ; to sink into the love of gain, the bands of a worldly mind, the blind worship of mammon.

With such dangers in our hearts, is it not well that we should remember who has said, even if He has not put it upon us in its literal sternness, " Take no thought for the morrow " ? Has it not all the more force for us because our way of life is one which necessarily has to take thought for the morrow ?—in which we should be neglecting our plainest duties if we did not take thought for the morrow? Yet is it not always and equally true that the morrow is not in our power? that the work and the labour are ours, but only with Him is the accomplishment and the reward ? All our thinking and care cannot do anything, unless He, whom we are so ready to forget and set aside, is pleased to grant His blessing.

To the Christian of eighteen hundred years ago, who left all to follow Christ, and to the Christian of to-day, who believes that he fulfils God's will by industry, saving, and forethought,—to both equally the morrow is not theirs ; the morrow belongs to God. Both have to do their duties, though the duties are so different ; both are equally told by their Master to

leave what shall come of their duty to-morrow to Him
to whom alone to-morrow belongs.   Do your work,
whatever it is, to-day ; then remember that it is really
in God's hands, and leave it in His hands.   To-morrow
will come to you, if it is His will ; and with to-morrow,
to-morrow's rewards, to-morrow's blessings, if you
deserve it.   If not, all you can do will not ensure
to-morrow.   Do not set your heart on it as if it was
yours, to make your own.

"Take no thought for the morrow" means now
as it meant then, *Trust God first, and wholly, and
honestly*.   And that is a lesson as needful for one
time as for another.

And so with other of our Lord's sayings, which
at first seem only to belong to the first days.   Their
meaning to us may not be in what they directly say;
but we shall find it, if we consider the reason why
they were said, and what it is which is implied in
them.   In what our Lord says of riches, He *does*
mean to say that riches are a real and dangerous
trial.   In what He says of turning one cheek to
him who has smitten the other, He *does* mean to
insist on the royal greatness of humility, and giving
way, and bearing injustice ; it was the greatness
which He showed Himself.   In what He says of the
blessedness of suffering and mourning, He *does* mean
that men are not always happiest when they have
what they like, nor always most to be pitied when
they are cut off from what is pleasant to flesh and
blood,—when their lot is sickness, and narrow means,
and earthly disappointment.

But, anyhow, now as formerly, the command of
our Master holds, "Be ye perfect."   Do your best.

Do not let yours be an irregular, up-and-down, half-and-half attempt to do God's will, to live according to your conscience and light. Do not use two measures, and false weights in what you do as your religious service. Do your best; do it with a whole heart; let all be thorough.

And surely now, if ever, this appeal ought to come home to us. For now God of His mercy has spared us the trials of early times. Now for the storms of those days God has given us peace. Instead of the absolute privation and forsaking of all earthly things, He lets us enjoy our homes in quiet; instead of persecution, He protects and keeps us safe; instead of the real, literal cross of shame and blood, forced upon us whether we will or no, He trusts our trial, our self-denial, our self-discipline to our own judgment, our own honesty. He has taken off from us the heavy load of outward suffering, which to the end of things men will always shrink from, even though it may not really be so heavy as many inward trials. But so it is. He has lightened what we feel to be a very heavy part of the trial which others have had to go through.

How much more reason for doing our part as we ought! How much more reason for doing our best, when it is made so much less hard and painful to do it! Shall we make it a reason for failing in small trials, that God has saved us from great ones? Shall we not rather desire to prove that our honesty, our thankfulness, will *bear* being put to a less severe trial; that we are not unmindful of the difference which God has made, in giving us times of peace and gentle quiet; that, even without the fiery trial, the forsaking all, the homeless life, the perpetual poverty, the martyr's death, men may yet hear, and answer to the Lord's call to be perfect,—may yet be in earnest in trying to do their best.

THE MIND OF JESUS CHRIST

"Let this mind be in you, which was also in Christ Jesus."—
PHILIPPIANS ii. 5.

ST. PAUL tells us that we ought to have the mind of Jesus Christ. We ought to try to have that mind—to think as He did, to have something of His Spirit and feeling—at all times. But especially when we are going to have before our minds His Cross and Passion—that in which His "mind" showed itself in so wonderful a way, we should wish to understand and share that mind. We cannot believe in the Cross, we cannot understand it, without having something of the Spirit which led to the Cross. Let us think what was the "mind which was in Christ Jesus."

The mind of Jesus Christ, as St. Paul speaks of it here, was His Infinite Compassion and His Infinite Humility.

Men were very miserable, and He took pity on them, and came here to give them comfort and hope. We do not want the Bible to tell us that, without the light and hope which He has brought us, man's condition, as a whole, is strangely miserable. Even with what the Bible tells us about how it began, we can understand but little of the reasons why it is so. But we want no one to tell us the fact that sin is in the world ; that sin brings on men unhappiness and ruin in every shape. We want no one to tell us, we know it too well ourselves, what sickness is, and pain, and weakness. We want no one to tell us what it is to have great hopes, and see them fail ; to put our confidence in what seems immovable and strong, and see what we trusted in break up and sink, like a wrecked ship. And though we have our turns of light and darkness, of joy and sorrow, and though there is indeed so much happiness in the world, and endless reasons to be thankful for all that we enjoy so bountifully, yet, after all, and at last, there comes one thing that there is no getting rid of,—that gives the measure of our condition here ; that turns the scale against every man in the end. The end of a man's life may be with all kinds of prosperity, but the end is, he must die. The closing scene is not, as in a book or a story, one of success and satisfaction ; in real life it is of mourning, of separation, and death. That is a man's condition ; and to make it worse, he tears himself and other men, and scourges them, and makes them still more miserable, by his sins— by his selfishness, his cruelty, his greediness, his wrong-dealing.

This was what Jesus Christ saw among men : the natural condition of the world ; its condition as men knew it by experience—a condition which, *without* the hope and salvation brought by Christ, is indeed dark and dreadful. Truly does the Apostle say, "There is none other name under heaven

given among men, whereby we must be saved."
For if not by Jesus Christ, then there is no hope, no
conceivable ray of light to be seen anywhere.   His
name does indeed clear up the darkness.   His name
does open to us hopes and promises beyond all
thought.   But take away that name, and there is
nothing left.

But He looked down on us, and had compassion
on us.   He beheld us in all our sorrows and sins,
and He loved us.   He, Perfect in Holiness, in
Happiness, in Glory,—He beheld our suffering and
struggling life, with its sparks of good and clouds
of evil, and His heart yearned to us in our misery
and low estate.   And He would be Himself our
Deliverer.   There was a sacrifice to be made ; there
was a great price to be paid ; there was great pain
to be suffered.   But the sorrows and evils of the
world filled His thoughts, and over against them He
set His infinite compassion.

This was one thing in " the mind which was also
in Christ Jesus ": His Infinite Compassion.   But there
was also something more : His Infinite Humility.

When we think of His Humility, we think at
once of His coming among us at all.   He, the
everlasting God, coming from heaven to narrow
Himself to the conditions of a creature ; to give up
what He was with the Father, that He might live
with men.   This is by itself a descent which we
cannot measure, for human thoughts cannot tell the
height and greatness of that majesty from which He
came down, or compare His Glory which He gave
up with the nature of even a sinless creature, which
He took on Him.   And this is not all.   He might

have come and lived with us as our Brother, or He might have come and ruled over us as our King. But He came, and was born among us, only to be poor and to suffer; He came not to rule, but to minister to us; He came, and died, He humbled Himself even to the death on the Cross. Yet, even so, we have not reached the point of His great humility.

Think what it was He came for. He came because of the sins of men; because the sins of men had made life hopeless, and without remedy; He came to cure the evils and miseries which men's folly and wrong-doing had brought about. He came to heal the diseases of the soul; to point out, to take away sin,—to reclaim men from their bad ways. It was because sinners had provoked God's righteousness, and brought such danger on the world, that, in His infinite compassion and love, He came to bring the great remedy.

And how did His creatures receive Him? "He was in the world, and the world was made by Him, and the world knew Him not. He came unto His own, and His own received Him not." It is of this great refusal and rejection that we are going to read.[1] He deigned to come, and in His own person, *ask* men to be reconciled,—*ask* men to receive His blessing,—*ask* men to return to their Father,—*ask* men to respond to His infinite compassion;—and they turned their backs on Him. He deigned to stand before the men whose misery had kindled His infinite pity, and to stand before them misjudged, as a criminal. He being what He was, deigned to

[1] During Holy Week.

stand before the public opinion of the Jewish nation, and to be set down by it as a deceiver and false prophet. He, the Judge of all men, the Sinless and the True, submitted to stand before the judgment-seat of fools and hypocrites to have sentence passed on His claims by blind and wicked judges, to be charged with blasphemy by His own High Priests. He would take the fate of merely any just man, unjustly accused.

We can partly measure what such humiliation means. We know what it is to humble ourselves before those who, we think, have wronged us. We know what it is to go and ask people to be friends, who, we think, ought to have themselves come and asked to be forgiven. We know what it is, being innocent, to be charged with guilt ; we know what it is, being innocent, to stand and have our case judged by those who dislike us,—by those for whom we have no respect,—by those who are incapable of giving an opinion about it. Yet the course of His work and ministry of self-sacrifice brought our Lord to this, to this deep bitter humiliation ; and to this, in His infinite humility, He submitted. " Consider Him," says St. Paul, " that endured such contradiction of sinners against Himself,"—the sinners whose needs and danger touched His heart so deeply, and brought Him down from heaven among them. " Who did no sin, neither was guile found in His mouth : who, when He was reviled, reviled not again ; when He suffered, He threatened not." Being the Lord and Maker of all things, He stood before Caiaphas, and was condemned as a blasphemer.

C.   G

This was the mind of Jesus Christ, with which He wrought out that Sacrifice by which our sins have been taken away ; by which the hope of a life that shall never end, and of which the prospects are boundless, has been opened, amid the perplexities, the sorrows, the disappointments of this mortal life. The Sacrifice began when in the secret of His Divine Will He chose to give Himself for man's redemption.   It began on earth, when He came to share our nature, and was born one of us, to inherit our lot.   It went on during all His life, when He was tempted like as we are ; when all day long He offered up His will and Himself that He might minister to men, and show them what it was to be perfectly good and true and loving.   And at last it came to its end, in the last Supper, in the Agony in the garden, in the Betrayal, in the mockery of the judgment hall, in the precious Blood shed on the Cross.   Then at last, when it came to the time to die, " He said, It is finished : and He bowed His head, and gave up the ghost."

Then was the Sacrifice completed ; for there was nothing more left, even to Him, by which to show what He was willing to undergo to reconcile man to God.   After that there was nothing more left but that He who had sunk so low should rise to the height of His victory.   " Wherefore God also hath highly exalted Him, and given Him a name which is above every name : that at the name of Jesus every knee should bow, of things in heaven, and things in earth, and things under the earth ; and that every tongue should confess that Jesus Christ is Lord, to the glory of God the Father."

This is what He has won for man.   This is what
man is meant for.   But it is by His steps that we
must go forward to His glory.   It is by His mind
that we must follow His victory.   Consider, then,
now when your hearts can hardly help being touched
by what this week is full of, consider the mind that
was in your Master.   Consider His infinite compassion and pity.   Consider His infinite humility.
Consider how He looked on the world, and saw the
troubles and miseries and sins that we know so
well ; how He looked on it, and heard the cry of the
poor, the simple, and the needy,—the publicans and
sinners whom no one cared for ; and how His heart
was, as it were, on fire within, and at last the fire
kindled.   "Then said I, Lo, I come to do Thy
will."   And yet, to do that will, and to exercise
that mercy, and to help those miserable sufferers,
He had to come down and be one of them :
"a body hast Thou prepared Me."   "He by whom
all things were made, for us men, and for our
salvation, came down from heaven, and was made
man. . . . He was crucified : He suffered, and was
buried."

Let us try to pray, when we read and hear of
that Cross and Passion, that "that mind may be in
us which was also in Christ Jesus."   That we may
have compassion one with another ; that we may be
above no offices of love and kindness ; that we may
be ready to forgive, and, if need be (what is much
more difficult), to be forgiven ; that we may set face
to face with our high thoughts of ourselves, Him
"who, being in the form of God," "made Himself of
no reputation, and took upon Him the form of a

servant " ; who suffered the provocation of those
for whom He had given up everything,—endured to
stand innocent, before the judgment of the unjust
and wicked,—refused not, for our sakes, not only
to suffer and die, but to be " reckoned among the
transgressors."

THE LESSON OF THE CROSS

" This is My commandment, That ye love one another, as I have
loved you. Greater love hath no man than this, that a man lay
down his life for his friends. Ye are My friends, if ye do whatsoever I command you."—St. JOHN xv. 12, 13, 14.

AT length the week is come almost to its end, and
the warnings which Christ has given day by day of
what was going to happen, have been fulfilled ; and
we are met here to bear witness, and to keep in our
own remembrance, that on such a day as this Christ
our Lord was indeed taken, and by wicked hands
was crucified and slain. And very suddenly it
seemed to come, notwithstanding those warnings.
It came after the fashion of most of Christ's dealings ; it came, not without preparation and notice ;
but it came suddenly at last. It had been foretold
in the Prophets. He had often spoken of it Himself
to His disciples. When the time drew near His
words became very solemn and very clear about it.
From the time that He had come to Jerusalem
scarcely a day had passed without something happen-
ing to force the thought of it on His disciples' minds.
From the supper at Bethany, where He had been
anointed for His burial, to the Paschal supper, in
which He had given to the disciples the sacrament

of His Body which was to be broken, and His Blood
which was to be shed for them, all His words and
actions pointed to death : a death which would not
be long in coming, and would be very terrible when
it did come.   The disciples felt it ; felt that they
were walking about with one who was marked for
death, who had of His own accord taken death as
His portion.   This was ample notice.   Yet when it
did come, it came upon the disciples unexpectedly.
It came suddenly, and in an instant, like a fierce
storm which bursts in a moment where just before
there had been calm and quiet.   On the Thursday
evening He was in the midst of His disciples, speaking with them His words of consolation and promise,
and free as yet from the malice of His enemies.
Later on in the Thursday night He was taken ;
early on the Friday morning He was before Caiaphas,
beginning His trial of cruel mockings and scourgings.
A little later He was before Pilate, sentenced to
death ; and then in the hall, in the midst of the
heathen soldiers, wearing the purple robe and the
crown of thorns.   At nine o'clock, the third hour of
the day, He was already hanging on the Cross ; at
three o'clock He was dead.   So sudden and speedy
was it all : not to Him, but to those who were with
Him.   A few hours before He had been calmly
supping with them ; and the next thing was, to see
Him who had washed their feet, naked and dying in
the hands of the scorners.   There was no time to
collect their thoughts ; no time gradually to get
accustomed to the great change, as there is when
death comes slowly and step by step on our friends,
and we can recover from the first stunning shock

that it really *is* death coming.   They had no time for this in the short hours from Thursday evening to the early morning of Friday.   They ought, indeed, to have been ready for it before ; they ought to have been prepared after all He had said to them. But they had not yet learnt Christ's lesson about being ever ready.   Though they knew He was to die, they did not imagine that it would be at that very moment.   So He took them by surprise (as He takes all who will not prepare at once when He gives them warning), by the suddenness and speed with which He passed from among them, through the agony of His Passion, to the grave.

And now the great day of the remembrance of it is come back to us again.   We have been a long time, outwardly at least, preparing for it.   We have been warned to keep it before our minds.   We have heard it spoken of beforehand.   We have known by the divisions of the year and the course of the Sundays that we should soon have to think of it— that the day was coming when it ought to fill and take up all our hearts.   And now it is come.   Are we fit for it ?   Are we in a state of mind fitly and with profit to read and follow and set before our thoughts the love wherewith our Master loved us ? Or has it come upon us by surprise, as His death came on His disciples?   It came to them in reality as the ruin of their hope and comfort, and filled them with dumb and hopeless sorrow, with selfish cowardice and forgetfulness of all their Master's love, and all His assurances.   It comes to us in remembrance ; and do we feel our hearts and souls in tune for it ?   Are we able and ready to devote our

thoughts to it, with the seriousness due to such recollections? Or do we feel that in reality we
cannot get ourselves to care much for it; that we
shall be glad when the day is over, which seems to
make it a duty to try and think about what has no
interest or meaning for us; that the recollection of
the history of this day does not really make us feel
more sorry for our sins, and more inclined to love
God, and to please Him by our obedience?

There is one test by which we may try ourselves,
whether we have sought to prepare our hearts to
contemplate and dwell upon the marvellous love of
our Saviour, which this day is meant to remind us
of. Our feelings are not always under our command,
and they are not always to be depended on. Many
a faithful soul is, perhaps, this day mourning, and
almost hopeless, because it feels itself dull and unmoved before the spectacle of the Cross of Christ.
Jesus Christ seems to open His arms to it, to show
it His wounds, to appeal to its devotion and love;
and that love seems cold, its heart will not move
towards its Saviour, will not give any response to
His tender call. And, on the other hand, there are
others who think that they are paying due honour to
their crucified Master, and are making a fit and
affectionate remembrance of His Passion, because
their hearts burn within them, and they seem to be
pierced through with quick and lively sympathy for all
the love and all the suffering of that great sacrifice:
who seem to see it all, as if they were actually
present, and to feel all, as *they* did who followed
Jesus, and stood afar off, gazing on His Cross. And
yet these same persons, though their feelings are so

strong and keen, forget them when they pass from
their secret chamber, and from church, to the society
of their brethren ; forget them when they are called
on to deny themselves in order to do good to one
of their brethren ; forget them when they ought to
sacrifice their own wishes to another's ; forget them
when something happens to ruffle their temper, or
try their patience, when they ought to do some disagreeable duty, or to take trouble to help others.

Many who are earnestly striving to follow Christ
in His life, do not feel as much moved by the remembrance of His death as they wish.   Many, too, who
seem to themselves to be deeply and strongly impressed with a feeling of the great love of Christ, show,
by their selfishness and want of care for their brethren,
that their feelings are vain and fruitless ones.   Christ
does not care about men being moved to tears, or even
to prayers, which for the moment are fervent and
earnest, if these feelings pass away the next instant,
and leave them lovers of themselves, and of the world,
instead of followers of His footsteps.   He has given
us the true test, to try whether we are really touched
by the greatness of His love to us.   He showed His
love to us not by words, not by feeling sorrow for our
lost and miserable state, but by doing something to
save us from it.   He showed His love by becoming
one of us, by putting Himself in our place.   He
showed His love by enduring all that was troublesome, all that was disagreeable, all that was hard, all
that was painful, all that to flesh and blood seemed
the worst evils that can happen to man.   He showed
His love by ministering to our wants, by healing
our sick, by feeding our hungry, by comforting our

mourners. " Himself took our infirmities, and bare our sicknesses." " Surely He hath borne our griefs, and carried our sorrows."

And yet that was not enough. Besides our sicknesses and our sorrows, we had our sins. Besides the comforts which we want here on earth, against our vexations and our sad bereavements, we have death, which comes to each of us, and seems to make all comfort vain. Who should take away our sins? Who should overcome death? Who should receive us after our weary pilgrimage through life, into the mansions of the Father? That, too, Jesus Christ did for us, out of that love of His for us " which passeth knowledge." But to do that something more was necessary than to heal the sick or to raise the dead. To do that for us He must needs go through all that sinners deserve; He must needs be, though sinless, yet as a sinner. God " hath made Him to be sin for us, who knew no sin." To take away our sins He bore our sins Himself. " He was wounded for our transgressions, He was bruised for our iniquities:" " the Lord hath laid on Him the iniquity of us all." To overcome death He poured out His soul unto death. To open to us the Kingdom of Heaven He endured the sharpness of death and the darkness of the grave. So He showed us His love. " Greater love hath no man than this, that a man lay down his life for his friends." That is the love of Jesus Christ. Who, indeed, can know it, and measure it to the full? But who can make any mistake as to what sort of love it was? We know what dying is; we know how we should feel if we had to die for another. " Scarcely for a righteous man will one die." We know how hard we think it when a death which a man might otherwise have avoided comes to him in the way of duty; when a man catches his death by attending on a neighbour who is sick; when, for the sake of others, we place ourselves in the way of mischief which would otherwise have struck down and destroyed some one else. Such things are, indeed, done among men, and, God be thanked, often submitted to cheerfully and bravely. But no man seeks them. Yet this is the love that Christ showed us, that He *sought* death for us. We can understand so much, at least, of His love, and know how hard we should have found it; how hard we should find it, even now that we know what He did for us, to do the like for His sake.

But He says nevertheless, " This is My commandment, That ye love one another, as I have loved you." And He calls us "His friends," if we do that which He commands us. If we would know whether we duly honour and are really moved by the great love of our Master on this day, let us see how far we are really trying to help one another; how far we are really trying to " bear one another's burdens, and so fulfil the law of Christ." There is no other way. The good thoughts and feelings which we have in church may deceive us. Let us go home and watch narrowly our tempers and our behaviour there. If we really understand the love of Christ crucified, the thought of our Master's suffering will be with us, to encourage us when we are trying to help our brethren; to reprove us when we are holding back from them in pride, or sloth, or selfishness; to comfort us when they meet our kindness with unkindness, or return evil for good ; to make us love them doubly when they receive our services as we give them.   When they are in pain and sickness the Cross of Christ will call us to their bedside ; will give us strength when we are worn out with serving them ; will make our voice gentle, and our step soft, and our hand tender, when we are ministering to them in their distress.

If they whom we are bound to help and please are rough and hard,—fretful when they ought to be satisfied, complaining and ever finding fault when we have done our best,—we shall think at once how our Master endured contradiction and vexation, and try to be silent and patient as He was.   When we are tempted to think that we are our own masters ; that no one ought to interfere with us, and claim our services ; that we have a right to think first for ourselves, and next for others, we shall feel ashamed before the awful spectacle of love dying for others on the Cross ; for " Christ pleased not Himself ; but, as it is written, the reproaches of them that reproached Thee fell on Me."   And how shall we dare indulge hatred and malice, how shall we dare vex our neighbour with bitter and cutting words, how shall we allow anger to burn up within us, how shall we dare to spread slanders and evil surmises about those whom we ought to love, even as Christ loved us,—how shall we dare, for very shame, endure in ourselves any of these things, before the thought of that Blessed One, who was afflicted and oppressed, yet opened not His mouth ; who, when the chief priests accused Him, and the multitudes wagged their heads, and the soldiers gave Him gall and vinegar, and the thieves railed on him, yet " answered nothing " ?

They only know and honour the love of Christ on the Cross who bear the remembrance of it about with them in the trials and duties of their daily lives. And if we would also come to feel it, to have such a sense as every true Christian must wish to have of its unspeakable greatness, we must begin by trying to imitate it. The reason why we feel so cold and dead on Good Friday,—why the reading of Christ's Passion seems so dull and tame to us,—is because we do not seek to catch the spirit of Christ crucified in our own actions. If you would know how to prize that love, and to enter into its sufferings and self-sacrifice, you must begin by practising the lesson of the Cross yourselves. Try and deny yourself some pleasure merely that you may give pleasure to another, and you will have made a step towards faintly yet really understanding the words and deeds of Him who pleased not Himself. Try and put yourself out of your way to do a service that you are not bound to do, and that is not expected of you ; try and bear in good earnest the vexatious and disappointing things which every week brings to most men. Do not shrink from them, but try and force yourself to go about your work as if they had not happened ; to keep down the heart that rises in pride, and restrain the tongue that longs to break forth into bitterness ; and you will be driven in time, for comfort and support, to that which was meant for our comfort and support, and on which alone we can safely lean,—that " anchor of the soul, both sure and steadfast,"—the remembrance of the Cross of our loving Master. So by degrees He will teach you Himself to know indeed the depth and the height of His love on Mount Calvary ; so by degrees you will see new meaning and new light in what the Bible tells us of His works and ways in those awful hours. It will be no longer dead and cold to you, but its words will seem to pierce to the very bottom of your heart, words so full of meaning, so full of comfort, so full of His heavenly peace. And so He will train you on, as He did St. Paul, to make it your first aim and chief happiness to try more and more " to know Him, and the power of His resurrection, and the fellowship of His sufferings, being made conformable unto His death."

XI

THE FEAR AND JOY OF THE RESURRECTION

" And the angel answered and said unto the women, Fear not ye : for I know that ye seek Jesus, which was crucified."—St. Matthew xxviii. 5.

THERE was, indeed, enough to cause fear to the boldest heart in what these faithful women found at the sepulchre of the Lord. They had come to do the last offices of love to His dead body. They had not been able to do them when He was laid in the grave, because the great Sabbath, which began in the evening, drew on ; and He had to be laid hurriedly in the tomb, before the setting of the sun should give the signal for resting from all work. But the Sabbath was now over, and they had returned, to do what they could not do then. They came to look once more on that gracious countenance. They expected to find much that would draw tears and sighs ; they expected to find everything in the regular course of nature. And in the regular course of nature there is not much to comfort those who go to visit the graves of their friends.

They thought only of their loss,—of a loss such as they had never seen repaired except by His hands :—

and now He was without power and life. The voice
which had said, "Lazarus, come forth," had spoken
its last words upon the cross. If even *He* had not
been able to save Himself from death, who could
have power to give Him life again ? True, He had
spoken of rising again, of seeing His friends again ;
but they thought not of these words of comfort now.
Their sorrow was too heavy ; after such an overthrow
of all that they had hoped for, it seemed like a vain
mockery to hope for anything more. There seemed
nothing left for them to do but to bow their heads
to God's will; to take their last leave of Him who
had been so dear to them, and then to go their way,
and bide their time, till they should be summoned to
join Him in the abodes of death.

That was in their minds probably when they
started, early in the morning, on the first day of the
week, to see the sepulchre. They expected nothing
uncommon now ; no more strange works of love
and mercy and power ; nothing but that sight which
they had looked at so long, and got but too well
accustomed to, on the Friday evening,——the pale and
still form of death.

They came, and they remembered as they drew
near that a heavy stone had been rolled to close the
sepulchre. "And they said among themselves, Who
shall roll us away the stone from the door of the
sepulchre ? " So little did they think of any change
in the course of nature ; so little did they expect to
find anything disturbed or altered in the stern law
of man's last end ; so little did they imagine of any
help, or any power, which could bring comfort from
the jaws of death.

They came ; but there was nothing at the sepulchre as they expected to find it. The stone was rolled away. The Lord was not there. Well might they be astonished and fear at this ; but the next moment brought the tremendous conviction that this was no work of man's hands ; that the power of Almighty God had been there ; that the law and course of nature had been disturbed, and some wonderful and mysterious thing had happened ; that the bonds which no man had ever broken before were indeed burst asunder. They had been think-ing of looking on a corpse without life and without power,—looking on it once more, before it was lost to them for ever in corruption and dust ; and, all at once, they found themselves standing on ground where the greatest of miracles had just been wrought, and the traces of God's hand were still to be seen ; and in the sepulchre, instead of the Lord's body wrapped in grave-clothes, they came upon the presence of mighty and glorious angels, filling the cave with light, and they heard voices of the other world. Truly, it was enough to cause fear and amazement thus to come suddenly from the thoughts and sorrows of earth, expecting to see only the common sights of this life,—the tomb as they had left it,—the everyday and familiar spectacle of death, —to come suddenly on beings fresh from the courts of heaven, and on a work of wonder and might such as no human eye had looked upon since the genera-tions of mankind had been upon the earth.

Their first thoughts would surely be of fear : fear to see that the death of Christ had brought down upon earth such an awful interference of the power

C.   H

of God ; fear to find that the Master, whom they
had known as so humble and lowly, was One to
whom the strong bands of death were as nothing,—
was One on whom angels in their glory were but
attendants and ministers. Well may they have
feared at the change so suddenly made in all their
thoughts and feelings and expectations. Well may
they have feared to find themselves so near to that
lighting down of the Almighty's arm from heaven ;
so tremendous, even when displayed for their deliverance and comfort.

The Resurrection of Christ was an event to make
men fear : all who were made to see its consequences
at the time feared greatly. When the angel whose
countenance was as lightning appeared to roll back
the stone, the soldiers who were watching the
sepulchre "for fear of him did shake, and became
as dead men." The women, when they saw the
angel, and heard his tidings, were sore afraid and
terrified, and bowed their faces to the ground. The
Apostles, after they had been prepared for the sight
of their risen Master by the reports of those who had
seen Him, were seized with awe and terror when at
length He did appear. "As they thus spake, Jesus
Himself stood in the midst of them, and saith unto
them, Peace be unto you. But they were terrified
and affrighted, and supposed that they had seen a
spirit." Cannot you well understand that it must
have been so ? If any one whom we had known
well were to be allowed to return to us from the
world of spirits, could we bear the vision ? Would
it not be too much for us to endure, even if he came
to bring us a message of peace from God, to comfort

us with the assurance of his being at rest, and of our certainty of joining him there? How much more awful to the disciples, when this was not a spirit, come back for a moment and then departing; but the very living body of Him whom they had seen crucified, and dying, and buried; come back to remind them of all that He had said to them of His power, and His care for them; come back to show them that He had indeed conquered even death; come back to tell them that all power was given to Him in heaven and in earth,—that He was indeed beyond all possibility of doubt the Son of God, in man's flesh and body, able to punish with a word all His enemies, and to save them to the uttermost who would trust His love.

But to them He said, " Fear not," as the angels had said to the faithful women, " Fear not ye." For in truth there were persons to whom neither Christ nor His angels could have said, " Fear not." There were persons who thought that they had got rid of Christ : that His reproofs and His threatenings, His holiness, which put to shame their lusts and covet-ousness,—His lowliness, which put to shame their pride,—His truth, which put to shame their hypocrisy, —His loving-kindness, His miracles of mercy and love, which put to shame their selfishness and cruelty, would never trouble them more ;—that all this was put an end to for ever, and buried in the sepulchre of the crucified Jesus of Nazareth. There were persons who thought that now they might go on as they had gone on before, outwardly religious and having the praise of men, inwardly serving divers lusts and sins ; that now they might take their ease,

and eat and drink and be merry, because He who
had troubled them was out of the way. If the
Jewish rulers had really known how utterly all that
they had reckoned on had been brought to nought,
they might well have called on the mountains to fall
on them, and the rocks to cover them, from the wrath
of Him whom they had mocked and crucified,—of
Him to whom they had been allowed to do their very
worst, and who was now alive again from the dead.

As it was then, so is it now. Easter is a time
of gladness and rejoicing, but it is also a time of
fear. For Easter is the time which, above all others,
reminds us that what Christ said He said in earnest ;
and that He has most certainly the power to do all
that He has said. And there must be many to
whom it can be no welcome news to be reminded of
this. There are many to whom it would be more
comforting to think that Christ had remained in the
grave. There are many who would much rather
think, if they could, that all that He said about the
necessity of being holy and about the punishment
of sinners had never been so confirmed and made
good. There are many to whom it would be much
pleasanter to remain in doubt for a while whether
they *are* to rise again, and whether Christ is really to
judge them,—to remain in doubt, to be able to
think that it is not quite assured to them, at least
while they have their fill of sin, and as long as they
have not got tired of it. To such persons, to be
reminded, as we are at Easter, that indeed Jesus
Christ did not stay in the grave, but rose again to
take His great power and reign, must be a troubling
and a depressing thought,—a thought that commonly

brings with it anxiety and dismay the more they take it in.

Easter is the time which, above all others, speaks to us of a great change from old to new ; from that which is of this world to that which belongs to the world to come ; from the corruption and death which belonged to the old Adam to the holiness and life which has been brought in by the second Adam. *He* was changed at His resurrection ; and each anniversary of it reminds us that if we are His *we* must be changing too. " If any man be in Christ," says St. Paul, "he is a new creature." " Christ our Passover is sacrificed for us : therefore let us keep the feast, not with old leaven, neither with the leaven of malice and wickedness ; but with the unleavened bread of sincerity and truth." But what must *they* feel at Easter, if they feel at all,—what ought they to feel, who are not a whit altered from the bad courses and bad tempers of last year ? What comfort can Easter give to those whom it finds without any improvement ? They hear once more the joyful sound, " Christ is risen " : " fear not ye." But are these words meant for them ? Should *they* not fear who have passed the year since last Easter in sin ; who have not made a step in it to please God ; who hate His holy ways still ? Is not Easter, as it returns, rather a fresh memorial and pledge to them that God will keep His word, not only to those who serve Him, but also to those who serve Him not ?

To those who feel that they are not improving, Easter must be a time of fear. They must feel that the great festival forces on their minds what they try, and probably are able, to keep out of them the

rest of the year,——how great a change there must be
in their souls before they can be like Jesus Christ.
They are reminded by it how little their ways of life
and their feelings chime in and agree with what
Scripture says of Christians rising from sin to holiness, as their Lord rose from death to life.   They
must feel that they have nothing to do with the
festival.   It speaks, indeed, of comfort, but it is to
those who have sought to follow Christ.   It speaks
of power to redeem and save, but it is not for those
who will not leave off crucifying Jesus Christ afresh,
by sins which they will not repent of and forsake.
And every fresh Easter Day speaks of Christ's resurrection, as the certain pledge that our bodies also
will be raised ; and what thoughts but those of fear
can any one have about the resurrection who knows
that he loves this present world, with its pleasures
and its pursuits, better than he loves the will and
the promises of Christ ?   To such an one every Easter
Day must be as one more melancholy and despairing
step to a resurrection in which he will see, indeed,
Christ's power, but will be cut off for ever from
sharing His love.

But such thoughts of fear are not what Christ
meant His resurrection to put into our minds.   He
meant it to say to us, as the angel said to the women,
" Fear not ye."   The women at the sepulchre, the
apostles in the chamber, were greatly afraid at first ;
but soon their fear gave place to great joy.   Jesus
Christ came and gave them His peace, and it took
possession of their hearts.   Surely that is what He
means for our portion still.   He means that after we
have fully felt the awfulness of His divine power, we

should go on to take comfort in the thought that
He who is so great and mighty is also our Protector,
the guide of our hearts, who watches night and day
over our souls and bodies, in whose hands they will
be safe through every trouble, through death itself,
till He makes us like unto Himself. " Fear not ye,"
He says to those who tremble at His word, and
humble their hearts before Him, in the deep consciousness how unworthy they have shown themselves
of such salvation, and of such a Saviour. " Fear
not ye," He says to those who are striving, by the
help of His Spirit, to purify their hearts day by day
from the pride or the vanity, the harsh tempers, or
the selfishness,—the old leaven which yet spoils and
embitters what must be made new and pure for
His presence. " Fear not ye," He says to those who
are waiting patiently, in sorrow or sickness, in old
age, in penitence, for the consolation of the Israel of
God. " Fear not ye," He says to those who, while
they love His appearing, and pray for the coming of
His kingdom, are content to remain in the calling to
which He has called them, doing whatever their
hand finds to do earnestly and quietly ; fulfilling
their homely tasks of charity and kindness, of peace-
making and of consolation, comforting the sick,
clothing the naked, teaching the ignorant, cheering
the faint-hearted. To such the joy of Easter Day
is indeed a new encouragement in their pilgrimage
—a fresh spring, from year to year, of blessed hope
and peace.

For what they feel to-day of calm and trustful
gladness is not, indeed, of this world. It is like the
peace which we may imagine God's servants to feel

when their course is finished, and they are preparing to depart. Please God, those who feel it now may humbly trust that it is a foretaste and first fruits of the comfort He will graciously vouchsafe them in their hour of departure. They may most surely believe that, if it shall please Him to accept and save them, it is a foretaste, feeble and poor indeed, yet not untrue and deceiving, of that love and joy which shall be in the resurrection of the just, when they shall for the first time see that Blessed One, and shall never more be separated from His presence.

XII

THE TREASURE IN HEAVEN

"Where your treasure is, there will your heart be also."
ST. MATTHEW vi. 21.

THE Ascension of our Lord into heaven, which we celebrate at this time, sets before our minds *where*, from henceforth, the treasure of Christians must be. It is the earnest to us, and the warning too, that what He has to give us is no earthly portion, but "an inheritance incorruptible, and undefiled, and that fadeth not away, reserved in heaven" for us. It lifts our views, our hopes, what we have to live for and to think of, from a course of things which must be all over in a few years, to one which shall have no end, of which the blessedness and glory will be such that man will have no cause to envy even the angels. Christ by going up on high has taken with Him our treasure, and removed it from where moth and rust corrupt to the everlasting throne. There He is,—all that we have to put our trust in, and to satisfy the desire of our souls,—all that we have in this world to calm our anxious thoughts of the future, to still our fears, to give us certainty and assurance that, amid the distress and sorrow of this present state, and the dreary end of death, we have a friend

who will never fail, a Redeemer whose love is
inexhaustible, a stay and hope on which we may
throw all our burdens.   Great, we all know, is the
value and blessedness of a friend on earth, but the
friend whose love and goodness are above that of
all friends is in a better place than earth : gone
before us, but not gone away from us,—out of our
sight yet ever seeing us, ever knowing our necessities,
ever hearing our prayers ; gone before us, that where
He is we may come,—that He may receive in
heaven those whom He has loved, and who have
loved Him in this short life on earth.   Our treasure
is not here.   Christ has made heaven belong to
men, as it belongs to the angels.

    And the angels look on, and see that it is true.
They see that something much greater than earth is
given us.   They see that what men are meant for,
are called to, and promised,—what is laid up in
store for them, is in heaven.   The angels see, and
wonder, and rejoice at the destiny, the inheritance,
which the Lord has won and appointed for us men,
—a throne in heaven.   Can they also see us, and
our thoughts and lives, as they see what is waiting
for us above ?   Can they see how much we think
and care about that glorious hope which lies before
us ?   Can they see how much our hearts are set on
that treasure in heaven, which belongs to us, as the
followers of our Risen and Ascended Lord ?

    We, my brethren, do not want angels to tell us
where our hearts ought to be.   We do not want
teaching to make us know that if our treasure is
indeed in heaven, our hearts ought to be in heaven
too.   If Christ is gone up on high, and if He is

gone to prepare a place for us, who can doubt that
Christians, though they have to live and work for a
while on earth, were meant to think of themselves
as persons whose main interests are, so to speak,
removed from this present world to heaven? Who
can doubt that they must be Christians to little
purpose if, with such hopes and prospects before
them, they never raise their minds to those hopes,—
if they live indifferent to those prospects? When
we keep in memory our Master's ascension to glory,
and His promise of His glory to us, surely the first
thought that must come into our souls is, that they
who have been so blest ought to bear a heavenly
mind; the first question that must strike us is,
whether our hearts and thoughts are indeed those of
persons whose portion is in heaven, who have heaven
in view, who have already their Master and best
Friend in heaven? "Where your treasure is, there
will your heart be also." But where are our hearts
now?

Surely, no one can be really a Christian who has
not something of a heavenly mind,—who does not try
to lift up his thoughts and feelings to that holy place
where he knows that his Saviour is, and is waiting
for him? And yet how difficult, amid the work
and troubles of the world, to bear this heavenly
mind; to keep ourselves from sinking down to
thoughts which never look a step beyond what we
see and do on earth; how difficult really to believe,
to remember, that we are citizens of a heavenly
country; that there is really another world of much
more consequence to us than this one, which now
fills up all our thoughts and takes up all our time;

how difficult to raise our eyes and wishes and hopes above the common daily circumstances, the cares, and business, and pleasures of this life, and to feel that indeed we have to do with something much greater, something that will last for ever—some one, a king, a master, a friend, a judge, whom we shall meet with when we are dead, either to be with Him in the light of heaven, or to live, cast away from His presence, in the outer darkness, with the worm that never dies.

And if it is so difficult to have this thought of heaven, what ought we not to do, what trouble ought we not to take, to remind ourselves of it,—to stir up and revive the faint and dim image of the treasure which we have in heaven, when it is clouded and almost blotted out by earthly cares? Is there nothing by which we may help ourselves in this? Is there nothing beyond our own weak wishes and intentions, which so often turn out vain? Many of us live a hard life of toil and labour, with no time to read, no time to shut ourselves up from the world and think, no time to be alone with God, and to shut out the pressing things of this world. Is there no help for such persons against the overwhelming cares and trials of daily life,—cares which wake with them in the morning and leave them no quiet till they lie down at night? Is there nothing to help in such a life as this? Is there no time, no place, to be fenced off from this world, for exalting, sanctifying moments, to help them to lift up their minds to their treasure above, and in heart and mind thither to ascend, and there continually dwell?

Is there such a time? Is there such a place? Is there a day out of the busy and weary week which belongs to God, which recalls the rest of heaven? Is there a place where the world has no business, where all that is said and done brings up the thought of God; where, as we hope, we may indeed meet with God, where we may speak to Him with more than usual solemnity and stillness; a place which reminds us of our eternal home,—the Font of Baptism speaking to us of an endless life begun and a heavenly inheritance bestowed; the Altar and Table of the Lord speaking to us of eternal life purchased for us by His Death, and nourished in us by His heavenly Food; the graves all round of friends and neighbours, speaking to us of death, and things after death? Is there any service and employment which may recall and refresh in our minds the hopes, the words, the work of heaven, where one day we trust our work is to be,—where one day we look forward to joining the songs of angels, and the hymn before the great white Throne? Oh, my brethren, is there such a work done on earth? is there such a place, is there such a time, which God has given us, on purpose that hard-worked men may for a little space re-member that they still are His children, heirs of His everlasting kingdom, sharers in the treasure which is in heaven?

You who feel that your heart *ought* to be where your treasure is, and yet feel that it is not; you who wish continually that you could bear a more heavenly mind, and yet feel that it has but a bad chance against the things of this life, which take up

your time and fill your heart ; you who grieve and
are vexed with yourselves that you cannot lift up
your thoughts to your heavenly calling, cannot make
this world give way for ever so little to the remembrance of the next, cannot keep before you
the hope of heaven to sanctify and raise your earthly
life,—have you ever fairly thought what helps you
have, if you would use them ? Have you thought
what Sunday might do for you ? Why does
Sunday come round, why is it fenced off and
separated from the six days of the week, but to
break the continual pressure on our thoughts of
earthly things, to give us a chance of escaping from
them, into a quiet and rest, in which heaven may
for a while open to our souls, to give us the
opportunity of shaking off what binds us to this life,
and of fixing our thoughts on where we are going
to, and on what we hope to have at last ? You
have your Sundays, week after week, reminding you
of God's rest, and of the rest which He has prepared
for you. In the midst of this world's labour He
gives you even here your day of rest. In the
darkest of this world's sorrow Sunday seems a day
different from other days, shining with a light and
place of its own, even into the chamber of sickness
and death. You have your Sunday ; and with
Sunday come also its calls, and invitations, its helps
and means of grace.

God has set in the midst of you, as the ever-
present witness and figure of heaven, His holy
House of Prayer. There it stands, built for no
earthly purpose, different in shape, and in all things
belonging to it, from earthly habitations, speaking

only of heaven, and heavenly uses, and heavenly
gifts, and heavenly blessings; the gate of heaven
when we are brought into it as little children to
Christ,—the gate of heaven, if so God grant us,
when we are brought to it, and pass through it the
last time on our way to our grave beside it.   And
here we meet our God.   Here we may come on our
day of rest, and be safe, if we will, from any
thoughts but those of the world to come.   Here we
gather together for no earthly business, but for a
purpose of one sort only; and that purpose is the
same for which saints and angels are met together
in that innumerable company before the throne of
God.   If there is a place on earth which, however
faintly and dimly, shadows out the courts of God
on high, surely it is where His people are met
together, in all their weakness and ignorance and
sin, in their poor and low estate, yet with humble
and faithful hearts, in His House of Prayer.   There
His Name only is heard, His law declared: His are
the promises, the warnings, the words:—all things
recall Him, all is done in His Name, to Him all
confessions, all prayers, all praises are addressed.   If
we only thought of what we were doing, we should
see that we are practising here on earth what will
be our life in heaven,—we are rehearsing the songs
which we hope to sing with the redeemed in heaven.
We are joining together, one with another, rich and
poor, young and old, small and great, into an image
and likeness of that great family of God hereafter,
which will know no will, no work, but His,—which
will be for ever in His presence, to whom He is the
shelter from all evil and sorrow, the Light that never

sets, their ever-satisfying and yet ever-increasing
hope.

We have, many of us, abundance of helps and
means of grace to set against the hindrances of the
works and cares of life, and to keep alive in our
heart the remembrance of our treasure in heaven.
But we have, all of us, even the poorest, the Sunday
of rest, to remind us of the everlasting rest, and to
give us time to think of God, and lift our hearts
without hindrance to Him. We have, all of us,
the Church open to us; open, because there is a
heaven waiting for us of which it is the present
memorial and figure; open, because there is a God
to be remembered, whom with united hearts and
voices we are called on to meet, and worship together. We have, all of us, the Church services,
morning and evening, speaking to us of God, and
all that He has done for us, stirring us up to listen
to and give attention to His gracious message,—
speaking out our thoughts for us, and putting words
in our mouths, when we would repent of sin, and
take hold of forgiveness; when we would ask for
grace and strength; when we would commit ourselves to our Master's keeping; when we would
sing our Master's praises, and, in singing them, rise
on wings of faith to the hallelujahs of that multitude
that no man can number, of the saints of heaven.

If we would use these means of grace and
memorials of our heavenly portion, and use them as
men use what they believe to be for their profit,
we should find that we were not without much to
help us in keeping up the recollection of that
heaven where our Master is gone, and the sense and

value of that treasure which passeth all understanding, which He has there in His keeping for us.
If the thought of it was driven out during the week-
days, there would be a hope that it would come back
naturally when the Sunday rest brought back its
remembrances of heaven, and the Sunday solemn
gathering of worshippers made us think of that
world for which they and we are preparing, to which
they and we are on our way. For God has given
us Sundays, set apart churches, and appointed the
regular unceasing round of services, where Christians
may meet to strengthen each other's faith and purposes of good,—where He, too, has promised to
meet them with His grace, and bless them with His
presence, and dismiss them with His peace.

And now I will tell you why I have dwelt on
these thoughts to-day. It is because I feel with
sadness that many in this place do not value as
they ought these memorials and helps to keep
religion and the fear of God in their minds ; because
I see, with distress and pain, that they do not use
them. It used to be a way of speaking, in
describing a good, earnest, humble Christian,—not
as if it were any such great praise, but as showing
that he really wished to honour his God and
Saviour, and try to be His true servant,—that he
never missed his church on Sunday. It meant, at
any rate, that he was a regular attendant at the
church which God had provided for him, and where
his friends and neighbours met together to worship
God ; where his father and forefathers had prayed,
and been taught God's Word ; where their graves
were round him, and where he might look to be

gathered to them. I am afraid that good old
feeling is very slack among us, of worshipping
together as one parish and congregation, of showing
God honour publicly by joining all together in His
House on His Day, of encouraging and stirring up
one another by each doing his part in keeping up
the remembrance of God's Name and fear. I know
that many of you are regular. I know that there
may be good reasons keeping you away from time
to time. I know that there are times when you
wish, quite rightly and innocently, to spend your
Sunday elsewhere. But, allowing all this, it is not
enough to account for the fact that many are *far
more* Sundays away from church here than they
are at it. It is not enough to explain the emptiness
of our church on Sunday mornings,—on Sunday
mornings, when the service is the most complete
and most beautiful, when the service of praise is the
most glorious and exalting, when the prayers for
all good are so fully and so touchingly set forth in
the Litany, when the Communion service reminds us
continually of that Holy Sacrament in which we
are called to be partakers.

Shall I tell you what is the most painful hour
of the week to me?—the hour that, week by
week, makes me feel that all I have said has been
wasted, and done no good? that makes me doubt
whether I am doing any good here? It is the time
when I come into church on Sunday morning and
see it so empty of worshippers, and think of the
reasons which keep them away, and of the dishonour
done to our Almighty Father. I know indeed,
better than any of you can, how awful is the

thought of that account and reckoning which I must
one day give, for you, before the judgment-seat of
God. But, dear brethren, remember this, that my
fault will not excuse you,—will not make it right for
you to do dishonour to God, and slight His means
of grace. I may suffer ; but it will not help you to
escape. If I have not spoken as well as I ought,
you know of your own selves that it cannot be right
to be negligent and irregular in giving God the
honour due to Him ; that it cannot be right, from
custom or fashion, or from laziness and want of will,
or for any other excuses, to stay away from God's
House on His Holy Day, when you might go there ;
that it cannot be right merely to go there when it
suits your fancy or convenience, instead of as a
matter of duty to God and your brethren.

I have never taught you that regular church-
going by itself would save you. But surely it is a
true and sad sign against a man having the
beginnings of the power of God, when He is a careless and seldom worshipper. The world soon puts
out of all our hearts the thought of our treasure in
heaven, do what we may. Oh, my brethren, let me
beseech you earnestly not to trifle with the gracious
means which God has appointed to keep up the
remembrance of His Holy Name, of His wonderful
benefits, of that unspeakable Peace, which He has
prepared for those who love and seek Him.

May He help us all, and may we all help one
another, to correct what may be amiss, to strengthen
what stands, to raise up what is fallen back. May
He, by His goodness, keep continually before our
hearts and minds the thought of what He has done

for us, and of what He has in store for us above ;
so that we may never lose it, never be false to it,
but find it brightening, enlarging, becoming stronger,
more real, more powerful in our hearts, as we go on
drawing nearer to the end ; till the days of hope are
over, and the treasure which we so often heard of,
and thought of, is made our own for ever.

XIII

THE WORK OF THE SPIRIT

"Thou sendest forth Thy Spirit, they are created : and Thou renewest the face of the earth."—PSALM civ. 30.

THE Psalmist is speaking in these words of that great burst of new life which is going on all around us at this time of the year. The Spirit of God, which once moved on the face of the waters, to fill the earth with light and life, still works ; still comes forth year by year to turn winter into spring and summer, to repair the waste of decay and death "Thou hidest Thy face, they are troubled,"—all things which God hath made upon the earth : darkness comes, and failing strength, and cold and winter ; and the year that was once so bright ends in gloom and sadness. "Thou takest away their breath, they die, and return to their dust." Then comes the change. "Thou sendest forth Thy Spirit," as at the beginning ; "they are created ; and Thou renewest the face of the earth."

But to-day these words sound in our ears with a deeper meaning. When we hear them now, they speak of a greater and more wonderful renewing than that wrought by the power of God working in the trees and fields, and all the tribes of living things.

To-day the thoughts which they awaken and the associations they bring with them are of the Day of Pentecost, and its effects upon mankind ; of the new life given to dead souls by the quickening power of the Lord, who is the Giver of Life ; of the springtide of goodness and holiness in a corrupt world ; of the changing of our decayed and ruined nature ; of the fresh growth in the heart of man, in faith and love and truth ; of the restoration to God, their Father and Saviour, of the creatures so long lost to Him, ruled over by sin, and swallowed up by death.

This was what was to follow, and what has followed, the " coming of the Holy Ghost ": the coming of the Holy Ghost, not merely into the world, not merely to be *with* men, but,—most blessed and wonderful thought,—to be *in* them ; to dwell in them, to give them a new life. To-day we call to mind the first beginnings of that coming down of the Holy Spirit upon and into man, which is the proof and pledge of reconciliation and peace between man and God. *He* was come who was to make all things new ; the new witness of God, not outside of man, but within him, to begin the work which has never stayed from that day, and never will stay till the Lord returns ; the work of purifying and restoring the generations of mankind.

" Thou sendest forth Thy Spirit, they are created :" one after another, age after age, the successions of Christian people, each in their own time born anew, and created to good works, running their race and doing their master's service. " Thou sendest forth Thy Spirit, they are created,"—the innumerable company of God's elect, who have given to the world a

life and beauty and glory which it never had
before. " Thou renewest the face of the earth."
This is that renewal of the face of the earth, that
new spring of holiness and hope and peace, which
we cannot help having in our thoughts when we hear
words which speak of all nature, once more quickened
into spring and life by the invisible grace of God.

That which we keep in mind to-day was the
coming into the world of a divine power, which has
acted, really though invisibly, on the hearts of men,
and made them different from what they ever were,
or ever could be before. It was the coming into the
world of a divine Helper to man, in the inward, secret
depths of his soul and conscience,—of a divine En-
lightener ; teaching him, as he never knew before,
the truth about himself, the truth about God, the truth
about righteousness and sin, the truth about his end,
his judgment, his destiny. It was the coming of a
Sanctifier and Purifier and Healer, who was indeed
Divine,—able to turn and raise man's thoughts and
will from what God hates to what God loves,—able
to give him power to do the good that he would do,
and resist the sin that he ought not to do,—able by
degrees, step by step, to give him victory over his
temptations, and to make him rise step by step to
understand, to love, and to follow the mind that was
in Christ Jesus. It was the coming of a divine
power, which has made the change between the
Jewish and the heathen world, as it was before, and
that which has been seen among men since they have
had the Gospel knowledge.

If our knowledge of God is clearer than that of
heathen ; if prophecies which were dark to Jews are

plain to us ; if a fellowship and communion with our
Father in heaven are granted to us which they could
not claim ; if the mystery of our sins and our forgiveness is declared to us in the Cross of Jesus Christ ;
if the hope of what is to come is opened to us, as not
even good and holy men under the old covenant were
allowed to have it ; if we know more of heaven, if
we see clearer through death, if we can trust more
surely in trials and temptations—it is because for us
the Spirit of God has been given.   If we have wider,
purer, higher views of our duty ; if Christians have
reached a standard of goodness and holiness of
which we have no examples before Christ came ; if
measures of obedience which satisfied Jews are seen,
even by the disobedient, to be utterly below what is
worthy of a Christian ; if conscience is more tender and
more far-sighted and speaks more strongly—it is that
Spirit of newness and light which has enlarged our
hearts.   And if we see in all ages since Christ came,
works of love and mercy, works of self-devotion and
self-sacrifice, care for the bodies and souls of men,
care for the humblest, the miserable, the worn out
and useless, care for the infinite varieties and shades
of human suffering, such as were never dreamed of
before ; if we see men giving all they have, and then
themselves, in the service of God and their brethren—
it is He who has kindled the enthusiasm and the
inventiveness of charity.   If we see purity, meekness,
tenderness, joined with fiery zeal ; if we see unworld-
liness with the spirit of forgiveness and forbearance
for others, as we see them in St. Paul, St. John, and
St. Peter,—and not in them only, but in so many
who in all ages have followed St. Paul's and St.

John's Master,—if it has come to pass that the Saints of the New Covenant have a higher idea of holiness, have walked by a more perfect rule, have shown forth a more excellent and lovely character, these are the fruits of that Blessed Spirit who has come to renew the face of the earth.

We may feel ourselves nearer to God than of old, adopted by stronger warrants into His family, and assured more certainly of our interests in His Kingdom ; we, instead of the sacrifices of bulls and goats, have the one all-sufficient sacrifice, oblation, and satisfaction of the only Son ; instead of the outward ceremony and seal of circumcision, we have the life-giving Sacrament of regenerating Baptism, in the name of the awful and most Holy Godhead, by which we can come to God as our Father indeed. We, instead of the sinful and dying High Priest entering once a year into the Holy Place, have ever at the mercy-seat above, the Priest after the order of Melchizedek, without beginning of days or end of life, who was tempted in all points like as we are, yet without sin ; we, instead of the Passover and the manna, speaking of Egypt and the Red Sea and the wilderness, have the Sacrament which tells of the victory over death, and we feed upon the food which nourishes us to everlasting life.   Whence is all this,—whence is it that our eyes are opened, and that we know truths that are behind the veil, and the powers of the world to come, but because the Spirit hath come and taught us, and given us life?   The Spirit of Truth, according to our Master's promise, has come, and has shown us all that was meant by our Master's words, all that was really done in what

He went through. The Spirit came, and threw light on the meaning of the Incarnation, the Temptation, the Agony, the Cross, the Resurrection. The Spirit made Christians understand what was in the words, " Go ye therefore, and teach all nations, baptizing them in the name of the Father, and of the Son, and of the Holy Ghost." " This is My Body ; this is My Blood : do this in remembrance of Me."

The Spirit brought to remembrance what He had said, and wrote it not merely in words and books, but in the tables of the heart, in the wills and affections, in the belief and deeds of living men. Knowledge and duty, and the grace to do it, and the face of life, and the worth of time, and the thoughts of death, are all new to us ; for the Spirit of God has come down to be with us, the Spirit of God is now in the hearts of men ; new things have been done, old things have been seen in a new light ; for the power and enlightening of the Spirit has come into the midst of man's life. " He has renewed the face of the earth."

And in the midst of this communication of power and light from heaven, we have our lot, we live our lives. We are not talking of things past and absent when we speak of the Spirit of God given to men, dwelling in the hearts of men, making them new, teaching, strengthening, sanctifying them. What was begun at Pentecost was to last for ever. Not in its first marvels and wonderful signs, not in its rushing wind and cloven tongues and diverse languages and gifts of healing. But in its real power, in its real influence on the soul of man, in its real comfort, in its divine communication of holiness and strength and peace. This was for all the world. This was for all time.　Heaven was once more united to earth not merely by the outward sign of the Lord's ascension, and by holding on its throne Him who had walked about on earth ; but by the invisible inward flowing forth of that Spirit, who is the power and love of God, from the Father and the Son to those for whom the Father had sent the Son to die,—to those whom the Son had loved with His Divine Charity.　And this knitting together of the visible and invisible, of heaven and earth, of God and man, —this was the very thing for which Christ had come and died and gone up again.　He had Himself done all His great works *outside* of us.　The Spirit was to come when He had departed, to bring the redeeming, restoring, and healing grace *within* us.

This is the truth : the awful, solemn truth.　The Spirit of God and Christ, the Eternal Spirit who came down in wonders at Pentecost, is with us now. He has been with us since our Baptism, when He received us ; He has been with us as we grew up, teaching us all the good we have ever learnt, and striving with us when we chose evil instead of good. He has been with us, showing us our danger and our sin, throwing His light into our conscience, inclining us—and we so unwilling and so obstinate—to pray in earnest ; delivering us from many a temptation ; giving us the thought, the strength, which perhaps just saved us on the edge of falling ; awakening us with disquiet and fear when we fell ; filling us with peace and calmness of spirit when we stood fast.

All that we have of good is from Him ; and how much more would He have given us, if we had not resisted Him, if we had not tempted and grieved

Him! To the greatest saints, to St. Paul, to St.
John, He has been all that made them what they
were ; and the same Spirit, the same Divine Person,
who was with them and in them, is with us, and in
us too. He met them where He meets us. Do not
let us think that it was in those extraordinary
visitations and open signs of His presence that His
grace and life-giving power to their souls was most
largely shown. He met them as He meets us,
in secret quiet thoughts, in prayer and praise and
sacrament, in the holy words of God, in Christian
communion and the assembling of the Church, in
thoughts that come with the night watches or the
dawning of the day ; in the secret strivings with
temptations and sins, in the fulfilment of duty, in
the zealous honouring of God, in unselfish services
of love, in the earnest endeavour after a better and
purer life. By this daily unseen training, by this
secret, unnoticed, but mighty discipline, and not by
outward shows of power or passing raptures of
feeling, He made them saints. As He dealt with
them, so He deals with us ; so He deals with all
Christian people, as they pass through their trial, and
are waiting for their summons.

This is the gift which our Master has left us.
Thus is He still ready to answer the prayer that He
will not leave us fatherless, and without guide and
protector in the world. Let *that* but come into
our souls ; and, if the world seems dark, He can
make it glorious and full of hope ; if religion seems
dry and unmeaning, He can pour light into all its
parts, making them start into brightness and reality
and comfort. If we are dead and dull and cheer-

less, His life can make us live.   He visits the souls
of men, in the truth and efficacy of His power,
unseen, unfelt by man ; known only by its fruit,
by the peace it leaves behind.   He comes from
heaven to be our guard and shield ; and without
Him nothing is strong, nothing is holy, nothing is
safe.   To His keeping let us commit ourselves : to
Him who gave us new life in our Baptism,—to Him
who was so solemnly appealed to in our confirmation
to be ever with us,—to Him who, if ever we have had
thoughts of good, or have been comforted and blessed
in prayer, has surely graciously come to us then.

Let us pray Him that He will mercifully continue
and finish His heavenly work in us ; that He will
wash away what is unclean, that He will heal what
is sick and wounded, that He will send His gracious
rain on what is withered, that He will bend our stiff
pride, and warm our coldness, and restrain our way-
wardness.   We have yet a while to toil and strive,
to pass through the fire of temptation, to mourn and
to be sorrowful ; but He came that to men in toil
He might give rest, to men in sorrow He might give
refreshment and consolation, to men in trial He
might give strength.   His stores of gifts and grace
are not exhausted.   Only let us have faith and will
to seek for them ; then we may hope to find Him
our stay and refuge, and the light of our hearts ;
then may we humbly look forward to knowing something of His sweet welcoming influences when all
things here are passing away.   For He, even in
the hour of death, can, to those who trust Him,
" renew the face of the earth."

XIV

THE DUTY OF HELPING MISSIONARY WORK

"As every man hath received the gift, even so minister the same one to another, as good stewards of the manifold grace of God."— 1 St. Peter iv. 10.

SUCH is the Apostle's rule, or rather God's rule, given through His Apostle, of the way in which we are to use what God has given us ; the rule of mutual service, by means of, and in proportion to, the power which God has given us to help one another. And of course the rule holds good of all the actions of our lives. Whatever we have, whatever we can do, is God's free gift to us, is God's talent committed to our stewardship,—to take care of and use for the Master's service, and for our brethren's good.

Manifold is His grace, manifold and different are the separate gifts which He bestows upon men. And what He gives He gives us not for ourselves alone, but for others also. He gives to us not that we may say in our hearts, " This is my own ; I may do what I like with it," but that we may be able, in the manifold wants and needs of our brethren around us, to contribute to their good or to their comfort. What different lives should we lead, what a different world it would be, if we really tried in ever so small

a degree to act upon this view of our place on the
earth, and of the reason why God sent us into it :
namely, that all we have is God's, and from God ;
and that His reason for giving us what we have,—
health and strength, or money, or skill, or understanding,—was not that we might use these things
only for our own profit or pleasure, but for the
profit and pleasure of others. We can none of us
do without one another. There is nothing, there is
no man, solitary and by himself, and needing no
help from others. God means all His manifold gifts
to be part of a common stock. He gave to others
for our sake ; He gave to us for their sake.

This is true of all God's gifts—that is, of all that
we have and enjoy and use in the world. If it be
true of the least of God's gifts that, according as
each has received, so ought we to "minister one to
another as good stewards," much more must this be
true of the greatest of His gifts. That great gift
we keep in mind to-day. That greatest of all His
gifts is that fulfilment of our Saviour's promise,
which began in the upper room on the day of
Pentecost, and has continued even to this day.
When God sent down His holy Spirit into the
hearts of men, He may almost be said to have done
all that could be done for sinful man on this side
the grave. He gave him that which was to turn
religion from something outward into something
inward ; which was not only to give him new
knowledge about God, about himself, about eternal
things, but also to light up and kindle this knowledge into faith and love and hope ; He gave him
that which was to change and make new his heart ;

to cleanse and purify it from the sin which had been born and had grown up with it; to put new strength, new thoughts, new desires, into it; to form a link and a bond between man and God, between earth and heaven, which no trials or sorrows or losses in this life could break, and of which death itself was but the seal. All that makes the religion of Jesus Christ different from all other religions,—all that makes it one not of forms and words, but of inward consolation and hopes,—all that makes it a worship of the Father of Spirits, in spirit and in truth,—hangs upon and flows from the gift of the Spirit. It is that which has raised our lot above all other men's; above the kings and prophets of God's ancient people, above the great and the wise men of the heathen. What has been given to us is not merely a revelation and unfolding of God's truth, but a power in our hearts to take in that truth; an inward fellowship with the Spirit of God, a living and life-giving grace, by which our spirits are brought near to God, and are taught His will, and are made to feel sure, with joy and hope, of the reality of things unseen.

Is then this great gift, this purifying and spiritualising and making inward of all religion, is it for ourselves alone? Has God sent it to us, to each for himself only? Has He sent it to our nation and Church for our own good, and for nothing else? Did He so send it to His first Apostles? Was it for them alone,—for their comfort and guidance and salvation only,—that the fiery tongues descended and lighted on their heads, and that under that power from heaven they burst forth into the praises of God in all languages of the earth? Was it for themselves, for a show of their new power, or for their own instruction, that the assembled multitudes heard them speak, each man in the tongue wherein he was born, the wonderful works of God? Surely, far from it. It was indeed, in all its fulness, a gift to them. It was the making good, to the chosen friends of Christ, of their Master's promise of His peace and joy and victory over the world, that the Holy Ghost came down to them: it was to them the arrival of the expected Comforter. But it came to them that, through them, it might stream forth to the world. It came to them that they might be preachers of the Word and ministers of the Spirit to Jew and heathen, to the ends of the earth. It came, that the fire kindled in their hearts might spread and embrace all nations of the world; as we said this morning in giving thanks for the great miracle of Pentecost, "whereby we have been brought out of darkness and error into the clear light and true knowledge of Thee, and of Thy Son Jesus Christ." It came to them, that from them it might come on to us. It has come from them to us; and do you think that it has come to us that it might stop here? Has it reached even to us, and have we nothing to do, think you, to send it on beyond us?

There is the plain broad ground for these efforts to convert the heathen, for which I am to ask your sympathy and help to-day. The law of the Gospel of Christ was that it was to be an ever-spreading religion. It was at first given and committed to a very few, and they were on all sides to hand it on

C.   K

to more ; and all, as they received it, received it
with the same solemn command from their Lord,—
spread it all round you wherever you go, wherever it
can reach. You know how that command was fulfilled by Christ's Apostles ; how they pushed forward
from land to land, from city to city, never thinking
that they had done enough while there was anything
still to do. You can follow St. Paul in the Acts ;
how he hastes onward from Jerusalem to Antioch,
from Antioch to Cyprus, from Cyprus to Lystra and
Derbe and Iconium, to Ephesus and the cities of
Asia ; then, following across the sea the vision calling him, " Come over into Macedonia, and help us."
Then, through the lands of barbarian and civilised,
through mocking Greek and persecuting Jewish
multitudes, preaching the Gospel where no one had
preached it before, lest he should be entering on
other men's labours ; passing from the great cities
of the Greeks, Athens and Corinth, cities of the rich
and the learned and the wise,—like our London
and Paris,— into the depth of the roughest and
wildest countries of his age, even unto Illyricum,
to preach the Gospel of Christ. Then, when he had
conquered for Christ in the east, pressing onward
to the west,—to Italy, to Rome, perhaps to Spain,
perhaps to the utmost isles of the west,—to our own
England. But how far he went we know not ; we
lose sight of him still pressing forward, as we lose
sight of a ship pushing out to sea, or a traveller
plunging into a thick wood or a wilderness. *Where*
he ended his course we cannot tell for certain ; all
we know is that, the last sight we had of him, he was
still pressing onward to carry yet to new hearers, to

hitherto untaught races of the Gentiles, his Master's message, his Master's gift of the Spirit.

St. Paul is but one of the Apostles whose history is more particularly told us ; but what he did the others did too. With them it was that " their sound is gone out into all lands : and their words into the ends of the world." With them it was always to fulfil the saying that " To whom He was not spoken of, they shall see : and they that have not heard shall understand." No one could doubt, in this case, how they had interpreted the great command of Christian communication of God's gifts, " As every man hath received the gift, even so minister the same one to another, as good stewards of the manifold grace of God."

We are not Apostles, it is true, nor entrusted with Apostles' work. But we are Christians. And while we have been called, by God's unfathomable counsels, to know and hope in Him, others—other nations and races of men, many times more numerous than ourselves—are not yet called. And as long as there are brethren in the world not knowing their God and Father, and sitting in the shadow of death, Christians can never shake off the debt they owe to God, and to their brethren, of handing on to them, as far as they can, what they have themselves received.

If there were no other reason why we should send missionaries among the heathen, there would be no escaping the obligation we are under, from remembering the way in which the Gospel was brought to us. The thought sometimes rises in our hearts, when we are unbelieving or indifferent, or out of humour, or grudge our money—What have we to do with all

these heathen ?   We have more than enough to do
at home.   God's providence has left them in darkness, and it is for God's providence to call them out
of it when He pleases ; but what have you or I, who
never saw them, who know nothing about them, to
do, to spend our money, or give our thoughts, to try
and give a little light to them ?   And after all (we
may go on to say), for the little that we can do, why
is it worth while to take so much pains ?   Missionaries do but little.   They work for many years, and if,
after that, they have gathered a few souls together,
they think they have done a great work.   And what
are these among the millions untaught, untouched
by the Gospel, who never can possibly hear a missionary's voice ?   It seems almost, as it were, like
counting the waves of the sea, or the leaves of the
wood, or the clouds of the sky, or the grass of the
field.   It is as if we were to try and remove the
sand of the sea-shore, by taking it grain by grain
away.   What a hopeless battle, what a vain and
useless toil !   Why not stay quiet at home and mind
our own business, and leave the heathen,——whom,
do what we may, we can do so little for,——to the God
who made them ?

I will say that I do not wonder at any one at
times feeling, and even saying, this.   It is natural,
and seems at first sight like the plain sense of the
matter.   But besides that we cannot get over the
plain will and command of God, that we should
spread His Gospel through the world, there is this
short answer to all this reasoning.   It is that if
people in former days had reasoned like this, and
acted on these principles, we here in England should

never have been Christians at all. If people in former days had said, " What have we to do with the heathen in that distant barbarian island? why should we take the trouble to convert and enlighten them ? " we might still have been worshipping stocks and stones. If people in former days had been frightened by the difficulty and hopelessness of the task of attacking the superstitions and idolatries of fierce thousands and ten thousands of barbarians ; if they had said, " What can we do,—we, a few scattered helpless men, with nothing but truth and God's Word to help us ; how is it possible that those fierce, wild men will listen to the call to be pure and gentle and loving ; or, if a few do, what are they in the crowds of their countrymen, strong and obstinate, and bigoted to the customs of their fathers ? "—if, I say, people in former days had, from fears like these, shrunk from the attempt to teach our forefathers the Gospel, where, do you think, at this day would be all the glory and peace and greatness which we prize so much ? Where would be the millions among us who do not name that Name in vain ?

I can assure you of this. Take any account which you may meet with now of the savageness, the ignorance, the terrible darkness and superstitions of the heathen tribes of Africa, or the islands of the sea, and it can be matched by what we read of the people who lived in England when the Gospel was first sent here. It is true that when we read the accounts given by travellers of the heathen, they seem like different creatures from ourselves,—as if God had not made of one blood all the nations

under heaven ; as if they were too childish, too
stupid, too debased and degraded, too cruel, too
hard-hearted, ever to receive our teaching, ever to
feel as we do, and love what we love.   I can only
say that those in former days who had the knowledge of Christ, when our forefathers were still in ignorance of Him, might have said just the same of our
forefathers.   The accounts of them are written down;
their customs, their doings, their fierceness and wildness
and bloodthirstiness, were well known.   And they, too,
were much more proud and terrible and confident
in themselves than the savages are, for the most part,
now.   But the Christians of those days, who lived,
as we live, in more settled and enlightened countries,
who could have their share of ease and quiet without
troubling themselves about distant barbarians, felt
that the Gospel was not to stop at themselves ; felt
themselves debtors even to these unknown barbarians,
to try and bring them within their Master's fold.
They came to us, and tried.   They did not shut
up their hearts to us, and refuse us their interest,
because we were so far off and so different.   They
were not daunted by the numbers of the heathen, by
what seemed to human reckonings the uselessness
of the attempt.   They came, and they sent their
preachers, in faith.   They trusted that God, who
had given His command to spread His Gospel, would
do what seemed impossible to man.

Here is, in a word, the *human* cause of the conversion of England.   A minister of God, living far
away from this island, was inflamed with love and
pity for its people, our *then* heathen countrymen and
forefathers.   He desired for them the heritage of the

angels in heaven. He could not go himself, but he got others to go. A few humble, helpless men, with the Cross of Christ and the Book of God, landed on our shores. There was opposition ; there was difficulty ; there was labour that seemed in vain. Over and over again all seemed lost ; over and over again the work had to be begun anew. It was not done in a generation, or in a century. But that good man who longed for the conversion of heathen England to Christ, and who dared to attempt it, has had his wish. He did not see it. He only saw what might have seemed then its feeble and hopeless beginnings. But his work went on and prospered. What could not be done at once has been done in time. And here is this great realm and Church of England, not the least among the kingdoms of the world which acknowledge the name of Christ, the mother of new nations, the planter of new churches,— where, through its length and breadth, in cities and cottages, the Light of the World is shining,—owing all its blessings, owing its knowledge of the Gospel, owing all to the warm love and far-seeing faith and hope, which refused to be frightened, of one old man far away.

Do you think that all you can do is so little that it is not worth doing ? that all you can give is so trifling that it is not worth giving ? That will not stop you if you listen to God's rule : " As every man hath received the gift, even so minister the same one to another." Nothing is more striking in the rules and commands of the New Testament than their equity and reasonableness and fairness. There is no laying of the same burden on unequal shoulders.

No doubt it calls on us to do our best,—to do it truly and honestly ; but the seriousness with which it makes this claim is shown in the just and even way in which it measures each man's duty by each man's ability.   But let us remember that if we could fairly do more, and do not do it, the equity, which does not claim from us more than we can do in proportion to our gifts and powers, will judge us.

And when, on a day like this, we call to remembrance, first, the great gift sent down from heaven of God's Holy Spirit ; and next, how wonderfully, by God's mercy, the knowledge and the admission to this gift of truth and comfort has been brought nigh to ourselves, we ought to feel that we owe some token of our thankfulness to God for His mercies to ourselves.   We owe Him, first of all, a thankful heart and a holy life as long as we live ; but, over and above this, we owe Him a special duty of endeavouring to do for others what has been done for us,—of handing on the light of His truth and salvation to men who have not heard of them.   We have received largely and bountifully.   We are accustomed to think that to no other people has God given the light of His truth more fully, and with less mixture of error.   In this we are all concerned ; we are all partakers.   Partakers therefore we ought all to be, according to our power, in the attempt to spread that light farther.   And, indeed, small as are now the beginnings of that work, and trying to faith, as it seems in our day, we know not what great things we are doing when we are laying the foundation of Christ's Kingdom in some heathen land.   No missionary undertaking in heathen countries now could be more unpromising than was the attempt to plant the Gospel here in England, and we see what this has come to. Shall we be less liberal, shall we have less faith in our cause, shall we be less able to look forward and foresee the final success, through many failures, and after long disappointments, than were those who in darker ages, and through greater difficulties, yet believed that they were not throwing away their pains in sending *us* the Gospel?

I leave this call of duty with you. I am sure that in helping it we are fulfilling our Lord's dearest wish. I believe that in it no labour, no gifts, no prayers, no self-denial, will in the end be wasted. I do not tell you that in our own day and generation we are to expect to see much fruit gathered in the heathen fields. It takes more time than that to convert nations, and overthrow a reign of darkness that has lasted for ages. But I do say that, in attacking this darkness, in sending men with nothing but their zeal and love, and the Gospel of Christ in their hands, to make their way among the heathen, we are doing exactly what was done when our own country was converted to Christ; we are doing what, in our case, has ended, after many days and many trials, in success. Therefore, I ask you to help in it; to help in it according to your means; to help in it according as your conscience tells you that you can spare something to be, as it were, a seed in the Gospel field. Here you will never see or hear of it more. It will go to swell the stream of gifts by which the missionary is sent abroad. But you know who will mark it; you know who can follow the least gift of the poorest, as it is lost to

human eyes in the multitude of larger gifts. You
know who watched and remembered the widow's
farthing, when the rich were casting in of their
abundance into God's treasury. That eye is upon us
still, to mark who might give and will not ; to mark
who gives, however little, according as each has
received from Him ability to give. As you have
been ministered to, so minister, as good stewards,
each in his own place, of the gifts of God, so manifold, so endless, in their differences. As others who
did not know you cared for you, so be generous, be
large-hearted, in caring for those whom you know not.

It is worth remembering, on an occasion like this,
that the first martyr who died for Christ in England
gave his life for his neighbour as much as he gave it
for the truth. His name was Alban. It was a time
of persecution, and a Christian priest came flying
from his pursuers, and took shelter in Alban's house.
Alban was still a heathen, but he hid the Christian
priest, out of pure kindness and pity for a hunted
man. When, however, he observed the devotion of
his guest,—how fervent it was, and how firm, and the
consolation and joy he seemed to find in prayer,—
Alban's heart was touched ; and he listened to his
teacher, and became a believer. Meanwhile the
persecutors had found out where the Christian was
hidden, and came to search Alban's house. Then
Alban, putting on the dress of his teacher, delivered
himself into their hands, as if he had been the fugitive ;
and in this way the man whom they had sought
had time to escape. But Alban, because he refused
to betray his guest, and say where he was gone, or
to offer sacrifice to the idols he used to worship, was

scourged, and led forth to be put to death. The spot was a beautiful meadow, clothed with flowers, on a little rising ground——a fit theatre for a martyr's triumph ; and there now stand a church and town which bear his name. There he was beheaded. And his example of noble generosity was followed on the spot. The soldier who was appointed to put him to death was so moved by his resignation and greatness of heart that he chose rather to suffer with him than to have the guilt of being his executioner. Let us remember this when we are tempted to be selfish. Let us remember that the first great deed of Christianity in England, the first instance in which it showed its power, was in making a man die to save a stranger's life, and draw on another to die with him. The first display of Christian grace was an act of loving others better than a man's self, and giving up for them all hope and reward in this world. It seems like a sign, a foreshadowing token, of what was to be the highest and noblest feature of English goodness and religion, the readiness to help others, to our cost ; the readiness to sacrifice every-thing to a call of duty, of which we cannot see the end.

May we not fall short of that of which we have such noble examples.

XV

TO KNOW GOD IS LIFE ETERNAL

" This is life eternal, that they might know Thee the only true God,
and Jesus Christ, whom Thou hast sent."—St. JOHN xvii. 3.

THIS is the great day of the year which reminds us
how much of the knowledge of God has been vouchsafed to us. By Trinity Sunday we are put in mind
that we have been graciously allowed to know God
as He is: God the Father, God the Son, God the
Holy Ghost, in three Persons, yet one God. How
highly favoured are we—how singularly chosen out
of all our race, to be brought near to our Maker, and
to know His name. Hundreds of thousands who
are alive with us at this day do not know Him at
all ; we may know Him as fully as He can be known
to man on earth. In former days He was known
only dimly and darkly ; all was not told about Him
that was to be told ; but for us the shadows have
departed, and the veil is taken away. We may
know Him as the angels know and praise Him.
Christ has shown us plainly of the Father, and of
the Holy Spirit, and of Himself. The mysteries
that were hid from many generations, which many
kings and righteous men desired to see, our eyes
have seen, our ears have heard. They have been

revealed so as to be understood even by babes. How great indeed is our blessedness, if we understand it ; how dreadful our blindness and our woe, if in the midst of light we still are blind,—if in the midst of God's love we still do not know Him. "For this," says our Master, "is life eternal, that they might know Thee the only true God, and Jesus Christ, whom Thou hast sent." Not to know God is to be in eternal death : and *for us* not to know God is, with eternal life before us, with eternal life offered us, still to be by our own choosing in eternal death. He who knows God truly is not merely waiting and hoping for eternal life : he has begun already to enter on the inheritance, to live that heavenly life which, except by his own sin and falling away afterwards, can never end.

But what is it to know God ? For in one sense there are few, among us at least, who have not some knowledge of God. When we speak of Christians who do not know God, we do not mean that they are like heathens and idolaters, who have never heard the blessed name. It would be better almost that *some* were as ignorant as heathens ; it would be better for them that they had not the additional sin of knowing their Maker and Saviour, and yet rebelling against Him. But this kind of knowing God cannot be what Christ meant when He said that eternal life was to know God. To know God in this way must be indeed a very different thing from knowing Him as even sinners and hypocrites may know Him.

Let us see what it does *not* mean. To know God does not mean to have heard of Him, and been

taught about Him, just as we may have heard of
some distant country, or some wonderful work, with
which we have nothing to do, except to hear of it.
Many people seem to think it enough to know God in
this distant, outward, formal way. It never enters
into their head that knowing Him by name, as it were,
and knowing Him as we know some famous person
who is far above us, whom we shall never see or
speak to, can never make God be to them what the
Bible represents Him ; can never make them take
comfort in Him, or rejoice in Him, or hope in Him.
How can we take comfort or rejoice in one whom we
know only by hearsay, and whose name is a mere
word to us ? How can we be saved or supported
by one whom we never bring near to us, with whom
we have nothing to do ?

Nor does knowing God mean merely knowing a
great deal of what the Bible tells us about Him. We
may know much about a person without knowing
the person himself. We may know much about a
business without really and truly knowing the very
thing itself, without having really entered into it with
our mind and made ourselves masters of it, and got
our hand into it. So we may know a great deal
of the Bible, a great deal about God, without knowing that God whom the Bible reveals to us. We
may take a great interest in searching out religious
questions without knowing God ; we may have
many texts in remembrance, and not only remember
them, but understand them, and yet not know God.
We may be able to speak wisely and truly about
God's nature, about His works and ways, about His
redemption and His promises, and yet but very im-

perfectly know and understand God as He is in His doings toward the children of men.

Nor even does knowing God merely mean being under the influence of religious thoughts and impressions. We sometimes hear persons speak as if knowing God was only one of many ways of describing in Scripture language a religious frame of mind and course of life. Doubtless, the man who, ever so imperfectly, tries in earnest to serve God,—the merest babe in Christ,—does know more of God really than the man who is most learned in the Scriptures, but whose heart is not turned to God. But at the same time the knowledge of God as Jesus Christ spoke of it is a great thing. It must not be supposed that every one has it whose conscience is really pricked for his sins ; nor even every one who has begun in earnest to think of eternal things, and heartily and seriously to seek to please God, and to gain the forgiveness and peace and strength of the Gospel. Such a man, if his faith is real and his heart sound, is in the way to know God. But we must not speak as if turning to God was at once the same as knowing God,—as if in the first days or the first years of a repentant sinner's new life he was to expect or to think that he had come at one step to what the Bible means by knowing God.

What then does knowing God mean ? It means, not knowing Him by name, not knowing about Him, not knowing Him as a stranger and foreigner, whose speech and ways we have not been accustomed to ; but knowing Him in the sense in which we know a father, or mother, or friend, whom we love and value above every one else ; whose ways and thoughts we are thoroughly acquainted with ; and who, we feel, knows us thoroughly, feels with us, cares for us, and longs for our being happy. This is really knowing ; and this is a thing not to be gained in a day, even among men. We may have a great deal to do with a person, and yet feel that we do not know him. We may like a person very much, and have much in common with him, yet feel that this is different from what we call knowing him intimately. We may be very good friends, and walk together pleasantly and profitably, and yet feel that there is very much of his heart which we have never come near,—that there are many of his thoughts which we do not understand,— that there are many of his ways which we cannot see the reason of. It is when we *do* feel that we enter into his wishes and thoughts, that our heart goes with his heart, that we feel the same way and follow the same things and act by the same rules,—then it is that we begin to say and to feel that we know a person.

And knowing God means nothing less than this kind of knowing : knowing not by the hearing of the ear, but by the heart and mind and soul ; knowing not by name or outward words, but by real experience, by having to do with Him in the course of life, in sorrow and in joy, in trouble and in success. Doubtless, we cannot know Almighty God as we know our fellow-men. We cannot understand the thoughts and ways of the wonderful Lord, who fills heaven and earth, who is without beginning and without end, whom no man hath seen or can see, as we can those of our brethren whose faces we have seen and whose voices we can hear. But what says the great God of Hosts ? " Thus saith the high and

lofty One that inhabiteth eternity, whose name is
Holy ; I dwell in the high and holy place, with him
also that is of a contrite and humble spirit, to revive
the spirit of the humble, and to revive the heart of
the contrite ones." And what says our Master also?
" If a man love Me, he will keep My words : and My
Father will love him, and we will come unto him,
and make our abode with him." He is in heaven
and we on earth, yet we may hope to know Him.
He is perfect and holy and we are blind and weak
and sinful ; but though we cannot know Him perfectly, yet we may know Him, though imperfectly,
and understand some part of His goodness, and
wisdom and love ; and even the archangels cannot
understand it all.

To know God is eternal life ; for, indeed, it is to
live continually in His presence, to have Him for the
witness and companion of our daily life. And what
else is eternal life than a life with God, a life led for
ever in the presence of God, and as God desires?
To begin to live so on earth is to begin to do here
what we shall continue to do in glory in the world
to come. Here we do it with pain and difficulty,
with many mistakes and continual sins, among
enemies and temptations ; and there enemies and
temptations will be gone for ever, and peace and
holiness and glory will have come in the place of
sin and pain. But the life will be the same,—only
the traveller will have reached his home,—the work-
man will have done his work,—the soldier will have
won his rest.

Compare the two lives : the life of him who does
not know God, and the life of him who does, and

C.   L

you will see that eternal life has indeed begun to
the man who really knows God—knows Him in his
walks and ways, about his path and about his bed.
To him who knows not God and His ways this world
may be very well as long as he is young and in
prosperity, and everything goes well with him.   But
when does the world go entirely right with any man,
even the young and the happy ?   Do not most days
bring their trouble and vexation—something that
goes wrong and cross ?   And what is there then for
the man who knows not God but to feel the bitterness
without anything to sweeten it, and to give himself
up to his sorrow and disappointment ?

And what, when real heavy grief and difficulty
come?   When he is sick, he must bear the whole weight
of it, without anything to brighten and soothe him, for
man cannot share it with him, and the comfort and
hope of God are strange and unknown to him.   If
heavy afflictions come on him, he can only see in them
unmixed misery and hopeless anguish, for he has not
been accustomed to God's ways, and understands
nothing of how God mingles mercy even with judgment, and how He chastises those whom He loves for
their good.   If he is in great straits, and cannot see his
way, he is brought at once to despair, for he knows not
that God is a light in the darkness, and that, to those
who trust His guidance, the time which seems most
hopeless on earth is the time when the seed of comfort
and light are sown for future years.   When earthly
things fail with him, when man fails to help and
support him, he has nothing beyond and above the
earth to give a stronger and more enduring consolation.   He knows not God ; he knows not God's

ways of dealing with those He loves.   He sees all
round him nothing but plagues and torments, which he
is not strong enough to get rid of and drive away.   He
sees all around, in heaven and earth, no one to pity
him, no one to take his part, no one who can feel for
his sorrows, no one to guide his steps, no one to bring
him right if he has gone astray, no one to tell him
that his sins are forgiven, no one to make up to him
for all that he has lost.   The name of God gives
him no hope, for it is merely a name to him.   He
has lived without God, in his real, actual life ; he has
not sought to understand and know God ; and when
none but God can minister relief and open the
doors of hope, the doors of hope remain closed, and
" vanity of vanities " is all that remains to him of life.

How different to be able to spend our days here
knowing God : knowing Him as our Father, our
Guide, our Friend ; knowing His way of dealing with
those He loves ; understanding His deep and abounding tenderness as it works, through outward troubles ;
seeing His hand and love in all things, and able to
commit our way to Him, sure that in the best and
most blessed manner He will bring it to pass ; feeling that He is with us, and that all things work for
good to them that love Him ; feeling that, as a dear
friend watches us in his kindness, so His eye is ever
over us, and He sees into our very heart ; sure that,
as earthly things depart, heavenly things will be
coming nearer, and, that whatever comes on us here,
nothing can take Him and His love away from us.

Those who thus know God have the thought of
Him with them wherever they are ; just as we think
continually of our friends whom we have long

known and tried and found faithful. Daily they learn, more and more, His mind and will. Daily they become more and more near to Him whom they have taken for their hope and reward. Daily their thoughts become more like God's thoughts ; they judge of things in the world as God judges of them ; they measure good and evil, blessings and losses, as He measures them ; they get to be one in feeling with Him,—able to take what He sends, and to be without those things which He sees not good to send. And daily, more and more, in what they do they think of what He would approve and like ; their first thought is not of what they would like themselves, but of what would please Him and help forward what He desires. Thus more and more, as life goes on, they live with Him, not by talking or profession, but in the real inward feelings and wishes and thoughts of their hearts ; and by watching Him, thinking of Him, trying to copy Him, they become more and more like Him, they are " changed into the same image, from glory to glory, even as by the Spirit of the Lord."

And then how different are earthly troubles to them. In pain and anguish they know that the smart is but for a while, and that it is not sent by chance and for no good ; for they know *God*, and they know His way of sending pain. When they are at their wits' end, and see no help anywhere, they still are not cast down ; they know who is secretly round about them, for they know God, and that it is His way so to try His children's trust and affection. And when it is all over with them here, and the silent and sure step of death is heard at the door, they know that, nevertheless, all things have *not* an

end with them; they know that the best part of
their portion and hope is yet to come,—yea, is at
the very doors with death itself. For why? They
know God; they know in whom they have believed;
they know Him who is Immortal, and strong above
death and hell; they know Him who is the Resurrection and the Life. Is not this, even here, eternal
life, to know Thee, " the only true God, and Jesus
Christ whom Thou hast sent"?

Oh how blessed above all are those who have thus
learnt to know Him. Pray and strive for it; for it
is not a blessing which comes by wishing for it, by
working ourselves up to strong feeling and heated
thought. It comes by degrees. It comes as the
wind comes—we know not whence. For, indeed, it
is the reward, not of the beginner in religion, but of
the tried and proved servant of God. It is the
reward of faithfulness and obedience. It can be
hoped for in no other way than from the earnest
and consistent endeavour to please God, to serve and
honour Him,—not here and there, not now and then,
but throughout the whole course of life. Thus by
experience shall we come to know God; thus shall
we find what we read about Him in the Bible made
good to our own hearts, to the joys and troubles of
our own lives. Let us live as if we desired to know
God. Let us earnestly strive, in thought and deed,
to keep His commandments; and surely we shall be
learning in very truth to know Him. For so is
Christ's promise, " He that hath My commandments,
and keepeth them, he it is that loveth Me: and he that
loveth Me shall be loved of My Father . . and we
will come unto him, and make our abode with him."

XVI

THE DANGER OF THE WORLD

"Love not the world, neither the things that are in the world. If any man love the world, the love of the Father is not in him."— 1 St. John ii. 15.

WE hear a great deal said in Holy Scripture about the world, the evil of the world, the love of the world; and we ought to take care that we understand rightly what is meant by these words. I do not know anything of greater consequence towards making our religion a solid and real thing than knowing what we mean, and having the right meaning, when we use common, familiar, religious words. And I do not know any habit that we are more apt to fall into than using them without thinking of what they mean. We hear them so often that we come to think that of course we understand them. Faith and grace, and sin and repentance, and forgiveness and salvation, and a number of words of the same kind, are for ever coming up when we read the Bible or hear sermons; and, I am afraid, we go on hearing them again and again, without ever asking ourselves whether we do more than hear these words with our ears; whether in our minds they stand for something which is more than a mere common sound, and of which we take in the meaning. And so we go on, hearing without profit, because we never ask ourselves whether we really know what is meant by these words, which seem so plain and easy only because we hear them so often.

Such a word is that which is so common in all religious books and discourses — the world. The world is spoken of as an enemy, a temptation, a danger. The love of this world is what we are continually warned against. Worldliness is one of the worst signs against a man—one of the sins which, in words at least, we all acknowledge to be inconsistent with true religion. Everybody can talk against worldliness. Every one allows and takes for granted that it is wrong to love the world. Ought we not then to know as clearly as we can what is meant by the world?

There can be no doubt or mistake that this is the true and right way of speaking. When in our baptism we renounce the vain pomp and glory of the world, with all covetous desires of the same; when in our Catechism we are taught to look on the world as one of the three great enemies of our souls; when in the Collect we pray to God to give us grace to resist the temptations of the world, the flesh, and the devil,—we are but speaking as the Bible has taught us, we are but calling the world our enemy, because the Bible has taught us that it is so. "Know ye not," says St. James, "that the friendship of the world is enmity with God? whosoever therefore will be a friend of the world is the enemy of God." "Love not the world," St. John says, "neither the things that are in the world. If any man love the world, the love of the Father is not in him." "The whole world," he says in another place, "lieth in wickedness ; " and the great victory of faith,—that in which it is like to the victory of Jesus Christ Himself,—is that it " overcomes the world." And our Lord Himself speaks in the same way about the world. Those who are not His are the children of this world. His and our great spiritual enemy, the devil, is called by Him the " prince of this world." Christ's kingdom is " not of this world." They who are His are " hated by the world "; they are said to be "not of this world, even as He is not of this world." The world, in all these passages—and these are but some out of many like them—stands for something confessedly evil, confessedly contrary to Christ's Gospel, confessedly inconsistent with His service, and fatal to men's souls.

What is meant by the world here ? What is this terrible world which rises up in the pages of Scripture as the mighty and dangerous foe of Christ and of His kingdom ? What is that ensnaring and corrupting world to which it is as much as their souls are worth, that Christians be not " conformed " ? What is this " present evil world " out of which their hope is " to be delivered " ?

I suppose, if we were asked what was meant by the expression,—if we were asked to explain, in other words, what it stands for,—our first answer would be something of this kind : that the world means all this present state of things which we see, with all the fine and pleasant and profitable things which men are so fond of, and with all the people who are fond of them and follow them. This present state of things, this present life, and what belongs to it—that is the natural answer of most to the question what is meant in the Catechism, or in

these passages of the Bible, by *the world*.   Must we
then regard this present state of things, and all that
belongs to it, with the feelings which the Bible tells
us Christians ought to have towards the world ?
Well then, but what a life are we all leading !   If
the world means simply this present state of things,
and if worldliness means simply the love of what
belongs to this present state of things, what are we,
one and all of us, doing ?   We have families and
family ties, fathers and mothers, husbands and wives,
brothers and sisters, and children.   Our hearts are
full of them ; we love them, and our hearts are
bound up with their lives and happiness ; and do
not family ties and interests belong to this present
state of things ?   We have our business and work,
one after this manner, another after that ; work
which takes up our time and thoughts, and gives us
enough to do to get through it, whether it be with
our hands or with our brains, whether it be our
farm, or our day's labour, or our merchandise, or our
learning, or our teaching.   Our days are given to it,
we think it right to be earnest and thorough in it,
and if we are doing it as we ought, we are finding
great and real pleasure in doing it to the very best
of our power.   And do not all the businesses and
works of man, works of his hand or of his mind,
every pursuit and calling in which he is employed,
do not they all belong to this present state of things ?
We have many pleasures and enjoyments ; we say,
when we speak of them religiously, that God has
graciously been abundant in His gifts to us ; we
enjoy the beauty and the bounty of His creation, the
beauty and the glory of the sun and the light, of the

trees and fields, of the sea and the mountains, of the
flowers of the spring and the richness of the summer,
of the ripeness and the golden harvests of the
autumn.   We rejoice in the great and wonderful
inventions of man's skill and power ; we find delight
in reading the beautiful and marvellous things and
thoughts which men with greater gifts than their
brethren have preserved and handed down to us
in their books.   But all these, — the beautiful
story, the grand history, the glorious poetry,—what
are they but of this present state of things ?   Yet
these are things among which our life is spent.   In
these is our chief employment, our chief pleasure.
As long as we are here we are full of them.   Well
then, are all these simply part of that world which
lieth in wickedness ? of that world which we have
renounced ? of that world which whoso loveth, must
of necessity be the enemy of God ?   These things, I
say, belong only to this present state of things ;
are they, therefore, necessarily of this world ? is the
love of them love of the world and worldliness ?

If so, I do not see what there is for us but simply
to go out of the world, and have no more to do with
what men in general engage in.   It is quite certain
that what we are all busy about is for the most part
of this present state only ; that it is but for a time,
that it must vanish and pass away, as we are told in
Holy Scripture that the world does, and the lust
thereof.   And if the world means all that belongs
to this present state, and if all love and care for
what belongs to this present state is worldliness, it
would seem to be impossible to live as most men
have to live,—to follow our callings, to love our

families, to rejoice in the pleasures which are the
portion of this life, and also to attend to the words
of the Bible, and to renounce the world and worldliness as we promised in our baptism.

But is it not much more likely that we have not
taken the trouble to think and understand what the
Bible means by *the world*; that we have used the
words at random, because we have heard them in
the mouths of others, and perhaps thought it a fine
thing to talk against the world, and perhaps condemn our neighbours as worldly? If what the Bible
means by worldly means everything which belongs
to this present state, which of us does not love the
world, which of us is not a worldling and servant of
mammon? But that cannot be the right meaning.
What it means we will try to see presently. But
in the meantime let us consider what comes of
using such a word as this without thinking of what
it really means. Either people put wrong meanings
to it, or they come to think that it has no meaning
at all. Either they torment themselves with scruples
and difficulties about what may be worldly, or they
get into harsh and uncharitable ways of denouncing
as the world or worldly some particular things
against which they have a prejudice, or which are
done by people they do not like, or which are not to
their taste; without thinking whether what they do,
and allow themselves in, is not just as much a matter
belonging to the present state of things. Or else,
looking at the inconsistencies of those who talk
much against the world and worldliness, and seeing
clearly that God did mean men to be busy with
the things of this present state, and to make them

glad with the blessings and gifts of His good creatures here, they persuade themselves that there is no meaning at all in what is said of the evil and danger of the world, and no such sin really as what is called worldliness. They flatter themselves that they need not be on their guard against what, perhaps, is their most deadly peril ; they throw off from their souls and consciences all that religion urges to awaken and alarm them ; and its sternest and most awful lessons fall dead on their ears and hearts.

What, then, does the Bible mean when it condemns and warns us against the world ? Not simply the things of this present state, or the love and care for them : for our families, which God bids us love and provide for, our business, in which He bids us to be diligent and earnest, the temporal gifts and enjoyments which He bids us rejoice in and give thanks for,—these are all of this present state, and of that only. And if they were " the world " against the love of which He warns us, He would be giving us with one hand what, with the other, He was beckoning us to refuse. The world which the Bible warns us against is not simply this present state of things, but this present state of things *set against and preferred to the world to come, and eternity.* If there were no heaven and no hereafter, we could have nothing to think of but this present state. But there is a hereafter, there is a heaven to be gained or lost ; and this being so, this present state, whatever be its goodness or desirableness, must of course be of very trifling moment when it is compared or weighed against that which is to come. So if we choose this present life rather than life eternal, we choose

what Holy Scripture calls *this world*.   If we are so
full of the things which belong to this present state,
however in themselves lawful and innocent and
right, that we forget that other world, then our
hearts are full of what Holy Scripture calls the *cares
of this world*.   If we, who are Christians, and have
the promise of an everlasting inheritance, live like
heathen, who know nothing of any promise of everlasting life, we are living a worldly life, a life conformed to this world.   If we love anything of this
present state so much as to drive out of our hearts
the love of our Father and God, and the wish to be
with Him, and to be like Him, for ever, we have
that love of the world which the Bible declares is
enmity with God.   He Himself bids us love our
neighbours, love our friends, love father and mother,
wife and children ; but if even *these* we love more
than Him, we choose our portion with this world,
and are not worthy of Him and His kingdom.

This, I say, is what the Bible means by the
world, by the love of this world, by worldliness,—
not simply this present state, in which we must have
our dealings, our interests, our deepest human love
and affection ; but this present state whenever, and
under whatever circumstances, it is the one only
thought and love of our hearts ; whenever it throws
the other, the eternal state, into the shade, shuts it
out and makes us forget it, and live as if it were not
to be ; whenever we sacrifice the hope of that
future blessedness, or the service of the God who is
out of sight, to anything whatever, hope or fear,
pleasure or advantage, care or love, that is of the
present ; whenever we shrink from denying ourselves

and our wishes now, in order that God may not
account us unworthy of His presence hereafter.   In
one word, the present state of things becomes " this
world " in its bad sense to us, with all its dangers
and evils, whenever this present state becomes all in
all to us, and whenever we use this world without
remembering that it is God's world.

It is not in the things themselves that we are to
look for that " evil world," which is one of our three
great enemies, and which, with the devil and the
lusts of the flesh, we renounced in baptism ; not in
the things themselves, but in our way of using them,
our way of looking at them, our way of loving and
following them.   They are in themselves what God
has made good, and given to us for this space of our
mortal life ; they are for our benefit, our comfort and
admiration ; we cannot do without them.   But the
moment that we lift them up to that exclusive possession of our hearts which something better and
greater than they are ought to have, we make this the
" evil world " to us.   The moment we put them in
the place of God, and make them the reason for not
obeying and serving Him as we ought, we turn them
into that fatal and poisonous world, to be bound to
which is to lose our souls.   If we find that, in fact,
they keep us from thinking of eternal things, we
may be sure that we are in danger from the world ;
not because they are bad in themselves, but because
our hearts are wrong.   It is the forgetfulness of
God's love and goodness and holiness, the dislike
to obey His laws, the turning away of the soul from
the remembrance of Him,—it is the fault and sin in
man himself, which finds snares where God placed

blessings, and which fills so widely human society with the sin of worldliness, that the Apostle speaks of the whole world lying in wickedness.

Now here is a meaning of "the world" and "the love of the world" which does not drive us from the employments of this life, or shut us out from its blessings ; but which certainly will not let any one say that *worldliness* is one of those empty words of which we cannot find the clear reality and substance in actual life.   For if worldliness is not simply the love of this life, but the love of this life better than of the other,—the sacrificing the hopes of the other to the good of this,—then surely most people's consciences must know what it means.   Most people must remember times when what was only of this world came into opposition with something that belonged to the other.   Alas ! and most people must remember times when the things of this life prevailed over and cast out all thought and care of the other. May there not be some who can hardly remember any time when, this life and the other being weighed against each other, the hopes of the other life made them give up what they liked or wished for now ?

But, at any rate, this any one can understand— that there is such a thing, over and above feeling interest and affection for the things of this present state, as loving them more than the will of God, more than the duty of a Christian, more than the prospect of eternal life.   If there is, then, that which we prefer to God's will and promise, is what the Bible warns us against as *the world*,—that love which will not let us obey God, which will not give way when it clashes and crosses with what He says is good and right, is *worldliness*.

If any one *so* love the world, surely, as St. John says, "the love of the Father is not in him." If he *so* love this present state of things that he deliberately shuts his eyes to that gracious and glorious promise of a better, which the Father, in His love to us, has revealed, the love of the Father cannot be in him. If he is so satisfied with this life that he deliberately chooses to have his portion here, it is no hard thing to say that there is enmity between him and his God. If he deliberately makes his religion give way to his worldly interests or earthly affections, he cannot be excused because worldly interests and earthly affections are not sinful in themselves ; he cannot thus escape the charge of serving mammon more than Christ, of being a "lover of pleasure more than a lover of God." And what a bargain is this love of the world ! "What shall it profit a man, if he shall gain the whole world, and lose his own soul?" What profit indeed?

This world, this present state of things, has its excellencies, its marvellous blessings, its marvellous perfections, its unspeakably gracious gifts. Great are they, greatly to be prized, greatly to be given thanks for. Let no one speak scornfully of them, lest he be found to speak foolishly and unthankfully. Let no one say that they are not meant for the use and profit and exercise of man ; for they are the gifts of our Father's love and providence for His creatures. But at the best, what are they ? They do not last ; they cannot be kept. And we,—*we*, undying and immortal spirits,—we last beyond them. We live on to find them gone ; we shall be living on when they

have been long forgotten. " The world passeth away,
and the lust thereof." Even so ; whether we use the
world rightly or abuse it, in either case it passes
away. The gifts of God, which we have sanctified
by thanksgiving, and so turned them into blessings,
and those which we have set up as idols against the
Giver, and so turned into curses, alike pass away ;
and leave us, the spirit and living soul which even
death does not kill,—leave us, who cannot pass away
into nothingness as they do,—leave us to receive the
fruit and reward of our use of them. And, then, with
this certainty before our eyes, to prefer *them* to God !

Oh, what reason to be watchful lest in our employment and use of the things of this present time
we forget all about that time which is soon to come.
We have no business to decline the things of this
present time. We have no business to fasten the
name of worldliness on a busy and occupied life, or
on the full and keen enjoyment of the countless
blessings which God showers on us. It is part of
our trial to serve and remember God in the round
and bustle of common workday life. But, after all,
it is but a short interest that we have in it all.
" This I say, brethren, the time is short : it remaineth,
that both they that have wives be as though they
had none ; and they that weep, as though they wept
not ; and they that rejoice, as though they rejoiced
not ; and they that buy, as though they possessed
not ; and they that use this world, as not abusing it :
for the fashion of this world passeth away." Can
we hear without being moved these solemn words ?
Can we resist being moved by them : and shall we
not lay them to heart ?

C.   M

XVII

THE NEVER-FAILING PROVIDENCE
OF GOD

"In thee, O Lord, have I put my trust: let me never be put to confusion."—Psalm xxxi. 1.

THERE are times in our lives when at the thought of all that we have to do, and of all that we have to fear, our hearts sink within us. Our duties are great and often difficult, and they are unceasing. There is no end of them. Doing them to-day does not relieve us from the necessity of having to meet new ones to-morrow. And so much hangs on these duties. There is mercy, there is considerate allowance, there is forgiveness; but yet so much hangs on these duties. And how can we be sure of always answering as we were meant to answer the call of God,—of fulfilling, as He requires of us, His will?

And our dangers, too, are great. We see in the Bible, we see in all experience, how common it is to fail, to be led from the right way into the wrong; how much there is in the world of secret, hidden mischief; how the path of human life lies among snares and pitfalls. We know that we must be tried; we know that we must be tempted. Things will happen which will put us to the proof, which will

show what we are and what is in our hearts.
And we know that we are weak, and have made
mistakes ; that we have before now been tried and
found wanting. And who can tell what is waiting
for us in the dark unknown future before us ? Who
knows what we may have to suffer ; who knows
what we may have to lose ; who knows what enemies
are lying in wait for us in the dark time to come—
enemies terrible, unseen, and unknown, of those in
the spiritual world which war against the soul ?
What may not be our appointed lot of trouble ?
What strange changes of our fortune may we not
see on our passage to the grave ? What may we
not have one day to choose between ?

We must feel that we are born into an awful
world,—awful in what it shows us and in what it
hides ; awful in its ever new beauty and ever new
opening glories ; awful in its undiscovered secrets,
and its darkness which no eye or mind can pierce
through. It spreads all round us and folds us round,
and we feel, as it were, lost in it. We are like children lost on a wide common on a dark night. Where
we are going, what may befall us, is hidden from
us. What has happened to others, why should it
not happen to us ? Where can we feel our guide ?
Who can feel sure that he will be guided safely ; that
help will come at the moment when it will be of
use ; that, when we are least thinking of it, the evil
day may not come ?

These things, I say, will come into our thoughts
sometimes. They do not come, perhaps, into the
thoughts of the brave, or into the thoughts of the
dull and insensible, who never look forward ; but

all of us are not insensible, and all of us are not
brave.

When these thoughts oppress us we are told, and
rightly told, to put them away from us.   They are
weak thoughts, vain thoughts, faithless thoughts,
useless thoughts ; and, taken by themselves as they
come upon us when they distress us, they are false
thoughts.   For besides that they cannot do anything
to strengthen and defend us,—besides that
all they can do is to disturb and discourage us,—
besides that all dwelling on what we can know
nothing of and cannot help is one of those wrong
things which we *ought* to, and which we really have
the power to drive out of our minds,—at the outside,
the thoughts themselves are but *half true.*

For if it is true that our duties are great, it is true
also that in their own due time and season they will
not be greater than we may hope to have strength
to do.   If it is true that our dangers are great and
manifold, it is also true that our safeguards and
means of escape are as many and as various, and
that we may wisely and reasonably trust them.   If
experience shows many failures, it shows too as
many triumphs.   So that to think only of what
is against us is to think of what is only half the
truth.   And half the truth becomes falsehood when
we think of it as if it were the whole truth.

But in our days of weakness and trouble these
fears and anxieties will not always go because we bid
them.   They will not always give way to what, in
calmer and cooler moments, we see to be truth and
reason and good sense.   And even if we do keep
them down, they do not lose their power to disquiet

and sadden ; their shadow falls across our path, and we cower and shrink before the unknown future and its unsearchable darkness, which looks so threatening because no one can tell what it may hide and have in store. To-day, perhaps, we can face it boldly To-morrow the awful "*may-be's*" of the time to come open out one after another with oppressive clearness, and rise up before us, challenging us to say that they are impossible. We have no covenant with pain or death ; we are not assured against what has visited other men. Who knows what news to-morrow may bring us ? Who knows what we may be called to go through before the month is past ? Who knows what accident may happen to us ? Who can say that, turning any corner, we may not meet our fate ?

Is there nothing but the calm, deliberate debate of unexcited reason, arguing about what is likely and what is sensible and prudent, to meet this pressure ? Is there nothing else to take off the burden on the heart and spirit ? Is there no present and immediate remedy against fears which are so trying just be-cause they are so dim and vague ? Is there any thought which can be set against these thoughts, strong enough to overpower them,——weighty enough to be put in the balance against them,——true enough to be matched against what is true in them,——real enough to be relied on, for the heart of man to lean on,——cheering enough to nerve our spirits to face the chances of our lot, and to quicken our fainthearted-ness into life and hope ?

There is such a thought. There is a thought, resting on which, and calling it up in our souls in its

simple, plain, living truth, we can endure, and feel
ourselves comforted and at peace, when a too vivid
sense of the risks and jeopardy of man's life threatens
to crush us.   It is the thought that God guides us;
that we are not walking and wandering unwatched,
uncared for,—helpless among enemies, blindly stum-
bling along a path in which no one directs our steps;
but that all round us, now and to-morrow, and each
hour until the end, are the watchful eyes of God,
are the mighty hands of God.   From the range of
those eyes we can never stray; from out of those
hands we can never fall.   Infinite wisdom is in that
foresight that never fails; infinite love and goodness
in that power which has no master.   Are we able to
trust that wisdom?   Are we willing to submit ourselves to that will?   Then we are within a shelter
where we can take no harm.   Then, come what may,
we are safe.

This is the belief which is the foundation of the
book of Psalms.   No men ever in this world felt
this truth so deeply and so unceasingly,—felt it as
the living and ever-present principle of each word
and thought,—as the men whose hearts the Spirit of
God taught to write the Psalms.   And it was to
stamp this truth upon all the ages and degrees and
changes of religious faith, to keep it clear and fresh
and strong, however men might otherwise differ from
one another,—rich from poor, learned from unlearned,
Greek from Jew, men of this day from the men of
hundreds of years ago,—it was to keep up among
them all this great truth, that in the hands of God
man may rest safe,—that the Psalms were gathered
into one book, and sung as the natural and familiar

expression of faith and trust, from generation to generation, from church to church, and have been adopted as household words of prayer.

This thought, this truth, that God guides those who trust Him, and never guides them wrong, is the mark, the distinguishing doctrine, the keynote, of the book of Psalms. Just as we mark in Isaiah, as that which is especially his own, his prophecies of Messiah and of the Gospel redemption ; just as we say that the ruling and leading thought in St. Paul's epistles is the doctrine of grace, and in St. John's the repetition of his Master's call to love,—so in the Psalms the leading and ruling thought, which makes them different from all other books, is the belief in God's unfailing guardianship. It is summed up in that verse which I have read as the text, and which, in a somewhat different shape, ends our great Christian hymn of *Te Deum*, "O Lord, in Thee have I trusted ; let me never be confounded."

It is the verse, of all others, which might be taken by itself to express the spirit of all the Psalms. In prayer, in assertion, in prophecy and promise—changed, it may be, in turn of language or choice of words,—nay, even in complaint, in expostulation, in misgiving and fear, in appeals in which are interwoven an agonised despair,—this expression of faith appears again and again, running like a golden thread, and mixing with colours dark and light throughout the Psalms. "In Thee, O Lord, have I put my trust ; let me never be put to confusion." "They put their trust in Thee, and were not confounded." "Be strong, and He shall establish your heart, all ye that put your trust in the Lord." "My God, my God, look upon me ;

why hast Thou forsaken me? . . . Our fathers hoped
in Thee ; they trusted in Thee, and Thou didst deliver
them." The verse, indeed, is one which has played
its sad, yet high and comforting part in many a
sorrowful history. Except, perhaps, that other verse
in the thirty-first Psalm, " Into Thy hands I commend
my spirit," no other verse of the Psalms probably
has been so often the last words on the lips of dying
men. The assertion of a hope, which the close of
all earthly hopes cannot shake, it has offered itself
as a stay to the spirits of men to whom hope was
over here.

To men of very different times and different feelings ; to men dying in their strength by violence, or
worn out by long years of toil ; to the missionary
on his deathbed in a strange land ; to the martyrs
of the rival creeds of Christendom ; to the victims of
deadly political strife, at the stake, on the scaffold,
and at the block,—these words have come back to the
remembrance of men who had but one gasp between
them and death ; and in them they have said their
last hope and prayer, each in his own language :
" *In te, Domine, speravi : non confundar in æternum.*"
" O Lord, in Thee have I trusted ; let me never be
confounded."

And what to them was the last comfort in dying
is the only sure stay and support to us in living.
They died feeling that, in spite of dying, they were
still in the hands of God. If we would, without distress and weakness, face our condition, we must open
our hearts to the belief that, living, we are also in the
hands of God ; that whatever we may live to see or
to meet, we are *never* out of the hands of God,

never out of the reach of His power to save and to restore. We cannot know our fate. We cannot foresee what may befall us. We cannot guess what we may be called upon to go through. We know that we are weak, and that deep and wide on all sides of us are the " overflowings of ungodliness," the forces of evil, the deceits of sin. We know not in what difficult position we may be placed, and with what weight of responsibility on our head. We know not what God may choose to take from us ; what light in our sky He may darken or put out ; what power in our souls He may cloud over or withdraw. We know not what a day may bring forth. But what we do know is, that in it all and with it all there comes to those who put their trust in God a Hand which wisely and strongly orders all things ; there comes the Providence which beholds all things from end to end ; there is present the same protection of that everlasting Goodness which has never failed those that hope in Him—which is able, through all appearances of loss and overthrow and perishing, to save to the uttermost what is committed to His charge.

Let us then turn to those great truths of God's Guardianship and Providence on which our souls were meant to rest and stay themselves, and be at peace. Let us make them our familiar thoughts, as they were to those who, in their trials, their dangers, their fears, their anguish, rose out of them into Psalms of hope and trust and sure success. So shall we be ready for what may come upon us. So may we look forward without terror. So may we bear the burden when it comes without losing patience. Let

us have that trust in God in our hearts; so will it
spring up in old, well-remembered words and texts,
which will come into fresh light and meaning to us
in our hour of necessity.

Let us now, in our day of peace and calm, learn
to commend into the Hands of God our spirit, soul,
and body, which He has created, redeemed, regener-
ated; and with it our whole course of life, and all
who are ours, and all that belongs to us. Let us
commend it all,—our life, and all its changes and
issues,—to Him, to whose Wisdom and Love and
Truth we may surely leave them. Let us beseech
Him now, in our time of health and strength, to be
with us at the end; that when the close is to be,
He would "direct it in peace, without sin, without
shame, and, if it please Him, without pain, gathering
us together with His Elect when He wills and as
He wills." So may we go forward in hope and
peace, committing all our ways to Him; casting our
burden on the Lord, who will not suffer the righteous
to fall for ever; casting all our anxieties upon Him,
for He careth and taketh thought about us. Then
the bright days of calm and sunshine will not be
treacherous, for they are the rest of God, and God
gives it to us, and guards it round. "The hills
stand about Jerusalem; even so standeth the Lord
round about His people, from this time forth for evermore." Then need we not fear in the days of darkness, for in them too God is there. "Behold, He
that keepeth Israel shall neither slumber nor sleep.
The Lord is thy keeper: the Lord is thy defence on
thy right hand; so that the sun shall not burn thee
by day, neither the moon by night." Then, when

one deep calleth to another; when trouble is heavy
on us, and all its waves and storms have gone over
us ; when we hear the voices whispering, " Where is
now thy God?"—we shall know how to fall back on
the thoughts with which the Psalmist once and again
cheered on his heart to hope : " Why art thou so
vexed, O my soul, and why art thou so disquieted
within me ?   O put thy trust in God, for I will yet give
Him thanks, which is the help of my countenance,
and my God."   So let us look forward.   " O Lord,
in Thee have I trusted ; let me never be confounded."
In all time of our wealth and peace let us learn to
say this with truth and earnestness.   Then, in all
time of our tribulation, will it become our fit and
natural appeal.   Then, at the hour of death, it will
rise to our heart and lips,—a prayer which is the
warrant and prophecy of its own fulfilment : " O
Lord, in Thee have I trusted ; let me never be confounded."   " O Lord, in Thee have I trusted ; I *shall
not* be confounded."

XVIII

TRUST IN THE LORD

*" Trust in the Lord with all thine heart ; and lean not unto thine own
understanding. In all thy ways acknowledge Him, and He shall
direct thy paths. Be not wise in thine own eyes : fear the Lord,
and depart from evil."—PROVERBS iii. 5-7.*

SPEAKING broadly and generally, there are two
ways in which people pass through life. They
pass through it *remembering* God, or they pass
through it *forgetting* Him. They go through it
with Him in their minds, though they cannot see
Him ; or they go through it as if they had nothing
to do with Him. They live as if this world were
all they had to think about, or they remember that
another life is coming, though they know they have
to die in this world. And, of course, in what they
do, this great difference shows itself. If people
have not God and eternity in their thoughts, how
is it possible that they should do anything as if
they *had*? how can they try to please God, whom
they never think of? and how can they give themselves any trouble to be prepared for eternity, when
eternity is nothing but a mere word and sound to them,
meaning nothing? But if they do really have the
greatness and mercy and judgment of God continually in their minds, they must either be openly rebelling

against the light, or else they cannot help shaping
their lives by the awful truths they believe, and
living as those who must soon pass away from here
to meet the Judge and Saviour of quick and dead.
Either they are "wise in their own eyes"—that is,
they trust themselves and the present world for
everything they wish and work for, and feel no want
of God, nor care for what He promises—or they
"acknowledge Him in all their ways"; they think of
His eye, His will, His hand, to uphold or cast down,
to guide or to chastise, in all that they undertake
through their life. Either they "lean to their own
understanding"; they are satisfied with what they
see and have learnt about the ways and wisdom
and good things of this present world, and will not
listen even to God, when He tells them a different
story about what men think so much of here; or
they trust in the Lord with all their heart, knowing
that "it is not in man that walketh to direct his
steps," and that it would profit a man nothing if he
were to "gain the whole world and lose his own
soul."

And so these two ways of going through life
come back to the old difference, which we have
heard of so often; one is walking by sight, the
other is walking by faith. One is caring only for what
we can see now; the other is caring for the things
which we cannot see, but which we know are true,
and which we shall one day see with our eyes as
surely as we see things of this world now.

These are the two ways in which all men are
now going through their days. God is out of sight
to us all: the difference is that to some He is out

of mind ; by others He is really and truly constantly thought of. The openly wicked, the sinners
who are not afraid to transgress with a high hand,
forget God—that we all see ; but I wish it was only
they. God is out of mind to many more besides
them ; to many who are not lawless and rebellious,
who are quiet and sober, industrious and respectable,
who get on in the world because they are so well
behaved, and hurt no one, and have such an excellent character, but who, alas! think of this world
only, and of nothing above it, nothing beyond it.
With them, too, God is really out of mind because
He is out of sight.

It is not, indeed, for man to say, except where
persons openly break God's laws, *who* is walking in
one way and *who* in the other,—who is secretly remembering God and who is forgetting Him. Men
are too much mixed up for that. God has given us
no command and no liberty to judge one another,
where only He can tell how the heart is thinking ;
for is there any one who tries to remember God, and
to trust in Him, but knows how often he forgets
God, and trusts to his own conceit and self-wisdom
instead ? Man cannot make the division, except
where outward actions make it plainly ; and even
then they leave it uncertain.

We are all mixed up together for the present :
those who are passing through the world looking to
God, and leaning on His arm ; and those who have
no help but what their own strength gives them, and
no hope beyond this world. We are all mixed up
together,—nay, the two ways are mixed up very
often in ourselves ; we seem to pass from one to the

other, from forgetting God to remembering Him,
from trusting Him to trusting only this world ; we
have Him in mind one hour—we lean unto our own
understanding the next. Yet in spite of all this,
there are but the two ways that I spoke of in which
we can pass our days ; there is no mixing up of
them in the eyes of God, who sees all clearly, however much to human judgment both seem sometimes
to be joined, and there seems to be a going backward
and forward from one to the other. God, who cannot mistake, or be perplexed and deceived by what
perplexes and deceives us, sees most surely that, *on
the whole*, we have each one of us chosen either the
one way or the other ; on the whole, in spite of
changes and inconsistencies, in spite of the better
mind which comes at times to some, in spite of the
mistakes and infirmities of others, we are all of us,
on the whole, walking through our earthly pilgrimage by ourselves, or with Him for our help ; providing only for this life, or providing for the next ;
trusting in the Lord with all our heart, and acknowledging Him in all our ways, and finding Him there
directing our paths, or else leaning on our own
understanding, and in all our doings wise in our
own eyes, and therefore not fearing the Lord, not
really departing from evil.

Now, to which is our ordinary course of life most
like ? Do not let us deceive ourselves. Do not let
us think that, because we often speak of God's hand
in our concerns, we are therefore really thinking
of His presence, and acknowledging Him in our
ways. Many persons speak of what it has pleased
the Lord to do to them, without at all feeling in

their hearts that *it is* the Lord ; they do it because they have heard others do it, or have been accustomed to use the words, or think it right in speaking to others to speak so. But it does not follow that they acknowledge Him in all their doings through the day, in small matters as well as great, because when they are moved by sorrow or gladness they feel the words come up to their lips. We ought to look close into our hearts and secret ways if we would not be deceived ; if we really wish to know, what is of such consequence to us, whether we are trusting to Almighty God's wisdom and strength to help and guide us through our day's walk, or whether we are leaning to our own poor weak understanding to guide our steps.

If you really want to know this better, you must go to some surer proofs than words and ways of speaking. One sure proof is in your private prayers. It is impossible that any one can really be acknowledging God,—can be thinking of anything but worldly things,—who does not pray by himself in secret, and pray every day regularly. Therefore, if any one knows that he does not take care to say his private prayers to God daily, there is a proof and warning to him at once that he is not acknowledging God,—that he is living without God in the world. He may be as industrious and quiet and respectable and kind-hearted as possible, but he is living without religion, as one who has only this life to pass through, and has no everlasting state waiting for him after he is dead. Private, secret prayer, offered to God daily and regularly, is the one great proof whether we believe and trust in God : if this proof is not there, then it is certain that, whatever we may say or do, we do not in our hearts believe God, or fear Him.

But even if we do pray thus in secret, this is not enough. *How* do we pray? Do we make a reality of our prayers by giving our mind to them, and keeping our thoughts from wandering,—by earnestly begging God to be merciful to us, and to take care of us, in soul and body, both here and for eternity? Or do we pray only because we should feel uncomfortable if we had not said our prayers, but yet without really feeling that we need what we pray for?

This matter of private secret prayer, not with others, but by ourselves,—whether we pray so at all, and *how* we pray, would settle the question at once, with many, whether or not we are worldlings, and how far we really in our hearts trust and lean upon God. Public prayer may depend on other things: on our wish to keep a good character, on our being accustomed to it, on our wishing to please and keep well with others; nay, the very earnestness of public prayer may depend on our feeling ourselves with others, and being carried away for the moment by *their* earnestness, and the stirring words or sounds of confession or praise. But prayer in private, where no one knows what we are doing, depends on whether we think it worth while to ask God's help and to acknowledge His goodness; and if we do not pray in private, it shows what is our real opinion of the good of prayer,—it shows that we do not believe it to be of use or value enough to us to make us do it, for ever so short a time, *for its own sake*, and

C.   N

when no one is by to see us. It shows that we do not believe that God really watches over us, or that we depend on strength or wisdom besides our own.

Another proof is our way of bearing disappointments, troubles, losses—the crosses and vexations which come upon all of us in our turn, as we go through life. Nothing shows more plainly than this whether we are indeed acknowledging the Lord in all our ways, for this discovers to us for certain whether indeed we believe that all things come from God's ordering ; and also, that there is nothing that He sends on us but He sends it out of love for our souls, out of the desire to do us good in the end. Perhaps it is the kind severity and sharp mercy of the Good Physician to heal what is amiss in us by the bitter but needful medicine of trial and distress.

Now, this is what comes at once to the mind of him who acknowledges God in all his ways : he believes in Him, and so believing, he tries to be patient, he tries to bear his affliction with thankfulness ; he thinks of it as coming not by chance, but from the hand of One whom he can trust, and who has said that it is necessary for men to be afflicted that they may be proved and purified by sorrow. But if we have not acknowledged God, or acknowledged Him outwardly only, and not in our secret thoughts, we think of such troubles as if they came at random and by chance ; we ask why we are tried, and not others ; we think ourselves hardly dealt with ; we murmur and complain at our trial ; we are angry or jealous with those around us, as if it were a shame that they should be spared when we

are not.   And thus we show two things : one, that
we do not really believe what God has said about
its being He who sends trouble, and sends it out of
love ; and the other, that all we really care about is
of this world, and when that is taken away from us
we have no other hope : nay, when it is cut short
and made less, by however little, we feel as if something which was our right, something for which we
had laboured as our reward and treasure, is lost,
without anything to make up for it.

Another proof is, the care we take to keep in
order our words and our secret thoughts as we pass
through the day.   "Acknowledge Him in all thy
ways," says the Scripture ; and how should we
acknowledge Him better than by showing how constantly what He loves and desires comes into our
thoughts, and keeps us from saying and thinking
what, if we sought only our own will, we should
think and say.   It is not by talking of Him that we
acknowledge Him, and prove to His all-seeing eye
that we are thinking about Him.   We may talk of
Him when others are by, and like to listen, and
encourage us to talk ; and then forget Him when
we are left alone, and go back in our thoughts to
the world.   It must be by owning Him where only
He can see that we do own Him.

When, for love and fear of Him, we keep back a
bitter or ill-natured word that no one knew we were
going to say, then we do nothing for the praise of
men, but we acknowledge Him in secret.   When for
fear and love of Him we not only set a watch on
our lips, but keep a guard also on our thoughts,—
drive away all things that we ought not to think

about,—check and keep down our passion when it is
rising,—then this is something which is meant only
for His eye ; for the eye of man cannot see what
was in our hearts, and would not have known anything about it if we had indulged our thoughts.
But if we let our thoughts run riot, and say
that no eye shall see them, and no one think the
worse of us for them ; if we prefer to say the first
harsh or unkind thing that comes up to our lips
when we are vexed and angry, instead of keeping it
under, though it cost us a struggle ; if we give our
hearts liberty to long for, and run after, the good
things of this world, and say that there is no harm
in it ; if we let our souls be burdened or surfeited
with the cares or with the pleasures of this world ;
if we have no time for thoughts about God and our
eternal state, and put them out of the way, that we
may give ourselves more completely to our worldly
interests,—if we do all this, how can any one deceive
himself with thinking that he is acknowledging God
in all his ways ?   How can he doubt that he is
in reality forgetting God, and giving himself only to
this present world ?   How can he doubt that he is
leaning only on his own understanding,—that he is
one of those who are wise in their own eyes, and so
think themselves wiser than God and His word ;
that he is going through life as if he did not belong
to God, and was left to himself to get what he could
out of this world, and then to lie down and perish,
without any hope, without any further reckoning
to come ?

   Will you trust yourselves to yourselves or to
God ?   That is the question.   I do not say, will

you have your portion in this world or in the next?
For no man would like to think that this was the
alternative before him ; and no man dares say even
to himself that he has chosen this world before the
other.   But, indeed, you can find out pretty clearly
whether you are trusting yourselves to God's wisdom
and guidance, or leaning to your own understanding,
and thinking that you can take care of yourselves
without God.   You can find out whether you are
now going through life, *keeping God in mind*, as day
follows day ; or whether you are going through it
without keeping Him in mind.   And if you are forgetting Him, where are you walking to?   What will
be the end of your journey?   Will your own understanding, to which you lean, deliver you from sickness, from tribulation, from death ?   Will that wisdom
of your own, which is sufficient for you in your own
eyes, which makes you, in your own opinion, sharper
and more knowing in worldly matters than other
men, and on which you depend to help you to rise
in the world,—will *that* wisdom stand you in stead
to get you out of the snares of death, to redeem
your soul when you are falling into the power of
the grave, to wash out your sins, to set you free
from the bands of a long worldly life to escape from
God's all-seeing eye, to deliver you in the day of
judgment, and to shelter you from the wrath of
God?   Will it serve to keep in your possession
what you have got in this world ; will it help you
to carry away your riches with you when you die,
and secure you from the loss you so fear now ?
Will it, as you grow on in life, help you to a peaceful and quiet old age?   Will it make your bed

easier when you are sick? Will it make up to you
for the waste of strength, and for the years that are
gone, and never can come back, when you are waiting in weakness and pain and anxiety for the call
to die?

There is nothing that will stand you in stead
then but feeling that you have trusted yourself to
God ; that you have taken yourself, as it were, out
of your own hands, given up your own will, renounced your own wisdom, and committed yourself
to Him, who can indeed keep that which has been
committed to Him against that day.   But if you
would have that blessedness—and there is no blessedness on this side the grave to compare with that of
feeling oneself no longer in our own hands but in
God's—it will not do to wait.   It will not do to put
your trust in yourself while you are strong and well
and young and thriving, and think that it will be
time enough to put your trust in God when you are
obliged to give up trusting yourself.

No ; it takes a long time to *learn* to trust in the
Lord, and to acknowledge Him in all our ways.
Those who most try to do it, who most wish to leave
themselves, and all that belongs to them, to His
manifest ordering,—who have most reason to hope
that they have given up trusting to their own understanding and wisdom in what concerns this life here,
—are reminded to the last how imperfectly they have
learnt the lesson ; how often, without knowing it,
they are setting their will before God's will, and
fancying that they know better than God what is
best for them.   And if this is so with those who try
to leave themselves in God's hands, how shall they

who never seriously try themselves at all be able to
do so when the time of trouble comes?

Oh, what light and peace would it shed round
our path if, indeed, we trusted in the Lord with all
our heart, and acknowledged Him in all our ways!
Such godliness had ever the promise of the life that
now is : " Honour the Lord with thy substance, and
with the first-fruits of all thine increase : so shall thy
barns be filled with plenty, and thy presses shall
burst out with new wine."   And those who have
trusted God's word, who have given up some present
worldly profit to honour God's law more fully, have
found the promise made good, and have not been
losers by their self-denial.   But this is the least
part ; for even the worldly prosperity which has
God's blessing on it must perish at last, like all
things earthly, in the day when we are too weak or
too sick to enjoy it.   The blessedness of trusting
God and not ourselves is higher and deeper and
surer than this.   When we are but our own guides
we can never be sure that we are not mistaken.
When we trust God we know that we are in hands
which cannot fail, and that, come what may upon
us, however painful, however much it may seem to
be against us, it cannot be evil, for it is God's doing.
Giving ourselves up to Him, we shall feel sure that
His love will never lead us wrong, though it may
lead us into sorrow and tribulation.   We shall know
and feel assured that there are ends of which we
shall one day, either in this life or the next, see the
infinite mercy, in the darkest and strangest dispensation of what, in man's eyes, is hopeless desolation.
Even then we shall be able to lift up our hands and

give thanks ; for we shall know that we are walking safely, although in darkness. " Then shalt thou walk in thy way safely, and thy foot shall not stumble. When thou liest down thou shalt not be afraid : yea, thou shalt lie down, and thy sleep shall be sweet. . . . For the Lord shall be thy confidence, and shall keep thy foot from being taken."

This is comfort which none of us can make sure of, by his own wisdom and strength, in the day of trouble. This is a stay and a peace for the soul, which alone can keep us from being overwhelmed when the great water-floods come upon us. And which of us can tell whether he may not need it to-morrow ?

XIX

THE CONSEQUENCES OF UNBELIEF

" And He did not many mighty works there because of their
unbelief."—St. Matthew xiii. 58.

WHAT a strange and sad state of things does this
verse bring up into our thoughts! Just think of
what is meant by it. There was, on the one hand,
the mercy and power of God present to help, present
to bless ; and there were, on the other hand, crowds
of men needing in all kinds of ways the help of that
mercy and power. There was the Redeemer, come
from heaven, to tell the glad tidings which all the
world had been longing for,—come from heaven, to
bring the long-promised deliverance which generation
after generation had hoped and waited for ; and there
were the men who were eagerly hoping for that
deliverance, whose one great thought was that of a
Saviour who was sure to come ; whose whole life in
the world, whose doings, public and private, whose
views of duty, whose schemes and prospects and
ventures were all shaped and governed by this
wonderful hope ; who at this very moment were on
tiptoe expectation, full of restlessness and agitation,
because they thought that the time was come at
last. There, on the one hand, was He in whom

God's promise was fulfilled, Jesus Christ, with His
hands full of gifts and His lips full of comfort and
wisdom.   There, on the other hand, were the children and heirs of the promise, thirsting, groping,
fainting, after its accomplishment; sick men wanting
to be healed, hungry men wanting to be fed, men
vexed and troubled with unclean spirits wanting
to be restored to liberty, sinful men wanting to be
cleansed, eager and anxious and perplexed spirits
wanting to be taught and enlightened and consoled.
That was just what He had come for; " The Spirit of
the Lord is upon me, because He hath anointed me
to preach the Gospel to the poor ; He hath sent me
to heal the broken-hearted, to preach deliverance to
the captives, and recovering of sight to the blind, to
set at liberty them that are bruised."   That day
was " the Scripture fulfilled " in their ears.   There
were the " poor," the " broken-hearted," the " captives," the " blind," the " bruised " ; and there, before
them, was the Healer, the Consoler, full of desire for
His work.   There was God's grace, ready to flow
over, seeking, striving to find those for whom to do
its mighty works ; and there were those whose days
were spent in looking out for its coming, and for
whose necessities and sufferings, in body and soul,
it was the only hope.   There they were both together,—the power and goodness of Christ, and
they who so deeply needed them.   But the two
could not meet.   It was as if there were an in-
vincible barrier between them.   Christ was with
His lost sheep, and we know what He could and
would have done for them ; but something kept
Him from them, and them from Him.

" He did not many mighty works there," says St. Matthew, " because of their unbelief." St. Mark is bolder still. " He could there do no mighty work, save that He laid His hands upon a few sick folk, and healed them. And He marvelled because of their unbelief."

The hindrance of their unbelief was the one limit to the Lord's power. He could heal the sick and cleanse the lepers and raise the dead. In the soul which was willing, which stirred itself up to attend to His word and look to His goodness, He could work wonders ; He could take away sin, He could give light, He could give holiness and strength, which were new in the world. But the soul of man is free. And when men use their freedom in re-fusing to bend to His grace and His power to heal them, even His grace and His power meet a barrier and check at which they must stop. Against the evil heart of unbelief God has many influences, many gracious persuasions, infinite ways of visiting and moving it ; but after all, and at the last, there is one awful liberty reserved for it which belongs to it alone, and which God does not touch,—the liberty of choosing finally for itself whether it will yield to God or resist Him ; whether it will see or whether it will be blind. With these Jews, there was Jesus Christ ready to heal, to save, to comfort them ; but at the last it must depend on themselves whether they would let Him help them. They would not, therefore He could not.

I suppose that it is true still that Christ does not do, *cannot* do, His mighty works,—the works which He came from heaven to do for men,—because of men's unbelief.

Christ came, indeed, to do yet greater works among men than even those which He was willing to do among the Jews. He came to work a work on earth greater even than healing the sick and cleansing the lepers and giving comfort to a few sufferers or a few mourners. He came to do a work in the souls of men, not in Judæa only, but throughout the world,—not in those few years of His presence here on earth, but throughout all generations of mankind to come,—compared with which the wonderful things done to men's bodies by His hands and by His word were little. He came to change, to fashion anew, the race of mankind. It had gone astray from God and His goodness, and He came to lead it back. It had fallen into miserable ruin and sin, and He came to restore it. It had taken an evil turn, which seemed past remedy, —it seemed to be sinking more and more hopelessly and widely into depths of sin,—struggling hard, but struggling in vain, to lift itself out of its corruption, and to escape from the snare ; and He came to show it the way back to peace, to take away its sins, to help it against its sinfulness, to bring men the grace and power by which they might in very deed correct and amend themselves, and rise up to the truth of a pure and holy life. He came to die for our sins, and to rise again, that men, who had fallen away so far from God, and had fallen so low, might die to sin, and rise again unto righteousness. He came, that is, to change our whole life ; to change the world ; to create anew the very nature of man, which sin and evil had spoiled so fearfully. He came to make men know and love the Father they had forgotten. He came to make them give up their sins, and recover once more the goodness which they had lost. He came to give us thoughts about ourselves, and about God's dealings with us, which it could never have entered into the mind of man to imagine. The shadow of death, of a death without hope and with many fears, rested upon our life ; He came that we might henceforth live our life here in the light of the life everlasting.

These were the mighty works which He came to do in the world ; and, as we know, He did them. His coming did change the world. His coming has made all the difference between what men have known and thought, and hoped for and tried after, and become, *since* He was with us, and what they were *before* He came. And that difference is indeed a great one. We may be disappointed that it is not greater ; that His grace, which has wrought such wonderful changes among men, has seemed to leave its work faulty and half done ; that the fruits of the Gospel have not been more perfect ; that the spread of His Church, and the conversion of nations to His faith,—so astonishing, so deep and lasting in its effects,—have been checked before the whole world was won, and have been troubled by so many scandals.

But if He has not done all that we might have expected, what He has done is clear and plain. He has spread new knowledge and goodness and hope in the world. He has brought a new law of holiness into the hearts of men. He has taught them heavenly lessons of love and truth and purity, and given them besides grace to learn them. He has

given success to repentance, and made it bear fruit
in deep and increasing improvement. He has
chastened and purified the inward thoughts and
wills of sinful men. He has put it into their hearts
to love and serve God in truth and sincerity. He
has strengthened the hands and enlightened the
eyes of those who were trying hard to become
better. He has made men glad to deny themselves, and to offer themselves a living sacrifice to
do His good work and follow His steps. He has
leavened the world, even the unbelieving, the indifferent, the disobedient part of it, with His Spirit,
and His higher thoughts of what is right and just
and good. Age after age He has kept up and preserved, amidst chastisements and deliverances, the
Church universal, which He founded to minister
grace and truth to men, and the visible lessons of
holy living, and a heavenly hope. Age after age
men like ourselves have been transformed by His
grace into very copies of His example, and faith
and good courage have been kept alive by the presence of His saints. These are the mighty works
which He really came to do, and which He has
done among men.

What He has come to do for men He has come
to do for each one of them to whom the knowledge
of His Gospel is brought. So He has come to do
all these mighty works among *us*. He means that
we, in our distant corners of the earth, should be
witnesses and partakers of that grace which has
won back mankind from evil to God ; which has
given new goodness, new hopes, new peace, new
strength, to men ; which has made them servants

and children of the Father, and led them through the darkness of this world and death to the everlasting light beyond.   Here, as elsewhere, He is spoken of and known ; He comes, He is ready, He is able to do for us what He has done so often for others ; to open the eyes, blinded by the glitter of present things ; to heal the sick—long sick with sins which have taken fast hold ; to cleanse the heart, which feels itself almost too deeply polluted even to attempt to repent and draw nigh to God ; to give strength and life to the feeble spirit, which knows that it is going on wrong, and is too dull, too hopeless, too entangled, to break through the snares which keep it from the good it would do. He comes to break the yoke of worldly custom and fear, which we feel with shame upon our necks ; to unloose the bonds which bind us captive to our bad ways ; to help us when we fall, and raise us up again, and keep us from falling ; to give us the good thoughts which we wish for, even when we have them not.   He comes to raise up our dead souls from the carelessness which we have let them sink into ; to give us an interest in those great hopes which we hear so much about, but which so often we bitterly feel are nothing to us.   These are the mighty works of Christ among men.   These is He ready to do for us.   Does He really do them among us ?   If not, why does He not do them ?

Blessed be His Name for whatever good is among us ; but when we think of what He came to do, and what He has shown Himself able to do, no one, I think, would like to deceive himself by saying that he was satisfied and struck by what he sees around him of the mighty works of Christ, in making new and purifying the souls of men, in raising them above themselves, and above what is merely of this world, to a better and holier way of living.   Christ is ready to save and bless us.   And we, with all our carelessness, with all our sins, feel in our hearts how much we want, how greatly we come short of what our conscience shows us ; what troubles and anxieties there are for which we have no remedy ; how painful and how comfortless is our want of settled peace, and our unfaithfulness to duty, and the dimness and uncertainty of our hope.   The Redeemer, the Deliverer, is there ; and we want help and grace and the Deliverer's power.   And yet we cannot come together.

For between Him and us there stands in the way our unbelief.   Not the unbelief which denies or doubts ; for we receive His word, and would not, I hope, speak against it.   Not the unbelief, like that of so many among the Jews, which could not get over the prejudices of a mistaken faith and the offence of a Redeemer on the cross instead of on a throne ; for we are accustomed to glory in those things which to the Jews were shame.   It is no matter of wanting signs and wonders from heaven, of disappointed expectation, or of reasons not strong enough to convince us.   The unbelief which is between us and Christ is of another sort.   It is that state of heart and feeling which dislikes the strain and trouble of thinking of things out of this present world ; which looks away from what is out of sight and to come, and is moved and impressed only by what is just before it—immediate interests, immediate pleasures, common customs.   It is the unbelief of carelessness, deadness of soul, lazy, selfish indifference ; which cannot understand how any one can be in earnest, so as to take pains and suffer trouble for the sake of things unseen ; which cannot bring itself to think that God is in earnest, and the work of serving and pleasing Him a real thing.   It is the unbelief which comes of wishing to save ourselves trouble, of not thinking it worth while to force ourselves to attend, to think, to remember, to lay to heart.

This is the unbelief which comes between us and the power of Christ to improve us, to strengthen us, to comfort us.   What we *will* not have done for us that He cannot do.   His Coming, His Passion, His Rising again, His Power, His Spirit,—those awful mysteries which have made all things new to man,— alas ! even they fail and lose their force to change and heal before the empty, thoughtless, frivolous soul, which will not rise up to think what they must mean.   We are not what Christians were meant to be ; we have only to read the New Testament to see that.   The great things which Christ said of His disciples are not fulfilled in us.   Nor need we be surprised.   We do not disbelieve them, we do not doubt them.   We only do not think them so serious and so real as to be worth going out of ourselves, going out of our old ways and fashions, to meet them,—as to be worth caring about and taking pains for in good earnest.

Do not let us waste our time in vain regrets, vain wishes, vain confessions of our weakness and folly. We need healing, and the power of Christ is ready

C.   O

to heal us. We need to be better men, and He is able to change and mend and strengthen us. We need comfort,—at least, we shall one day or other sorely need it,—and He is ever calling, "Come unto Me all ye that labour and are heavy laden, and I will give you rest." He is able to do all this for us ; He is ever making it all known to us. Let not that one barrier of our own unwillingness keep us from sharing, each in our own place and measure, in that light and goodness and comfort which have gladdened and transformed this world, and made it a new place for men to live in, to work and to die in. Let it not be that, simply from our slavery to custom and to things before us,—from our idle trifling with the truth which we confess,—from our blindness to the greatness of what has been done for us,—from our dull shrinking from the real meaning of our own words and the convictions of our consciences,—we are none the better for our Lord having come ; none the better as men ; none the better in our hope of what is to come.

Let us pray, and not only pray, but do our best, that it may not be said, in the long run, of our religious history, that Christ "did not many mighty works there because of their unbelief."

XX

THE CHRISTIAN RACE

" Know ye not that they which run in a race run all, but one receiveth
the prize? So run that ye may obtain."—i CORINTHIANS ix. 24.

ALL run, for the race is human life ; and all must
run it somehow, whether they will or no.   But there
are many ways of running it, and many endings to
the race.   All must run, but many run without
hope of the prize, and many throw it away.   Many
run because they cannot help it, and never try at
all ; and many try hard, but find at the end of their
running that they have run in vain.

All run, but the prize of human life is not for
all running ; it is not the mere running which ensures
the prize ; it is the running " so as to obtain."   All
run, but the prize is for those who win.

What is our life for, and what are we doing with
it ?   What are we living for, and what good do we
expect that our having lived here will do us at the
end ?   Here we are all of us together, running our
appointed race, the race of which much has been
run, and of which the remainder is quickly shortening,—shortening as quickly as the hours pass, and
bringing us ever nearer to the point where we are to
stop, having either won or lost.   The race of life,

and the race for what life is worth! What do we see around us of the running and its success?

We see much idle running; running without a thought of what the running is for; running without end or purpose; running carelessly, without trouble and at random, as if all were play and nothing were earnest,—a game for passing the time, with no duties. nothing to be serious about.

We see the slothful servant, with the only talent by which he could do his Lord any service, wrapping it in the napkin and putting it away out of his sight, that even the sight of it might not trouble his laziness, and quietly making up his mind that he had nothing more to do than to sit idle, and play and sleep, till his Lord comes back.

We see the foolish virgin go forward to meet the dreadful hour—the coming of which no one knows —gaily and lightly, and scorning to trouble her mind with thinking of what may be, and of what one day may run short. She has lighted her lamp, and the Bridegroom will come in good time; the lamp will take care of itself for as long as it is wanted. Her careful sister may be over-cautious if she likes,— over-anxious, and burden herself with the supply of oil which never may be needed; she will not vex herself with these too busy cares; she will trust her luck, and take things as they come.

We see the great company of the thoughtless, the selfish, moving on recklessly towards the fearful Left Hand. All around them are the hungry, the thirsty, the sick, the naked, the prisoners; all around are the piercing cries for help, but they hear nothing; their eyes are blinded, and see not Christ needing to be ministered unto ; they only ask why they should not do what they like with their own—harming no one, helping no one.

The prodigal son takes his half of the inheritance and goes forth, with the world before him ; the time goes lightly and easily, and he crowns it with idleness and amusement, and then darkens and defiles it with sin ; and he cares nothing where it is bringing him, or what he is on the way to become.

To such running, to such runners, what good has their life brought them ? Some vain delights, they may say, they caught at while the time was hurrying by ; it was sweet to taste the pleasures of sin for a season ; it was sweet to take things easily, and not to look forward ; it was sweet to do nothing,—to spare oneself the drudgery, the responsibility, the struggle. But all that is soon over, and the end must come. The prize of the running is at its end ; the gain and success of life is what it brings at last. *All* are in the race ; but what chance of the prize for those who will not look where they run, who stop to pick the flowers in their running, who lie down and go to sleep ?

There is much earnest, patient, serious running too : running which succeeds and gains its triumph, —a triumph which all can see. The world and this life has much to give and much to win, and many runners gain it ; much, no doubt, that is base and bad, and not worth running for ; but much, too, that God Himself has given men to run for here, and meant them to strive for, and given them a reward for winning it. But of all that man runs for, and wins here, the best, the most innocent, the noblest, there is this to be said : it is of this world, and this world passes away ; it belongs to this life, and this life ends in the grave.

And it is of the prize of human life and human running that the Apostle speaks. Can *that* be its prize which, when we have reached it, we must lay down and give back again ? If riches and honour reward our running, is it any great success to have got for a moment what the next moment we must leave behind ? Is it so great and delightful a lot to have what we have longed for put within our hands, only for it to be at once torn from them ? Is that our prize which, as soon as we have got it, we must have done with for ever, and be as though we had never had it ? Is that the worth of our life ? Is our running, our care, our toil, our waiting, so easily repaid that we think ourselves well satisfied by just touching what slips from our fingers and perishes in the using ? Do we not feel at last that to have to leave our great prizes behind us, not knowing what shall become of them, turns those great prizes into little worth ? The end to which we must come fixes their real value. If *then* they are nothing, and we have run all our lives for them, then, just when our running should win its reward, it has won nothing. If there was any reward in them it was really in the running, in the living, in the having life.

But surely God made us to live for some purpose ; He did not give us this wonderful life of ours merely to live while we lived. He gave it that something might come of it ; that at the end we might feel that we had not lived for nothing ; that life had given us something of our own, something not to be lost or taken away. Are we really to run these our Christian lives as men used to run when they had no hope beyond? Are we content to pass our days as blindly, and is it enough for us to be in our aims and ends no better for that incredible change in the prospects of human life, of which eighteen centuries has not yet worn out the wonder, which was made when the Word became Flesh; when the Son of God was crucified for our sins; when He overcame the sharpness of death, and " opened the kingdom of heaven to all believers "?

No ; when we come to the end, and think what we have run for, and what we have won, it is not the things which we must leave behind us which will satisfy our hearts, and seem like the prize. It is not our success, our riches, our name, our family. They are ours now. But let a few days pass, and what will they be to us and we to them when death is between us? No, it is not in those things that we shall feel that we have not run in vain.

Doubtless there are things at the end, at the very end, when all here is departing from us, and going for ever, which, even while we are here in the flesh in this world, keep life from seeming a failure, and glorify its very last steps with peace and triumph. But it is not the thought of what we have gained and are now going to lose ; it is not the thought of what we have long enjoyed and are now to see no more for ever. It is not this.

But there are deathbeds where all is still, holy, calm ; where what is coming is not feared, but only waited for with hoping, patient, trusting solemnity and awe ; where loving hands are always ready in their ministries of comfort, and loving lips are ever whispering words of peace, and the last sight to dying eyes are the loving eyes which watch them ; where the air seems full of unearthly thoughts of the Great Sufferer, and all hearts are bursting with such memories as they never had before of His agony, His passion, His dying ; where, once more, the leave-taking before the hour of death between him who is going and those who stay is kept as He kept it in the breaking of the bread and with the cup of suffering and salvation ; where all feel entering under the shadow of the world to come, and over all broods with new and strange power the hope of the resurrection of the dead.

That is a time, awful as it is, when we feel that life is not vanity ; that God has indeed given them something worth running and waiting for. *That* is worth living for, even on this side the grave.

We have all heard of men whose last act on earth was love to their brethren. They have died giving their lives for others ; they have put themselves in the way of entire destruction, that by perishing themselves they might keep others from perishing. With unmoved eyes they have seen their death drawing nearer and nearer, and have only thought of helping the weak and comforting the miserable : with the alternative of life and death between themselves and another, they have quietly chosen death ; they have stood fast and let the fire burn them, or the fierce sea bury them, that others might escape, or because it was their place and their duty.

It is a blessed end of life to die in a Christian

home, and to meet death in the way of duty and for
duty's sake ; much more to be, in however distant a
way, made like to Him who said, " Greater love hath
no man than this, that a man lay down his life for
his friends." This is indeed to part with life amid
light and triumph. In such endings of the race
surely there is a victory, surely there is a hope full
of immortality.

But can we say with truth that they are the prize
of our running,—that they are the prize of human
life ?

No ; the prize, the real prize of human life, can
be nothing on this side of the grave. All on this
side is the running ; the running, with many partial
encouragements and rewards to those who run faithfully, with great and enlarging hopes to the end.
But the prize of it cannot be here ; for the things
that are seen are temporal,—but for a time,—and the
things that are eternal are the things that are not
seen. And that for which man was made, that
which he is called to run for and to obtain, is
eternal. It is out of our reach and sight, and above
our thoughts,—" that which God hath prepared for
them that love Him." It is in the everlasting world,
free from change, safe from loss and decay, that
" eternal weight of glory," which is " the prize of the
high calling of God "; that unfading crown and incorruptible inheritance which the Bible hangs up before
our sight and hopes. It is in the other world that
man's destiny is to be fulfilled, and that for which
he was created and sent into this world to fight his
way and learn his lesson, and be tried and buffeted,
chastened and disciplined, is to be at last made

manifest. Then, and not till then. Here we only run. We all run, wisely or not,—after what is worth running for, or after what will fail us even when we have gained it. There it is that it will be made manifest how we have run, and who has not run in vain.

Let us look then to that end. Let us try to run so that we may obtain. An Apostle was not absolutely sure how he was running ; and if St. Paul felt at times misgivings, I am sure that we may well put some sharp cross-questioning upon ourselves. The question is whether our life at last shall have been in vain, and shall have been thrown away ; or whether we shall have used it as God meant it to be used, and so shall be ready to blossom forth into something infinitely greater and more glorious after this world—into something which will not be unworthy of a life and a kingdom which God and Christ assure us are to be for ever.

For ever : that is what you are running for ; that is what you are preparing yourselves for. For ever. You know what is not for ever, even this present time ; but when this is done, and death is passed through, then begins for ever.

Even if we had no such prize in view, it would be better not to be idle, not to be frivolous, not to be wasteful of our chances,—to do our best. But if this were all we know but too well what the world and its success must turn out, even when men have run well and not in vain for its rewards. But now we know where we are going, and why we are called to run. The other world is opened ; that is why we are here. Corruption shall put on incorruption, and mortality be swallowed up in life ; that is why we are called to run and work, and become fit to begin the life of angels, and that endless service of which we can understand so little but that it is only for the holy.   Men run bravely, men work hard, and suffer long for this world.   Oh let them not put us to shame who believe in another.   They do it for a corruptible crown ; and with the incorruptible crown within our reach, shall we lose it ?   Oh, my brethren, let us run, let us live in earnest ; not without aim and hope, but looking forward by faith to that which one day must be.   Let us not be slack, faint-hearted, self-indulgent, in that race which is at once so easy and so difficult ; so easy because, with God's grace, it wants nothing but a true heart in earnest ; so hard because it *does* want the true heart in earnest.

Let us hear our great teacher : " I therefore so run, not as at random ; so fight I, not as one that beateth the air ; but I keep under my body, and bring it into subjection : lest that by any means, when I have preached to others I myself should be a castaway."

Do we look for the resurrection of the dead and the life of the world to come ?   And has not Some One said, " Many are called, but few are chosen " ? Strive—strive as if for your life, to enter in at the strait gate ; " for many, I say unto you, will seek to enter in, and shall not be able."

XXI

GOD'S VISITATIONS TO HIS PEOPLE

"Because thou knewest not the time of thy visitation."—
ST. LUKE xix. 44.

JERUSALEM, the chosen city of God, knew not the
time of her visitation; did not understand what
was going on, and what she was called to do, when
her Lord came with mercy and judgment to try
her heart. And, therefore, that sad prospect of
ruin which made the Lord weep when He beheld
the city. He saw that the city and people which
had been so highly favoured had after all missed
the great prize which God had set before them, and
for which He had been so long preparing them.
The Hope of Israel,—that for which they had been
waiting for hundreds of years,—that for which they
had endured so much,—that which they had all
believed in, and trusted to so earnestly,—the Hope
of Israel, the long-promised Saviour, had actually
come, and they would not know Him, they would
not receive him.

"If thou hadst known, even thou, at least in this
thy day, the things which belong unto thy peace."

Here was the moment come for the fulfilment of
God's promise; here was given them, here before

their very eyes was set forth, favour and mercy and grace, far beyond all that their fathers had ever dreamed of. If in former generations they had misunderstood God's dealings, here was a day of redemption and glory, which, if they accepted it, would make up for all that had gone wrong before.

"If thou, even thou," the nation whom God had chosen and enlightened and blessed above all other people ;—" if at least in this thy day," when the Son of God had come to bring His message of salvation and blessing in His own person, to speak to them face to face, to do the works of the Father among them ;—" if thou," after all thy former sins and failures, had now at last, now in this greatest of all thy chances, only known how near thou wert to peace and glory, how great the blessing within thy reach, how easy to stretch forth thy hand to receive it ;—" if thou hadst but known !"

But Jerusalem would not know her hour of mercy and acceptance. It passed away ; and the Lord saw, and wept as He saw, that it was gone. It was too late. God had promised great things ; the time for them had come ; but Jerusalem had not known the time, and now they were hid from her eyes. Now there was nothing left but to meet the disasters and punishments from which her Saviour had come to deliver her ; the disasters and punishments which come on those who are too proud and careless to mind when God means to save them. Her enemies were to come and destroy her, and her children within her, and were to leave not one stone upon another ; " because thou knewest not the time of thy visitation."

Not to know the time of our visitation means not to know when God is giving us opportunities of good ; not to feel and be alive to the blessings which His providence is putting within our reach ; not to see when the time comes, as it comes to all, which is meant specially to suit our necessities, and to open for us the door to peace and mercy.

That time of peace comes in very different ways to different persons : the time which brings with it advantages and chances of a special kind for escaping from sin, for turning in earnest to God, for making fresh steps onwards in goodness and holiness. There are many different sorts of these visitations of God to the souls of men. They are always the openings and beginnings of new mercies, more than had been vouchsafed before. But there is about all of them this danger—that those to whom they come should not know the time of their visitation.

And there is additional danger of so failing when these visitations of God's providence and mercy are not, as they were to the Jews, accompanied by strange outward marks of God's power. If, in spite of the wonderful works of Jesus Christ, the Jews mistook Him, misunderstood Him,—did not discern the tokens of His heavenly grace and power, and so missed the opportunity which He gave them of peace and glory and blessing,—how much more easy to miss it when it comes to us in the common course of our lives, without any appearance of what is extraordinary and wonderful !

The days were when God's presence was revealed by visible miracle and sign and judgment. He was

known to be near us by the earthquake and the
wind and the fire ; but now those are passed away,
and it is only the still small voice in the secret heart
which tells us that the Lord is nigh.   And if men
could be heedless of the manifest and open sign of
His presence, they are in great danger of not hearing
that still small voice.

The real dealings of God with our souls are out
of sight. We cannot now, as in the days of miracles,
lay our hands on them and say, Lo here, or Lo there.
We cannot make certain of each particular movement, each separate call, each undoubted instance of
Divine working.   The Spirit, when He witnesses
with our spirit, does so in ways that are secret
between our heart and Him, and to no one can we
really reveal that secret and make it plain. If, then,
the blindness and selfishness of man were able to
resist the outward call and the manifest token,
much more the whisper of conscience, and the
solemn but gentle appeals of Providence.   If men
were not persuaded that the time of their visitation
was upon them when they beheld the Lord heal
the sick and raise the dead, we may well fear for
ourselves lest we miss our opportunity of mercy,
lest we do not perceive and heed God's visitation,
which comes seeming to be nothing more than the
common things which happen to us ; seeming to be
clothed and veiled in the ordinary changes and
chances of our mortal life.

There is one sort of visitation from God which
many of us are going through now.   How many of
us are leading a quiet and peaceful life, without anything apparently to try us greatly, anything greatly

to disturb and trouble us ; no great sorrow, no great pain, no great fear, no great disadvantage to struggle with, no great care to weigh us down. There are the common temptations and burdens which belong to the lot of all men. But those surely are little to speak of when we think what men have had to go through, what might have come upon us and has not. And in this kind of life we go on undisturbed from year to year perhaps. No great change happens in it for worse or, for what the world calls better. It is even, quiet, safe. We do what we have to do. We work, if we must work ; we have our time to ourselves if we are not bound to work. We look out on the course of other men's lives, on the ups and downs, the wonderful success and the wonderful ruin, which go on round us ; on the wars and commotions of other lands, the "distress of nations, with perplexity ; . . . men's hearts failing them for fear, and for looking after those things which are coming on the earth." But we look on at a distance ; none of these things come nigh us to touch us. Peace and quiet is our portion, the regular unbroken order of our lives.

I can well imagine people sometimes being almost frightened at the perfect peace and stillness in which their lives flow on, with everything given them that they can really need, kept safe from all that they fear, and that seems to come so easily on men like themselves. I can almost understand people thinking that something dreadful must be coming on them some day to make up for the long time that they have been left free from trouble and pain.

This is faithless fear. God does not deal with

us in this way. He does not make a certain amount of evil weigh against and balance a certain amount of good. He gives us good and evil by a different rule ; one which we cannot understand, but which we may be sure is not one of cruelty and delight in disappointing us.

Let us enjoy the blessings which He gives us : our quiet days, our health and peace and safety; and let us hope on in the mercy which has been with us so long.

But there are two things to be remembered, which we are apt to forget. One is, that, without superstitiously vexing ourselves with the thought that God must bring evil on us in proportion to the good, it is yet true that all this quiet cannot go on as it is for ever—that we must expect one time or another some of the trials of life. It is not likely that we shall always escape pain or vexation or sickness so entirely as we are doing now ; we are still men, and the covenant of sorrow and death is not given us. This is one thing : and the other is, that this time of quiet, of leisure, of freedom from the burdens of sorrow and pain, is a time of visita-tion ; a time when God is visiting us,—visiting us as truly as He visited Jerusalem when He sent His Son to tell of the kingdom of heaven,—visiting us by many a blessing as truly as He visits and searches other men by His chastisements and judg-ments. In this time of peace and regular work, and quiet days and nights of sweet sleep, He is pre-paring us, He is trying us. He is giving us time, full ample time, to fit ourselves to meet harsher and heavier ways of His providence. He is seeing what is in our hearts, whether we have it in us to

C.   P

be thankful to Him, whether so much mercy and favour will draw our hearts to Him, and strengthen our purposes and efforts after goodness ; whether *we* can be made better in the way in which He would make all men better if it were possible, by giving us the desires of our hearts, and keeping us in safety from the evil we are afraid of.

This is our time of visitation ; and how do we use it ?   Do we even think as we ought that it *is* a time of visitation ?   When some great trouble or sorrow comes upon us, then, if we have any religion at all, we have no difficulty in understanding that God is visiting us.   Then we feel it to be natural to recognise His searching and trying hand.   Whether we bow to it or resist it, it at any rate sobers and solemnises us ; and we feel—to our cost, perhaps, we say—that the Lord is near, that the hand of the Lord has touched us.   But do we remember that the hand of the Lord is upon us, that His eye is beholding us when He goes on keeping us safe day after day, driving away sickness and death from our door, giving us time and strength and spirit to go on doing our work and our labour till the evening, blessing our basket and our store, doing good to us and to our children ?   Do we remember that surely He is observing how we take all this ?

Surely we *may* take it very ill.   We may be all this time growing more and more selfish, more and more thankless, more and more turned away from God, more and more in love with the present world.   We may be lazy, and think it too much trouble to stop and think what we owe to God ; too much trouble to examine ourselves whether we are receiving our good things as Christians and religious men, or as those whose hope and portion is in this life ; too much trouble to see whether we really say our prayers in earnest, and are asking God to help us not to abuse our blessings.

Surely it is but too easy, in the midst of peace and mercy, fenced in from trouble, and with mind and body at ease,—it is but too easy to forget the great seriousness of life : where we are going to, whom we have to deal with, what He has given us to do, how we shall one day have to give an account of what we have had and enjoyed. And if we do, we are missing our day of visitation ; we are hearing without heeding the call of God ; we are failing under our appointed trial, just as if that trial were one of sorrow and suffering, and we murmured and resisted it. The time of our visitation is upon us, and we are not knowing it.

Remember this too. Now, in this time of peace, and probably more or less leisure, is the time to fit ourselves to meet trouble when it comes—to arm our souls with that faith and trust in God which will alone keep us up when the weather changes and the storm and winter come on us. It is not when we are sick that we can expect to learn how to bear sickness. It is not when death darkens our doors that we can hope to be taught at once the thoughts and feelings which help the believer in Christ to keep fast his confidence, and not to sorrow as those who have no hope.

It is those who have learned beforehand to believe in God who are able to put forth their belief when the moment comes when it is wanted. And now is the time given you to gain this firm, quiet, real trust in God. Now nothing disturbs you. Now you have no pain to take off your thoughts, to weaken your body. Now you have no bitterness of sorrow to fill up your heart. You have time to think, to read, to consider, to give quiet, calm attention to the things which most concern your peace. If anything strikes you in what you read or hear, you can turn it over in your mind till you have become accustomed to it, and it has become part of your very self.

The soldier who is to fight well must learn his exercise in time of peace ; and now is your time of peace, your time of learning. Oh, see that you use it. See that when the time of real trial comes it does not find you unprepared, and only beginning to think about putting on your armour when you want in good earnest to have it on and ready for use. See that with so much goodness and mercy appointed for your lot in life ; with so much grace offered you ; with the promises and redemption of the Lord of Life continually before you ; with the choice blessings of the kingdom of heaven made your heritage, not only without money and without price, but, so far, without the sacrifices and the tribulations which had to be endured by our elder brethren in Christ, and which still have to be en-dured by so many now alive,—with all this lot of loving-kindness and peace appointed you,—with your trial made so easy and so gentle, instead of being painful and difficult,—see that you do not miss recognising, as it passes over you, " the time of your visitation."

NO DIVIDED SERVICE TO GOD

"No man can serve two masters : for either he will hate the one, and
love the other ; or else he will hold to the one, and despise the
other. Ye cannot serve God and mammon."—ST. MATT. vi. 24.

THE Gospel for this morning is one of those passages which are very hard to preach upon. To
preach upon, I mean, wisely, faithfully, honestly,
making the words mean what they do mean, re-
fraining from making them seem to mean what they
do not mean. It is easy, very easy, taking them as
they stand, and putting a strain upon them, to draw
lessons from them which should be very startling
and very impressive. It would be very easy, taking
their simple literal expressions, to show how great
is the difference between the way of thinking and
living which they hold up, and that which we are all
accustomed to. It would be easy to ask, How is it
possible to reconcile the life of business and worldly
employment, the life of money-making, which is the
ordinary one in our world, with the saying, " No
man can serve two masters ; . . . ye cannot serve God
and mammon " ? It would be easy to set side by
side the care which we all of us think it right to
have about the time to come, the value and the
praise which we ascribe to the habit of looking

forward, of being provident, of laying up against
the evil day, or for those who are to come after us ;
and, on the other hand, the words which sound like
a condemnation of this very spirit of painstaking
thought and care for the future.

"Therefore I say unto you, Take no thought for
your life, what ye shall eat, or what ye shall
drink ; nor yet for your body, what ye shall put
on. . . . Take therefore no thought for the morrow : for the morrow shall take thought for the things
of itself."

It would be very easy, I say, to push home these
solemn sayings ; to show the inconsistency of the
ordinary ways of life, and of what we are all doing,
with our Master's words : to enlarge upon the
separation from the world which may seem to be
the only way open of obeying them. Very easy :
and some have so heard and understood them that
they conceived themselves bound to separate altogether from the common course of life, in which
men in general earn their bread, and carry on the
business of the world ; they could see no point
where they could stop, short of giving up all
concern with the world, giving up friends and
neighbours, wife and children, lands and houses,
and every earthly possession, and living as long as
God left them to live, without anything that they
could call their own, without any employment
besides what was directly and immediately and
exclusively religious employment. Very easy to
bring out from these words the stern and sweep-
ing condemnation of all earthly employment ; and,
in doing so, to put extreme and strong ways of

speaking into people's mouths, which they satisfied
their conscience by repeating with their lips, and
dwelling on in their thoughts, while in their daily
and real life there was nothing approaching to the
way in which they professed to understand our
Lord's words.

It would be very easy, I say, to make a very
solemn and impressive sermon out of them, simply
following and applying the unstrained literal sound ;
it would be impossible to say anything more sharp
and clear about the little business that Christians
have with the world than is said in these words.
And, on the other hand, it would not be difficult
to preach about them in order to show that they
have been often misunderstood and misapplied ;
that they cannot mean that complete separation of
Christ's disciples from the business and the employments without which human things would come to
a standstill ; that they cannot be meant to condemn
industry, prudence, the diligent and faithful labouring to get our living in the state of life to which
God has been pleased to call us.

As it is easy to preach about them so as to make
them mean what seems extreme and extravagant
and impossible, so it is equally easy to preach
about them, to soften and smooth them down, so as
to make them have no meaning at all.   But what
is difficult is to remember that they are the very
words of God Himself ; for He who spoke them was
Almighty God, who made us, who will judge us ;
and, remembering this, and therefore not daring to
take liberties with them, or explain them away, or
say that they do not mean what they plainly do,

to apply them, honestly and wisely, to guide our thoughts and our behaviour in a state of life which, we are perfectly certain, it is God's will that we should live.

Jesus Christ, who made men to live together, and to live by their work and their labour, and who so ordered the world that men should have to lay up to-day what would be wanted to-morrow,—to sow, in order to reap,—to gather in summer-time what would not be given in winter,—Jesus Christ, who appointed and knew all this, spoke these words for the instruction of men, who, He knew, would have to live by their business and by their looking forward. He spoke them for the use and instruction of all generations to the end of time, and not only for those who first heard them, and who had indeed, for our sakes and the Gospel's, literally and entirely to give up their work and business with the world, their families, their homes, their possessions, everything which makes the ordinary employment and ordinary interest of life. To them, indeed, those sharp stern words, " No man can serve two masters," " Take no thought for the morrow," " Take no thought for your life," had the utmost literal meaning which the words could have. For they were called to give up life, and everything else, for the one single object of following their Master in His work of bringing the good news into the world, and setting up His Church, the kingdom of God, among men. For that purpose it was not wonderful that they should have been obliged to give up every other thought and care, when we see that, even now, any great and difficult work which has to be done requires the same sort of exclusive and entire surrender of every other claim, and devotion of every thought to the great end. He spoke these words in the shape in which they would be most impressive and most striking to those who were first called to be Christians. Unless those words had been realised and fulfilled to the very extreme of their literal meaning, the Gospel never could have made its way ; we should have had no Christianity, no universal Christendom of eighteen hundred years, among men. But also, unless the spirit and real principle of those words is kept up among Christians, Christianity will die out among mankind.

But Christ did not mean His Gospel to be always beginning. He did not mean it to be always a time of first introducing His religion to the world. He did not mean it to be always a time of persecution, of wandering missionaries, of martyrs. He meant that the preaching of Apostles should have success ; that nations should be con-verted ; that His Gospel should take root, and be established as the religion of mankind ; that it should be the mustard seed, at length springing up into the greatest of all herbs ; that it should be the leaven which in time should change and fill the whole mass. When the Apostles' work was done, when the Gospel had taken possession of whole nations and their society, when Jesus Christ was recognised as our Lord and Saviour, and His word as the truth by which we were to live and die, it was plain that things could not be as at the beginning. The Gospel work was to be done otherwise than as it had been at a time when no one believed in it, and all the world was against it. The labours, the wanderings, the entire giving up of all earthly business, all earthly ties, all earthly possessions, which had been necessary in St. Paul and St. Peter and St. John, gave place to another manner of life. Men, when they had learned the great lesson about Christ and ever-lasting life, were to return to their work and their ordinary employment. The world was still to go on ; and it can only go on by men being busy and being provident, by their labouring each at his trade or calling, by their carrying on the business of life, and, as it is called making money. There were still to be different employments, different ranks and stations, among men. There were still to be families and households, husbands and wives, masters and servants. Servants were still to obey their masters on earth, though the Lord had said, " No man can serve two masters." Fathers were still to lay up for their children, though the Lord had said, " Take no thought for the morrow ; " for the Lord had not meant to abolish or destroy human society, in which busy employment, hard work, looking forward and preparation for the morrow, are things without which it cannot go on. Our Lord had not meant to abolish labour and business, the good sense and wise care which make life go straight, which give men power to be useful and to do good service in the time of need. He did not mean to destroy and condemn all this : what He meant to do was to fill it all with His heavenly Spirit, to purify, to sanctify, to direct it to its true and right end.

But He did not speak in vain when He said,
" No man can serve two masters ; " " Seek ye first the
kingdom of God, and His righteousness ; " " Take
no thought for the morrow." He did not speak
these words merely for those who were to have
the hard and painful work of setting up the beginnings of the Church and Gospel of Christ. He
spoke them for the Christians of quiet and settled
days as much as for those whom He called to walk
literally in His footsteps, to drink of His cup, and
be baptized with His baptism. And I do not know
if they are not, in their living and eternal meaning, more solemn to us, who cannot and are not
meant to fulfil them literally, than even to those to
whom it was plain and simple enough what they
meant. Worldliness was not likely to be the temptation of those who had given up all they had, and
were going to die for Christ.

To those who are called to live in a state of
things where it is their duty to be busy in the
world, to arrange and guide its affairs, to make
money, to provide for their families, their wide
unlimited meaning, leaving on us the responsibility
how far we take in, and live by their true spirit, is
like a test and touchstone continually trying what
is in their heart, and making proof of the honesty
and earnestness of their conscience.

For if they do not call us straight out of this
world's business and engagements ; if they leave its
ordinary course and necessities as they find them ;
if they say nothing against men doing their work
with all their might, fulfilling their obligations with
all their ability, throwing their strength and heart

into their employments; if they really leave us to
our own responsibility, in laying up for the future,
in making money, and providing for our families,—
and all sober men will agree that they do all this,—
yet they bear witness to certain truths which, be our
interest in the world what it may be, are at the foundations of the Christian life. They remind us that
the Gospel is a religion which was founded on the
sacrifice of all that the world values and makes
dear. Sacrifice, sacrifice of self, sacrifice of will,
sacrifice of pleasure, sacrifice of hope, was at the
bottom of that life and example, of that work of
atonement and reconciliation, by which God's kingdom has been opened to us. Say what we will
about the necessity and obligation of worldly works
and worldly claims, the fact remains that the first
step in what was done for our salvation was absolutely to give up this world. And on each thing
that was done, on the gradual working out of God's
great plan, on each moment and action of our Lord's
ministry, on each point of the apostleship of those
who took up His commission, sacrifice, the sacrifice
of this world, is stamped. If ever we forget that
sacrifice, self-denial, the giving up of what flesh and
blood would have, the willing surrender of what
the Gentiles seek after, is of the foundation and
essence of Christ's religion, we forget our Christian
profession.

Another thing which those words hold up before
our thoughts continually is this : that our religion
is one in which this world is absolutely as nothing
in comparison with the world to come. It is quite
true we are called by God to take our part in the

world and its concerns.   For the time we are in it
we must work as hard in it and take as much
trouble about it as if it was our only and final
home.   But our home it is not ; we are in it, in
comparison with what is to come, as players are in
a game, compared with the work and business of
their whole life.   While the game goes on they
must do their best, and keep their thoughts on it ;
but it is but for an hour or two, and then comes
what is serious and lasting.   And such is our life
to that state of things which we call eternity ; of
which all that we really know is, that it is beyond
exception serious and lasting, and that nothing
that can happen to us here can be of such consequence as what will happen to us there.   The will
of God *will* be done, *must* be done, there.   No one
there can serve two masters ; and the time during
which it is possible to try is not worth speaking of,
considering the time afterwards in which we shall
have to take the consequences, and lament the
folly of our mistake.

And, again, they remind us that, after all, after
all our diligence and labour and prudence,—which,
in such a state of things as we live in, the Gospel
does not forbid, but commands,—yet, after all, what
is the simple truth ?   Is it not *that* told in the
words, " Which of you by taking thought can add
one cubit unto his stature " ?   " Consider the lilies of
the field, how they grow ; they toil not, neither do they
spin : and yet I say unto you, That even Solomon in
all his glory was not arrayed like one of these."
All we do and all we have, our possessions and our
plans and our hopes, the world about us and the

days which we are appointed to see,—all is in the
hands of Him who feeds the fowls of the air, and
clothes the grass of the field, and does what He
thinks fit with the works and the years of men.
In His hands we are. He bids us trust in Him.
With all our doing, with all our wisdom, this ever
remains at bottom,—that what is His good pleasure, ·
that, and that only, is to come to pass.

Let us read His words with manly, sober, serious
hearts ; not carelessly, as if Jesus Christ, our Maker
and Judge, could have said His most solemn words
in vain ; not foolishly and perversely, as if He did
not know the various generations and different
states of society which would have to hear and
apply them, and as if His words would have to be
explained extravagantly, or turned into a snare ;
but in faith, that He who spoke the words, who
appointed our circumstances, planted in His words
eternal truths, fitted in all times to instruct, to warn,
and to console us, be our circumstances what they
may.

XXIII

THE CONSEQUENCES OF FORGETTING GOD

"Because that, when they knew God, they glorified Him not as God, neither were thankful."—ROMANS i. 21.

THE first chapter of the Epistle to the Romans contains the most terrible picture of human sin and degradation that, I suppose, was ever written. There is, as far as I know, no other chapter in the Bible that is so dreadful to read. A darkness and horror seems to come over our minds, seems to clog our words, as we read it. It is not only a description, but a history. It not only tells what human nature had come to be, but the steps by which it had sunk deeper and deeper into the horrors of sin. There is no fine writing—no trouble and art used to dress up the account. Verse after verse rolls on with its increasing burden; but what makes it so terrible to listen to is, that it is nothing more than the plain matter of fact of what men have come to, and why and how they came to it. It is the plain story of what has happened in this world, happened with this race of mankind, who were meant for something so different, who might have been so different. *This* is what they are fallen to; this is what the history of the world shows. And in this chapter it is summed up with a plain-spoken force and clearness which seem to bring before us the judgment of eternal justice, when, once for all, on the Great Day of Christ, it pronounces the doom of the world.

But now let us try and draw a practical lesson from it. It is, as I said, not only a description of known sin, but a history of the way in which human sin grew up to such a frightful height. Whether or not the same picture could be drawn of the society in which we live now as St. Paul drew of men in his days, there is no doubt at any rate of this : that the same germs and seeds of sin are to be found within it still,—that the same causes are at work to corrupt and degrade, and to lead men on deeper and deeper into evil—nearer and nearer to that frightful state which is described in this chapter. Let us see what were the steps by which men came to be so lost to shame and dead to conscience, to truth, to mercy.

The first step was, that knowing God, "they glorified Him not as God, neither were thankful." God had made Himself known to them. It matters not *how*, and to what degree. St. Paul here talks of the very world in which we live, making known to us God, its Maker. "That which may be known of God is manifest to men ; for God hath made it manifest unto them. For the invisible things of Him, from the creation of the world, are clearly seen, being understood by the works which He hath made (the invisible things of Him, that is), His eternal power and Godhead ; so that they are without excuse."

He is speaking of the lowest and least knowledge of God which can be among men ; and there is a great difference between such knowledge, the first notion of God, such as the works of creation ought to have taught to a heathen, and that knowledge of Him and of His will which came directly from Him, which is the inheritance of those to whom He has revealed His word. But, wherever this knowledge comes from, or of whatsoever kind it may be, St. Paul is here speaking of such knowledge in itself—more in some and less in others ; but, wherever it is, leading men on to draw nigh to God, to glorify Him, and be thankful. And, he says, the first step in the downward course of sin is to know God, and, knowing Him, not to glorify Him, nor to be thankful.

Now let us ask ourselves the truth about this. If God is known in the world, He is known among us. In a sense, we all know Him. We know His greatness and power; we have heard of His righteousness, His goodness, His love. We have all heard of Him at least by the hearing of the ear. His Name is nothing strange to us,—far less strange than it was to the men of other days, whom yet St. Paul declares to be without excuse. And what is God to us ? What is He in reality to our thoughts and feelings ? Do we own and know Him in our secret souls ? Do we acknowledge Him with the eye of faith, as One who, though we see Him not, is over us, is with us, is in us ? Is He to us as a real person ? Knowing Him as we do, accustomed to the thought of Him all our lives long and every day that we live, does this knowledge make any difference to us in what we think and wish and do ? Do

C.   Q

we remember Him in the real work of our life?
Do we live differently, because we know Him?
Do we "glorify Him as God,"—let Him be the
true King of our hearts and desires,—the Master,
the Father, whom we wish to please and serve?
Knowing what we owe Him, knowing all His
benefits to us, knowing all that He has done to
redeem and bless us, are we thankful to Him as our
God?

Because, see what happened to men before us,
who "knowing God," yet knowing Him far less
certainly and far less nearly and well than we know
Him, yet "glorified Him not as God, neither were
thankful." Forgetting Him, living without the belief and remembrance of Him, they fell away into
the folly, the vanity, the utter failure and disappointment of those who have nothing but an earthly life
to live and an earthly hope to trust to. They
"became vain in their imaginations, and their foolish
heart was darkened." Forgetting God, they forgot
heaven; forgetting God, they forgot the high and
glorious things which man was made for, but which
he can only have when he is with God, and God
works with him; forgetting God, their hearts and
hopes and desires and thoughts fell down to earth,
and became of the earth, earthy—childish and vain,
and foolish and fruitless. Knowing God, and yet
forgetting Him, they lost their guide and measure
of what they were meant for, and what they might
hope for. Their mind ran on follies; their heart
lost its light and became darkened, and could no
longer see the things which belonged to its peace.

But that was not all. That was not the worst.

They could not stop, even in this miserable loss of truth and hope. From being fools they went on to be sinners. From wilfully casting behind them the knowledge of God, which was given them to inflame their hearts with His love,—from wilfully forgetting Him, whom all living souls were created to glorify and praise,—it was a short and swift step to rebelling against Him, and setting up evil and falsehood to worship instead of Him. Man must have *some* God to worship and believe in ; and if he will not believe in the true one, he cannot stay long without worshipping a false one. So they " changed the glory of the uncorruptible God into an image made like to corruptible man, and to birds, and four-footed beasts, and creeping things." They " changed the truth of God into a lie, and worshipped and served the creature more than the Creator, who is blessed for ever." They thought it a weary and unprofitable thing to retain in their knowledge and thoughts that High and Holy One who inhabiteth eternity, whom no mind can comprehend, no words express, no service of created being fitly praise. And so they fell down to the unutterable madnesses and infatuations of superstition. The living man bowed down to the dead stock and stone, and saw his God in the beast and insect without reason, which his foot could crush.

And *this* was not all either. There was something deeper and darker in degradation yet to come. From forgetting the God they knew, they had come to be drowned in falsehood and vanity and ignorance ; they had, like crazed madmen, persuaded themselves that there was more hope and comfort

and advantage in making idols with their own hands
than in serving the living God who made the world.
" Wherefore "—mark the word, the terrible word,
which shows the connexion between the sin and
the punishment, which shows what the wrath and
judgment of God can bring on those who, having
the power to know and do better, dishonour God—
" Wherefore God also gave them up to uncleanness
through the lusts of their own hearts, to dishonour
their own bodies between themselves. . . . For this
cause God gave them up to vile affections. . . . And
even as they did not like to retain God in their knowledge, God gave them over to a reprobate mind, to
do those things which are not convenient ; " gave
them up to become instances of every conceivable form
of sin that is known ; gave them up to become at last
such sort of men as those " who knowing the judgment of God, that they which commit such things
are worthy of death, not only do the same, but have
pleasure in them that do them."

Now here is the state of things to which the
world had come when our Lord Jesus Christ came
into it to arrest the course of sin and the ruin of the
world by once more setting before the eyes of men
the form of perfect goodness, and by shedding His
blood, that the sin of the world might be washed
away in it, and a new world and a new hope begin.
Here was the state of things to which the world had
come, and for which, if the Son of God had not died,
the only remedy was the fire of consuming judgment. This is what it had grown to and blossomed
into. And now, what had it all come from ? What
was the seed from which this crop of sins had

bloomed and thriven, and become so thick and strong? Was it something which has now utterly passed away from the world? or is it something which is in us still?

The beginning of it all, according to the Apostle who speaks the words of the Holy Ghost, the beginning of it was only that forgetfulness of God, as our real living Lord and Father and Judge, which, you know only too well, is a state of mind we all are accustomed to—a state of mind in which many people live on from day to day. Knowing God, and forgetting Him : knowing God, and not glorifying Him as God, and being thankful. It was this, only this, and from this, as from the fruitful and unfailing seed, came to pass in time that monstrous growth of sin which it is frightful and shocking even to read of.

The world is very different in many ways from the world as St. Paul knew it. But the differences are, after all, surface differences—differences in the shape and form of what, at bottom, is the same. Idolatry, superstition, and sin take different appearances, but the same causes run the same course ; and wherever there is a knowing God and forgetting Him —a knowing Him and not glorifying Him as God— there is the seed of that idolatry and superstition and degradation of all that is true and pure and good in men, which St. Paul describes. The plague has begun ; it may not have got so far—it may be only in its early stage ; but the plague has begun, and will go on unless it is checked in time. If you know God and do not own Him in your conscience,—if you know God and do not glorify Him as God, nor are thankful to Him,—you are on the way

to become darkened and blinded, and fast bound in
vanity and falsehood. You are on the way to lose
the truth ; you are on the way to being let alone by
God, whose grace alone can save you,—let alone to
do those things " which are not convenient." Oh, who
can tell where that may bring a man ? Who can
tell where that dark, slippery, downward road may
end which begins in simply forgetting God, not
owning as Lord over our life the God whom yet we
know full well ?

Take warning : take warning from the Apostle's
words—words which we could hardly dare read anywhere except in the presence of the God of holiness ;
and remember that the whole history of mankind,
with its terrible experiences, bears them out and confirms them. Let us tremble when we find ourselves
trifling with the thought and fear of God. Let us
fall on our knees and beseech Him to save and help
us, and give us light and life, when we find that we
are forgetting Him, living without Him in the world ;
knowing Him, yet not glorifying Him as God ;
knowing Him, yet not liking to retain Him in our
knowledge.

XXIV

THE CONVENIENT SEASON

" When I have a convenient season, I will call for thee."—
ACTS xxiv. 25.

MOST of you know the occasion of this famous answer. Felix, the Roman governor, made it to St. Paul, who had been talking to him of religion : and when Paul " reasoned of righteousness, temperance, and judgment to come, Felix trembled, and answered, Go thy way for this time ; and when I have a convenient season I will call for thee." The words, as I said, have become famous. They have passed into a kind of proverb, when we want to signify the self-deceit with which we put off what we are afraid of, and do not like, but yet cannot altogether resist and deny. Felix felt the truth of what St. Paul said : he felt it so much that it made him tremble. A powerful ruler, and master of St. Paul's life, and able with a word to put him to death, yet he was afraid of him. He was a bad man, and could not hear of the righteousness and temperance which he had set at naught, and of the judgment which his conscience told him *must* come, without alarm and distress. He could not shut his eyes to the fact that he stood in serious danger : he felt convinced in his secret heart that what St. Paul said was the truth. But he soothed

his conscience by saying that he would think of his
words another time. Now it was not "convenient."
There are all kinds of reasons why an unrighteous and
unjust man finds it, at the moment, inconvenient to
learn and follow righteousness—why the sinner and
ungodly finds it inconvenient to look in the face the
tremendous certainty that he is one day to answer
before the judgment-seat of God. But perhaps a
time might come when it would be convenient.
Felix would wait till then, and in the meanwhile go
on as usual. The looking forward to the fancied
convenient season kept his conscience satisfied and
cheated for the present. He even seems to have
liked to hear St. Paul ; he was able, in spite of his
trembling, to find pleasure in listening to words
which were his own condemnation : he sent for
Paul often, we are told, "and communed with him."
But the time when God awakened his fears and
made him think seriously what he was, and where
he was going to,—that time had passed away unavail-
ingly. We have no reason to think that Felix
ever repented.

And that convenient season, in which Felix, to
his own ruin, cheated himself into believing—how
many of us believe in too. It is the great delusion
which cheats us all more or less ; which has gone
on cheating men from the beginning of the world ;
which has been warned against, and preached against,
and found by universal experience to be the most
lying of delusions ; but which is yet, and will continue to be to the end, as strong as ever. What is
it that enables us to listen unmoved to things which
we know to be true, and, if true, most terribly im-

portant to us, but the convenient season, which never comes? How is it that people can hear the things that they hear, Sunday after Sunday, in church——things which, so far from denying or contradicting, they *like* to hear,——they would be uncomfortable not to hear,——how is it that they can hear them, and agree with them, and yet still go on living as if they were mere words and meant nothing,—— if it were not for that other time which they trust to find, when they will attend to them in earnest? How is it that the words of God are received as most true, and yet produce no effect on the hearts and lives of those who receive them, except that they are able, while they hear them, to fancy to themselves a time when it will suit them not only to agree with them, but actually to put them in practice,——a time when they please themselves with thinking that all those beautiful and striking things which they hear in God's Word, and which even now, while they do the opposite, still seem so taking, so much to be wished for, so fit to make them happy, shall be really felt, and seen, and worked out, in their own lives : a time when they shall pray in earnest, though they do not care about praying now ; a time when they shall be gentle and loving, and heavenly-minded and pure, whatever to the contrary they may be now? What is it which enables them to bear the reproaches of their own conscience, the conviction of religious truth, the calls and visitations of God's providence, but that they can manage to persuade themselves that they can let the whole matter stand over to another day, when they will be more in the mind to think about it, more free from what tempts them than they are now, with more time to give to it, with less business and trouble to interrupt them?

It is not open refusal to believe and obey the Gospel which is so dangerous among us ; it is not the corrupting it, the excuses by which men make what is false seem true and what is wrong seem right. These, no doubt, are dangers ; but the great danger of all is seeming to agree with the truth, and to be persuaded by it, and putting off to another day the really attending to it. We listen, perhaps sometimes we tremble ; but we think that a more convenient season will come in time, and that we may wait till then before we begin to change our ways in earnest. And *when* do those who trust to it find that the convenient season ever comes?

There is really no greater practical snare than the putting off religious duty until another day. We do not want the Bible to warn us against its folly. Its warnings are striking enough against leaving such things to the last, against leaving them to another day at all when we are called to think of them to-day. You remember the foolish virgins finding it too late to enter in ; the guests, called to the feast, and choosing rather to look after their worldly interests, and thus shut out from the kingdom of God ; the people whom Christ called, and who wanted first to attend to their friends and business, and with whom Christ would allow no delay. But we do not want such warnings to show us what risks we are running, and how plainly we are deceiving ourselves. Our own experience is enough. There are people who are given to putting off and waiting till another time, not only in religious matters but in matters of this world. Well, what do we think of a man of this sort? a putter-off, who leaves till to-morrow what he ought to do to-day, whose common way it is to wait for a more convenient season, whose way of getting out of something that is troublesome, or that he does not like, is to leave it to another day? Your worldly wisdom tells you that when a man has once got into this way of putting off, there is no depending on him; that he goes on amusing himself, and dreaming, and looking forward, but that it is little use hoping that he will bring anything to perfection. You know that he is not a man to get on, or to succeed in what he takes in hand. You know that his plans are likely to come to naught, that the convenient day to which he is ever looking forward never comes, and never will come, as long as he goes on cheating himself in this way of waiting for it. You know that the secret of it all is that he is lazy and indolent, and dislikes the work which he has to do. You see through and smile at his excuses for trying to put off a difficulty which he is afraid to face. You smile when he thinks he is making you believe that he is in earnest when he puts off something, and you remember how often he has put off and waited for a more convenient season before. You find no difficulty in taking the measure of such idle putting off things in matters of this world, in the dealings between man and man. Well, then, you have the character, as it appears in God's eyes, and as it is in truth, of so many who are putting off the day of repentance and earnest religion to a more convenient season; who are leaving the

peace of their souls, and the preparing them for death
and judgment and eternity, to the last ; who think
that they need not be in a hurry in doing those
things which yet they hope to do sometime or other
before they die.   You see how such a character looks
in the world.   Can you suppose that it can look any
better in the eyes of God as respects the most solemn
things that man can have to do with ?   Can anything good come from such idle looking forward in
religion any more than in business ?   Is it at all
more likely that the convenient season, always
waited for and never found, will at last be reached
by these putters off of repentance, any more than it
is by the putters off of necessary work in their earthly
callings ?   If it is the mark of a man who cannot be
depended on, who will not do any good in his work,
that he sees what he ought to do, and is always
meaning to do it, but never can find the convenient
time, what can we hope that this same spirit will
ever bring us to in religion ?   Can we, when we think
for a moment, really believe that going on in this
way we *ever shall* find the time to which we are
looking forward ?   Can we help seeing that what
makes people put off in worldly business and put off
in religion is exactly the same thing, namely, a dislike to what has to be done, and that the dislike is
not likely to become less by this waiting for a more
convenient season ?

We can see, too, what has come of this putting
off of religion in our past lives.   If we will but
remember, we shall see plainly enough how, a few
years back, we were doing just as we are now.   We
were feeling the truth of religion.   We were promis-

ing to ourselves that we would change our ways—
only, not just yet, not at this very moment, which
would be so inconvenient, but at some time, soon
perhaps—at any rate a better time than just now.
Years have gone over us since then.   Have we found
the fitting time?   Has the convenient season come
yet?   Has the change begun which we were looking
forward to, perhaps counting on for certain, then?
Are we the same, or different from what we were
then?   Year after year has gone, summer and winter
have brought their changes ; but, among them all,
the convenient moment for changing our lives, for
giving more heed to the Bible, for thinking more of
eternal things,—that long looked-for moment,—has
not yet arrived.   Still we are looking forward to it.
Still we gladly listen to God's words and warnings ;
still we feel them to be the words of life.   Still we
wish that we followed them more.   Still we hope
one day to find them our portion.   But still we are
waiting for the convenient season.   Still we are
putting off the time of real examination of our lives
and condition in God's sight.   Still we are not yet
preparing ourselves to die.   Still we are the same
sort of people we were when, years back, we were
looking forward to the time when we could con-
veniently begin to say our prayers more regularly
and carefully, to be more constant at church, to come
to the Holy Sacrament ; the same sort of people as
then, when we were purposing to do what, in fact,
we never have done ; too good to give up our hope,
our intention to obey God's word and commandments, but not enough in earnest to make the change
at once which we know must be made some time if

we are to be saved ; to deny ourselves in order to obey God better, to force ourselves to begin the great work of life, the getting ready for what is to meet us after death.   That is—if we look back on our lives during their late years—that is what has in fact come to many of us from putting off and waiting for a more convenient season.   Things are as they were. Nothing has been begun in the way of improvement. The convenient season has seemed always near, yet has never been reached ; it has fled before us like our shadow, but we have never got hold of it.

Shall we never reach it ?   Not if we go on for ever looking forward to it, and in the meantime doing nothing.   The convenient season will never come if we are for ever passing by the season which now is because it is not as convenient as we wish. It will never come if we are for ever to leave till to-morrow what we may do to-day, if we cheat ourselves by thinking that it will be easier to do next week, or next Christmas, or next Easter, what we think hard and are not inclined to do now.   The easier time is not the time when things that have been long neglected have at last to be made up for. The easier time for paying a debt is not (though so many deceive themselves by thinking so) when it has mounted up by being put off, and we are grown older.   The easier time for getting through a serious and important work is not when, by being left untouched for years, there is more to do to it, and we have not grown stronger and more fit for trouble. And the easier time to turn to God, to break the chain of sin, to change to a better life, to begin to make trial of Gospel obedience, is not when years have stiffened us in our way of life, when we have got accustomed to thoughts and ways which are only of this world, when the mind begins to flag, and the body to droop, and we begin to find that we have already worked out the best of our health and strength.

Is it *ever* so easy to change from anything that we have been accustomed to, that we should venture to think that a distant day will be more convenient than now to do what we know we ought to do, but have not been accustomed to as yet? You know how little a matter, different from what you are accustomed to, makes you uncomfortable ; a change of house, a change of persons about you, a change in the way of doing what you have done in the same way for many years : you find these unpleasant, and the more so the older you get. Then, if you are not accustomed *now* to religious thoughts and principles and ways, can you suppose that some time hence you will find some method, some contrivance, by which, when it is convenient, you will become accustomed and reconciled to them ? If you are putting off saying your prayers regularly because it is not convenient now, do you really think that the time will come when it will be made easy and natural for you to say them ? If you are still putting off, as so many have been putting off for years, what yet you acknowledge to be a Christian's bounden duty, the coming to God's Holy Table, can you really expect that anything will happen to you which, somehow or other, will be the opportunity you cannot find now of drawing near to that blessed Communion ? Have you not had trial of yourself ? Chances, as we call them, have come, and touched you for the time, and gone. They might have helped you, but they did not seem to help you as much as you required,—you missed them, and they are passed away. You have had a serious talk ; you have heard a sermon which impressed you ; you began to think that now you would make up your mind and come, but you had not the heart—the opportunity passed, and you have not come. Perhaps you were sick, and looked forward that if you were raised up again you would make the effort to obey your Saviour's call, and seek His blessing. You got well, you returned to your work, but you have not come. Well, then, judging by the past, can you really expect that your future condition will ever in any way seem to you more convenient for coming to the Holy Table than your present condition seems to you now ?

No, my brethren. It must be *in yourself* that the change must be. It must be you yourself and not outward things, sickness, or calls, or impressions from others, which is to make the step and fulfil the duty. It is you who must *make* the opportunity, not wait for it ; or rather, I will say that God will most surely give you the opportunity, but you must seize it for yourself. You must make the convenient season, and make that convenient, which is the only season you can make sure of, the present. And be sure that there is no truer word in the world than this, that he who waits for the convenient season in matters of duty will never find it.

You know the folly of leaving things to the last in matters of this life. Words are not enough for you to express your scorn of the stupidity, the miserable weakness, of those who in any matter, be it only in starting for a journey or doing some common household service, leave things to the last; much more when the matter is a high and important one. Will you laugh at and scorn men for leaving things to the last in their worldly concerns, and will you leave things to the last when the everlasting destiny of your soul is concerned?

Men have two short words by way of excusing themselves when they are warned to think of God. "Not now," they say; "it will be soon enough by and by." And God has two short words, too, to set against them, which He is making good each day that we live—who can tell how awfully? To man's "not yet," God's answer is, "then, never." To man's "soon enough," He answers, "too late."

C.   R

XXV

GOD'S ALL-SEEING EYE

" Neither is there any creature that is not manifest in His sight : but all things are naked and opened unto the eyes of Him with whom we have to do."—HEBREWS iv. 13.

THERE are some things in religion which are among its plainest and most familiar teachings, but which yet, when we come to think what they really mean, seem almost too awful and tremendous to be endured by the mind of man. Among these, is the truth that the eye of God is always upon us. The Bible everywhere takes it for granted, and appeals to it. " Thou God seest me." " The eyes of the Lord are in every place, beholding the evil and the good." " The eye of the Lord is upon them that fear Him, and upon them that put their trust in His mercy." And, as it is said in the 139th Psalm, which is all about it, " Thou hast searched me out and known me. Thou knowest my downsitting and mine uprising. . . . Thou art about my path, and about my bed, and spiest out all my ways. For lo, there is not a word in my tongue but Thou, O Lord, knowest it altogether. . . . Whither shall I go then from Thy Spirit, or whither shall I go then from Thy presence ? " All this is manifestly the plain and simple truth. It could not be otherwise. Almighty God must behold all we

do, and know all we think.   It is as certain that
God must see us as it is certain that God made us.
We must be ever before His eyes, because He is God
who made all things to be, and without whom all
things would cease to be.   It is a thought which it
is impossible to get rid of; for the moment we
think of God at all, it comes with the thought of
Him.

And yet, as soon as we begin to say to ourselves,
" What does it mean, what does it come to?—how
does it touch me, and my life and thoughts ? "—how
unspeakably awful does it become!   To what
terrible greatness and meaning does it swell out,
just in proportion as we get hold of all that there
is in the simple, well-known words, God sees me
always.

God sees me always.   It must be so, it must be
true.   Then how awful is the very difficulty which
I feel in getting myself really to believe and feel as
if it was so!   Here I am, standing before His all-
seeing eye, never out of its sight, never for an
instant hidden ; and yet to think that I can hardly,
by trying, get myself to feel that it is so!   How
awful that even when I am on my knees, and
speaking words of prayer to Him, I yet so often fail
to remember that He is listening,—that He knows
what I am saying, and whether I am thinking of
Him or not.

God sees me always.   Then, to think of all that
He knows of me, of all that He has seen ; I, who
should fear to let my best friend know all that I
am ; I, who cannot bear to think of the secrets of
my heart being broken into by man ; I, who claim

to have a life of my own, privileged and reserved for myself alone, into which no prying eye from without may enter ; I, perhaps, who take so much trouble to keep up appearances, and to keep out of sight what, I feel in myself, will least bear the light ; to know that all this secrecy and pains are vain,—that all that I am is known to Him who takes the measure of us all. The world may not know it, but it is all "naked and opened unto the eyes of Him with whom we have to do."

God sees me always. And then to think of the things which I have done without remembering that He was looking on ; to compare the number of times when I *have* remembered that He was seeing me, with the number of times that He was utterly out of my thoughts and recollections ; to think how differently I should often have spoken, if I had only had it in my mind that He observed me, and knew what I was saying ; to think, I say, not only of all that He has seen, but of all the times when I entirely forgot that He was by ! To think of the vain devices and pretences by which I excused myself to myself, and hid from myself something which I did not like to see and acknowledge to myself. And then to think how all this must have looked in the eyes of One who saw through it all ; what He must have thought of me, how I must have been put to shame in His presence ; how He must have despised me, for the vain fool that I was. Is there any one of us who can steadily fix his thoughts on the simple words, "God sees me always," and who in proportion as the meaning of them opens on him, can help having some such feelings as these ?

It is naturally difficult to us to keep in mind
things that we never see ; and, of course, there are
many other reasons which make us not care to keep
this thought in our minds.   Those who like to do
what God hates, naturally do not like to retain God
in their knowledge, or to torment themselves with
the perpetual remembrance that He is seeing what
they do.   They will forget it as long as they can,
and will keep their eyes shut to His presence till
they cannot help opening them.   But there are
many who feel their weakness and sin, and yet wish
to do better, who do not like to let their thoughts
dwell steadily on this great and real thing, that they
are ever under the eyes of God.   They shrink,
because they feel that it is so certainly and unavoid-
ably true, and because they feel, too, that they
are not fit to bear such watching, or able to endure
the thought of it.   It is in itself so awful, that it
seems easier and more comfortable to get rid of it
by forgetting and shutting our eyes, and letting the
world blot it out of our minds, than to face it, with
the consciousness of an utter weakness and utter
unfitness to be observed all day long by the pure
eyes of the most Holy God.   And so, many people,
without the direct and deliberate meaning to do
wrong, keep the thought out of their minds, or,
what is almost the same thing, take no trouble
to keep it *in* their minds.   For, certain and plain
and true as it is beyond a moment's doubt, it
is, without question, one of those thoughts which
will go out of minds like ours of itself, unless we
hold it fast.   Go out of them, at any rate, for a
season ; for no one can tell in what terrible strength

and unbearable vividness it may return, when we least expect it.

But let us consider this. In the first place, we all know that if there is anything true in the world, it is that Almighty God, who made us and keeps us alive, must see and know all that we are, and all that we do. What is the good then[1] of fighting against what is so certainly true? What is the use of stiffening and hardening ourselves against what all our wishing and all our thinking will not make otherwise? What is the use of accustoming ourselves to dream that something is *one* way when all the time we know it is *another* way?

We ought to learn to live all day in the thought that God's eye is upon us, if for no other reason, at any rate for this one,—that this is the truth; that it is the real condition under which we must live, and that we cannot change it, or run away from it. "If I climb up into heaven, Thou art there; if I go down to hell, Thou art there also. If I take the wings of the morning, and remain in the uttermost part of the sea; even there also shall Thy hand lead me, and Thy right hand shall hold me. If I say, peradventure the darkness shall cover me, then shall my night be turned into day. Yea, the darkness is no darkness with Thee, but the night is as clear as the day; the darkness and light to Thee are both alike." There is no escape from the truth; and why should we vainly try to escape from it?

But, in the next place, consider this. The thought of God's eye upon us is generally looked upon as a thought to restrain and bridle us in, with the fear of His awful strictness and holiness of

judgment.   And so, of course, it is.   It is a terrible
thought to have hanging over us when we are
inclined to do wrong, and to play with sin.   But is
this all ?   Does that awful eye of God, ever fixed
upon us, speak only of severity, of warning, of
reproof?   Is it fixed on us only to condemn us,
only to make us feel our infinite distance from Him
who is our Father and God ; only to make us shrink
and tremble before Him ?   Is this the reason why
you are afraid to face the thought of God's continual
knowledge of you, that you find in it only what
disquiets and presses down your soul ?   I believe it
is the reason very often ; and so, in our cowardice,
and with our slavish love of forbidden things, we
miss what is surely meant, not merely to restrain us,
but to be the greatest of our comforts.   For if the
thought of God seeing us, and knowing us through
and through, to our hearts' depths, is a very awful
one, it is one on which, if we really take it in, we
can stay and rest with hope, and encourage ourselves,
as we can on nothing else.

If there is any truth whatever in man, God also
is truth itself, and it is to God that he can look up,
to be sure that the truth about him is fully known.
He knows that God sees him just as he is ; that it
is no use to hide his sin and unprofitableness and
falls ; but also that God sees too every step, every
effort, which he makes in trying to do better.   We
live in a fool's dream about ourselves, and it is not
the outside world only, but our own imaginations
and judgments about ourselves, which we cannot
help feeling convinced, from time to time, are utterly
wrong and mistaken.   It seems to me that it is a

great comfort to be able to fall back on the thought that there is One who knows us really, knows us without mistake ; who has no temptation to mis-understand or misrepresent us ; no temptation to think us better, nor yet to think us worse, than we are ; who judges us, justly indeed—oh, how awfully justly—and yet makes every allowance, with the continual desire to help us, tenderly and lovingly watching over us, and caring for us. Surely this is a thought to retire into for refuge, not only from the " provoking of all men," and " the strife of tongues," but from our own perplexities and doubts about ourselves,—our own questionings and uncertainties whether, after all, we are in the right way ; whether our wishes and attempts to do right are not all useless and thrown away.

For we are what we are in God's sight ; not what men think us, not what we think ourselves, but what He sees and knows that we are—nothing more, nothing less. There is One to whom we can always reveal our cause, knowing that it will be perfectly understood and fairly weighed. To His absolute and perfect knowledge we can make our appeal, even if we can only make it with shame and self-reproach and bitter abasement. In the certainty that He knows all our case, we can find comfort, even above that of the testimony of a good con-science ; when feeling that our heart does not condemn us, we can lift up our thoughts with con-fidence to God, who is greater than our hearts, and knoweth all things.

We are ever in God's sight. Let us not dread it as cowards and slaves now, only to be overwhelmed

by it in that judgment which must surely one day
come ; but let us learn, awful as it is, to welcome the
thought, and make it real to ourselves ; to believe in
it, to face it steadily as often as we can.   And so shall
we find it, what it is meant to be,——God's great
encouragement and help to His creatures and His
children in doing right.   *There* is His eye—not of a
Judge and Ruler only, but of a Shepherd, a Father, a
Giver of all good gifts, a Promiser of all blessed
hopes, the Lover of the souls of men, even to the not
sparing His only Son for them.   So shall we find
something to rest upon—a sure and true and just
judgment, to fall back upon, in the difficulties, the
temptations, the mistakes of our lives ; a judgment
which it is hopeless to imagine deceived by any show
on our part, but which is sure to give us credit for
all that is good and faithful and honest.   So, in
pain, in sorrow, in those bitter times which seem to
shut out all remaining hope to us while we are here
we shall know and feel that we are being watched
by an eye of tenderness and sympathy, deeper and
truer than that of any friend on earth to his suffering friend.   So shall we come to feel that, unseen
though it is, in the brightness of the sky or the darkness of the night, there is an eye which meets
ours when we turn to it for support and guidance.
" I will inform and teach thee in the way wherein
thou shalt go : and I will guide thee with mine eye."
So, whenever we will, whenever we want it to help
us, to reassure us, to give us hope, we shall have that
constant presence to appeal to, whom none can really
doubt, none can hope to deceive ; to appeal to in
our prayers, even when they are miserably cold and

wandering ; to appeal to in our striving against evil and temptation ; to appeal to when we are by ourselves, and dare not trust our suffering thoughts to any one ; when perhaps we do not know the cause of our trouble.

So may we prepare ourselves, by the continual thought of His never-ceasing though invisible nearness to us now, for that day when our eyes shall be unsealed ; and He, who has all along been walking unnoticed at our side, will be manifested to us "as He is,"—" that when He shall appear, we may have confidence, and not be ashamed before Him at His coming."

XXVI

THE CHRISTIAN'S DUTY AS MAN TO MAN

" Be ye therefore merciful, as your Father also is merciful. Judge not,
and ye shall not be judged : condemn not, and ye shall not be
condemned : forgive, and ye shall be forgiven : give, and it
shall be given unto you ; good measure, pressed down, and shaken
together, and running over, shall men give into your bosom.
For with the same measure that ye mete withal it shall be measured
to you again."—ST. LUKE vi. 36-38.

OUR Lord sets before us, in these words, two things :
the pattern of mercy, of justice, of forbearance and
forgiveness, of generosity, which we ought to take ;
which is the example of Almighty God,—" be ye
therefore merciful," because, as it is said in the verse
before, " the Highest," of whom we call ourselves
the children, " is kind unto the unthankful and to
the evil :"—and next, the rule of God's government
and judgment in matters between man and man ;
" with the same measure that ye mete withal it shall
be measured to you again."

Thus we see that, for the present, God is to us
all, even to the unthankful and to the evil, what
He would have *us* also to be : He is merciful,
He is gracious, He spares, He condemns not, He
forgives, He gives to us all " good measure, pressed
down, and shaken together, and running over."

But this is only true for the time that we are here on our trial, preparing for the other life. Between this life and that other life comes the day of judgment, when we must give up an account for this life, and receive the things done in the body. And of this judgment this is one of the great rules : with what measure men have measured to others, it shall be measured to them again. Mercy will follow mercy, and he shall have judgment without mercy that hath showed no mercy. By the rule by which we have judged and condemned shall we, in our turn, be tried. There can be no looking for forgiveness, if forgiveness has on our part been denied. And, according as we have shared our Father's bountiful gifts with our brethren, will our Father's bounty be poured upon us in infinite increase ; or else be restrained, withheld, taken from us for ever.

We all know that the great practical rule of life, that in which the meaning of God's law about our duty to our neighbour is summed up,—the second of the two great commandments,—is, that we should do to all men as we would that they should do to us. And, answering to this great rule of duty, is God's great rule of judgment and recompense. As we have done to others, so, in the end, shall it be done to us. This, which our own consciences and feelings bid us to expect from a God of righteousness, God's word to us, by His Son our Lord, and by His Prophets and Apostles, fully confirms. In all things as we sow, so shall we reap.

And in our behaviour to other people, and our treatment of them,—not only in our deeds to them, but in our judgments and words about them,—we must expect nothing more from our great Judge than what we have been willing to give to them. We are now choosing the rule by which we shall be dealt with by and by ; the rule of just severity, of which we little know yet the tremendous meaning and searching righteousness ; the rule of forgiveness, of allowance, of compassionate love, of which we cannot measure or imagine the depths and treasures of mercy.

God, who has planted this law of His kingdom deep in our nature, has again solemnly declared it by the voice of Jesus Christ : the law of being done to, as we did to others. "With the same measure that ye mete withal it shall be measured back to you in return."

My brethren, I do not know with what feelings you hear these well-known familiar words, but to me they always seem some of the most awful words in the Bible. For, in the first place, they are so plainly the words of that justice which all men acknowledge, that we not only believe, but we *feel*, that they must be true. They are not a matter of faith to us, which we receive on the authority of God. The moment we trust ourselves to think at all of the matter, we feel sure that so it must be ; we cannot help seeing that it could not be otherwise ; we cannot, if we would, doubt them, if we believe in a judgment at all. In that judgment men must look to be dealt with in the same spirit, by the same measures, according to the truth and righteousness and generosity which they have shown when it was their turn to be the judges, when it was their turn to show mercy, to pass their opinion, to help and share and give. Can we imagine any one claiming to be judged by a different measure? Can we imagine that the forgiveness, the allowances, that they would not grant to others, they may count upon for themselves? Can they imagine that they may deal with men harshly, but that God ought to deal with themselves tenderly?

This is one thing which makes these words so awful, that we see for ourselves that it *must* be as they say. And the other is that, while we feel the certainty of the law and judgment, we cannot see or guess *how* it will be carried out. It lies in the awful darkness of the time to come; and there, in due time, in ways that we know not, at a moment which none can tell, the sentence will have its effect, the measure will be measured back. All we know is that, some time or other, a man's deeds will be returned upon him, and he will find out how he dealt with his brethren, and what God, his Maker and Judge, thought of his dealings, by what happens to himself.

And the fearful thing to think of is that, for the most part, this is to be in another world,—another world, where all things will be different,—another world, where all things will be so much greater, for blessedness and for anguish, than they are here,— another world, where what is to be is to be for good, and for ever. It is there, for the most part, that the law, which cannot be broken, will have its fulfilment, and the measure be measured back to men. Here it only is so partially and sometimes. It *is* so sufficiently to awaken our thoughts and fears. We do see, from time to time, strange and sudden instances of a man being overtaken by a trouble and humiliation, answering in a wonderful manner to his own manifest wrongdoings, and rolling back on his own head that same measure which he had measured to others. And do we not, in our own consciences, sometimes trace dimly with surprise and awe, in the things which God's providence brings upon us, in the trials which are become the accustomed portion of our life, and meet us daily, the very likeness to those things which, long ago, were the sins and offences of our lives?

Men see, in the harshness and looseness of the unfair judgments passed on them, the reflection and likeness of the judgments which they once so carelessly uttered. Men see, in the disappointment and unkindness of their own children, the remembrance of what their own parents once had to grieve over in them. These things do happen. The awful rule of the measure measured back does show itself in our real life and experience here, partially, though often with overwhelming force and evidence. But it is only partially for this world. This life is a life of preparation, of waiting, of grace, of possible repentance and change and amendment. The rule is put off here, because here all things are imperfect and but for a time, and of very short continuance. We do not see it fulfilled here. If we only judged by this life, it would seem to be sometimes fulfilled and acted on, but more often not. Where it is to be fulfilled and accomplished completely and universally, is in that unknown world to come, to which we are all hastening.

But whether here or there, this is the rule of God's government; this is the rule by which we shall all

have our lives and doings tried and judged. " With
the same measure that ye mete withal it shall be
measured back to you in return." That is the clear
plain rule.

If a man wants to know how his life, with all its
imperfections and inconsistencies, and weaknesses and
sins, will be dealt with, let him first consider with
himself how, in serious business and disputes, and,
still more, how, in the common talk of life, he has
been in the habit of judging others. What has he
shown of care and anxiety and trouble to be fair,
really to do justice to another man's case, to know
the whole truth, to make no charge before he was
sure, to keep from all malice and ill-nature, to make
allowances, to pay regard to the rights and feelings
of others, to guard against harshness, violence,
passion, and bad temper?

We must, all of us, judge often, and sometimes
condemn. We must sometimes condemn with un-
shrinking severity. The harm and sin is not in
judging and condemning, but in judging and condemning without reason,—carelessly, unjustly, ignor-
antly,—condemning for the pleasure of condemning,
condemning without mercy and without fear. Now,
if our conscience tells us that we have dealt this
measure to others, we have here before us the
announcement of what we have to look for. What
we have refused to others will be refused to us. If
we have taken judgment and condemnation into our
hands needlessly and harshly, there is the same
harsh and unsparing judgment waiting for us. If
we, who need so much indulgent allowance for ourselves, made none for others, it is vain to look for it

when we are judged. If we have made the worst of things against others, we know that things will not be made the best of for us.

Is there any one who can look back on all his past life, and venture to say that he could endure the judgment, if the measure which he knows he has measured to others were, in God's justice, exactly measured back to him? Yet that is God's rule; the rule we must stand or fall by; the rule from which there is no escape. Can we hear the rule and doubt it,—doubt of its fairness, doubt of its certainty? Can we hear the rule and not tremble?

If there were nothing else to drive us to take refuge in God's offers of mercy in Christ, surely this alone would be enough. To be done to, by the infinite and perfect justice of God, as we have done to others so often and so carelessly—who could stand it? What hope is there for us, but that great mercy and patience and forgivingness of our heavenly Father, which we care so little to copy? If we can venture to look forward to that day of trial, surely it must be with the hope that what we have so justly and righteously deserved may, for the sake of Him who died for us, be after all *not* meted out to us. It must be with the hope that we, who have so often refused to forgive, may be forgiven our unforgivingness, which we have confessed and repented of at God's mercy-seat before the great account was closed. It must be with the hope that we, who have so often judged so lightly and condemned so harshly, may, now that we see and are sorry for our harsh judgments, yet find, for Christ's sake and goodness, a mercy which we once would not show.

C.   S

If, I repeat, there were nothing else, this alone ought to bring us to earnest and serious thoughts ; that, for our past dealings with our brethren, there is nothing but true repentance to save us from being dealt with exactly by the same measure which we dealt to them.

Let us live with the remembrance of this awful truth about the justice of God. God repays to men what they do. God measures back to them by their own rule. God judges them by the standard they apply to their brethren. Then, if we feel ourselves getting slack in our obedience and careless in our repentance, let us ask ourselves how we can look forward to facing it if we neglect the promises and grace of Christ to offending men, whom the law condemns. Let us beseech Him not to enter into judgment with us who never can be justified in His sight. Let us believe with thankfulness that there *is* mercy with Him, even for those who have sinned against mercy ; but let us also believe, as is most true, that it is only for those who *now* desire and try to be merciful,—who try not to provoke God by judging carelessly and unjustly,—who fear when they condemn lest they should be condemned ; who, in the hope of God's forgiveness, are ready with all their heart to forgive their brother ; who, in the hope and knowledge of God's unmeasured goodness, are glad to follow the example of their Father in heaven.

May God help us all to share in the spirit and mind of His Son, that we may hope for the " good measure, pressed down, and shaken together, and running over," which His Son has to give to those who love Him.

XXVII

THE UNJUST STEWARD

"And the lord commended the unjust steward, because he had done wisely : for the children of this world are in their generation wiser than the children of light."—St. Luke xvi. 8.

"THE children of this world:" that is, the people who plainly and entirely live for this world alone, and do not care, or profess to care, for anything beyond it. "The children of light:" that is, those whom God's grace and calling has enlightened and drawn to the light of goodness and truth; whose hearts and consciences feel and acknowledge what is right and lovely and of good report; and who in various measures try to follow it,—wish to be on the right side and in God's favour,—hope in the end to attain by His mercy to the light of His countenance and the blessedness of His kingdom. And the lesson which our Lord means to teach by the remarkable story of the unjust steward,—the dishonest servant who did his evil work thoroughly; and, having begun by cheating his master, and not being willing to repent and do better, did not stop half-way, but carried out his cheating to the last, and made the most of it as a provision against the evil day ;—the lesson, for the sake of which our Lord is not afraid to represent the master as praising the unjust

steward, because he had done wisely, is this, that
the men of this world, in the sense which they
show, and in the thoroughness and consistency with
which they live for the world, outstrip and put to
shame the men with consciences.

That was the general sight when our Lord was
among us : it was never different before He came,
and has never been different since. The world is
served more perfectly, more wisely, more successfully, than God. Men think, and look forward, and
take trouble, and even suffer for the world, in a way
in which they will not think and act and suffer for
the sake of the world to come. The children of this
world do their work with a whole heart ; the children
of light do theirs with only half a heart.

"In their generation," with a view to the object for which they choose to live and work, "the
children of this world are wiser than the children of
light." They are wiser, more prudent and sensible,
in what they do, because they are more in earnest
in what they want, and use the proper means to gain
it. If the unjust steward wants still to enjoy himself, and to have friends to receive him into their
houses, he knows that he must think beforehand of
the most likely way to gain his end ; and when he
has thought of the means, he must use them. He
knows that he will never reach what he wants by
dreaming about it, or wishing it, or talking about it,
or beginning and then drawing back. Bad man as
he is, he has no thought of such folly.

Yet this is the way in which "the children of
light" seem to think that they may gain their ends ;
may fulfil the will of God and please Him in their

lives ; may gain the witness of a good conscience, and the peace of a holy life, and the sure and blessed hope of the rest which is prepared for God's children. The children of light are not in earnest in the way in which the children of the world are in thorough earnest.

There are two points worth noticing in that wisdom of the unjust steward for which his master commended him,—in that wisdom of this world, which is indeed folly and vanity as regards the things worth living for, but which, so far as it goes, and for its own purposes, is to be seen on all sides of us, steadily successful, and obtaining all that it seeks after. One is, that the unjust steward had the sense to look forward. The evil day, he knew, must come ; the day when, unless he had something wherewith to meet it, things would go hardly with him. He knew it was no good shutting his eyes and wishing and hoping that it would not come. He knew that it was before him, and he must meet it. So he faced it. He did not try weakly and foolishly to escape from what cannot be escaped from. But he knew that he had certain means of preparing for it. He had time still ; he had that knowledge of the business of his master's debtors and their affairs that gave him the opportunity of doing something for himself before the evil day came.

We are not talking, as the parable does not talk, of the right and wrong of what he did. The point is, that there were certain things to be done, and he did them. He had the sense to look forward and make ready, and do what his sort of wisdom taught him to do, beforehand—before the day of evil over-took him.

In the next place, he went through with what he had begun. Wicked and unscrupulous at first, he was wicked and unscrupulous to the end. A less bad man might have seen his fault, and repented of it, and taken the consequences, ruin and beggary, as the just punishment of it. A weaker man would have been frightened, and faltered, and hesitated, and have been afraid to go on in the bold bad path he had entered on. He would have been cowed at having been found out. He might have wished still to cheat, but he would have been afraid of what might come of it if he were found out ; afraid lest he should provoke his master further. He would have gone backwards and forwards, willing to do wrong, and yet not wholly daring.

But the unjust steward saw that, to save himself at all, he must act boldly. Nothing could be gained by being a coward, and shrinking from using the opportunity which lay open to him. He had had no scruples about cheating his master before, and he had no difficulty about it now. He was consistent ; he would not lose the fruit of his past life by giving way to discouragement, or shrinking from the courses which he had followed.

So does wickedness ; in the resolute earnestness with which it follows its bad ends, in the trouble it takes about them, in the risks that it is willing to venture for them, in the forethought and patience with which it compasses them, in the thorough and complete mind with which it sticks to them, it rebukes and shames the coldness, the half-heartedness, the cowardice, with which most of us serve our Master, and follow religion and goodness. Alike in the worldly-wise idolaters of mammon, who astonish us by their success and prosperity, and in the daring criminals who venture too far, and whose craft and boldness cannot save them from their fate, we see the counterpart of the scheming of the unjust steward ; of his courage in looking forward and facing the day of difficulty and trial ; of his steady perseverance in the path which he had chosen.

In them there is no going backwards and for-wards, at one time wishing to do right, at another time swept away by temptation. In them there is no having only half a mind to what they do. In them there is no being frightened by trouble and difficulty. In them there is no being afraid to go through consistently with what they have begun. Those who have made up their minds to do wrong know that this kind of hesitating foolishness will not succeed in the world. They take care to avoid it. It is left to those who have made up their minds to try to do right. If only the good were as good, as thorough-going and resolute in their goodness, as the bad are bad, the world would be a very different one ; the cause of the kingdom of God, of right and truth, would be winning its victories in a very dif-ferent measure.

This is our Lord's solemn lesson to those who, in whatever degree, may hope to claim the name of " children of light." What goes on in the world, what succeeds in the world, is a rebuke and con-demnation to them. Nay, their own pains and trouble, their own careful thought for the future, their own wise management of their worldly busi-ness, their own spirit and courage, their own industry

and perseverance, their own success, condemn their
feebleness, their ill-success, the poorness of their
attempts in what they do as the servants of the God
of holiness and everlasting life.

Take the two points which I mentioned in the
case of the unjust steward : his looking forward to
the day of trial and difficulty, and his steady, unflinching, thorough carrying out of the unscrupulous
manner of life which he had chosen.   Compare that
with the way in which we so often act as regards the
claims of God and the next world, as regards our duty
and the principles which we profess.   As to looking
forward—how little does that come into the common
ordering of our lives.   We know that we have to be
prepared.   It is the very thing for which we believe
that we are on earth.   We are here to be prepared,
to be ready for something.   We have to be prepared
for trials and temptations which may meet us ; sickness, pain, losses ; the breaking up of all that makes
life happy.   We have to be prepared for occasions
which may try our principles, whether they are
sound, or only fair on the outside ; our honesty, our
tempers, our unselfishness,—who knows how our
souls and spirits may be tried ?   We only know how
terribly men have been tried in this world, and *are*
being tried every day.

At any rate we have to be prepared for the awful
day from which there is no escape ; we have to be
prepared for the judgment-seat of God ; we have to
be prepared for that wonderful new life beyond the
grave.

Are such things to be met without preparation ?
Can we really expect that, without looking forward,

without taking any trouble to be ready when they
come, they will cause us no difficulty, they will all
come straight of themselves? And yet, how much
do we attempt to face the fact, and to prepare for it,
that we may have to be severely tried, and that we
must have to die, and to be judged, and to live
again afterwards? Can we really think that these
things can be safely left to take their chance, to find
us as they may? Can we really think that it is safe
to let our tempers, our thoughts, our tongues, run
riot now, and that in the day of temptation we shall
be able to keep them in order without difficulty?

St. Paul says, " If we would judge ourselves,
we should not be judged." What trouble do we
commonly take by examining ourselves, by finding
out what is amiss in us, by passing sentence in our
own consciences, on our own evil and perverse
ways, to condemn beforehand what God must condemn ; to meet His judgment with that deep sense
of all that has to be pardoned in us, which alone is
fit for guilty creatures appearing before their most
merciful, yet most awful Judge ?

We do not look forward and dare to face what
yet we know must soon be upon us.

And so with the other point. We are not
thorough. We have only half a heart in our wish
to do right. Else why is it that when we know
the sins and temptations which beset us, we take so
little trouble to escape from them and conquer them ?
Our conscience makes us see and wish for what is
right ; we follow it to a certain point ; we follow it
while it gives us no trouble. Nay, we follow it up
to a certain point in spite of difficulties ; we follow

and keep to it for a certain time, in spite of attempts
to lead us wrong ; and then, just when we have half
gained our victory, we give way, we let ourselves be
shaken, we slip back again into the mire from which
our steps were all but delivered ; and all our en-
deavours, all our progress, all our good resolutions,
are wasted and thrown away.   Thrown away for want
of a little more thoroughness, a little more resolution
to carry out what is right, and what we have begun,
to the fair end.

The unjust steward ended as he began ; he began
by cheating, and carried his bad ways through.   And
so he gained what he cheated for, an idle living.
We begin well, and spoil it all by stopping short ; by
slackness, by want of faith, by want of serious belief
that we have to live and work in earnest for God,
and in the ways of goodness, as much as people
work in earnest for the world and its rewards.   He
went through and faltered not.   We do things by
halves.   We check our tongues, but not regularly
and always.   We say our prayers, but not always.
We do not neglect our church, but we do not make
a conscience of coming.   We come to church, but
stop short at the Holy Sacrament.   We say our
prayers, sometimes taking trouble to attend, sometimes taking none.   We make a rule against some
bad habit, keep to it while it is new and fresh,
get tired of it and give it up when we are accustomed to it.   All the care, all the patience, all the
perseverance, all the consistency, which men find
necessary for success in the world, we think may be
done without, when we are running the awful race of
life on which depends the salvation of our souls.

Remember, our Master has warned us. Do not let us think that, because we may hope that by His mercy we have been made "children of light," we are freed from that care and trouble which we all see to be so necessary in the world. The world, and all that goes on in it, its great movements, its wonderful schemes, its astonishing successes, its endless labours, all witness against us, that with such heavenly and lasting hopes we are so far below those who only serve the world, in earnestness and seriousness and consistency. Wickedness itself, in its thorough-going, unflinching steadfastness in wrong, rebukes the faltering and hanging back and cowardice of those who wish to do right.

Let us hear the Lord's warning, and see it confirmed all around us, and recognise our danger. We hope that we are on the side of our Master Christ. Let us not be on such a side, and yet betray it. The world is ashamed of folly and faintheartedness in its servants. Let us pray that we may not, by folly and faintheartedness, bring shame on what is right; on the service of the Master who spared not to give His own life for us.

THE CHRISTIAN'S LIFE A PILGRIMAGE

" Strangers and pilgrims on the earth."—·HEBREWS xi. 13.

THIS is the description which the Bible gives of the old saints, such as Abraham and his family. They passed through things temporal on their way to things eternal. They lived in the world like travellers on the road. The world was even more to them than it has been to the children of faith and promise in later times ; for God's especial promise to them was that land of inheritance which was to be given to them, and their children after them. Yet, even " in the land of promise," they " sojourned as in a strange land, dwelling in tabernacles," that is, living, not in fixed strongly-built houses, but in tents put up to-day, taken down to-morrow, such as wayfarers and soldiers use on their passage through a country. For they had not yet reached home, the city where they would dwell, but they " looked for a city which hath foundations," which could not fall into ruins or be overthrown, " whose builder and maker is God." That was their feeling ; and their life, as it was appointed them of God, was such as to keep up this feeling. For though other men in their times built houses and lived in them, had their own proper country and home, and passed their lives in them,

Abraham, on the contrary, was in fact, as well as in faith and thought, a wanderer. He was called to go out into a " place which he should after "—but long afterwards, and only in the person of his children —" receive for an inheritance ; and he obeyed, and went out, not knowing whither he went."

And, as it also says, if he had chosen to rest, and be quiet in a home of his own, he might have done so ; he had only to go back to his kindred and to his father's house, and stay there. " If they had been mindful of that country from whence they came out, they might have had opportunity to have re- turned." But they never thought of turning their faces backward, or returning, for " they desired a better country, that is, an heavenly." And so they went on through life, and to life's end,—waiting, and pressing onward from tent to tent, from well to well, from one stage of the journey to the next, literally and in fact, and also in mind and heart, till the end of the journey here was reached ; and they " all died in faith, not having received the promises, but having seen them afar off, and were persuaded of them, and embraced " and greeted them, saluting and making them welcome in their hearts, " and confessed that they were strangers and pilgrims on the earth."

Our life, at first sight, does not look like that of " strangers and pilgrims." A settled home is what most of us get accustomed to ; and in our thoughts we feel about things present as if they would always be the same. It is difficult to throw ourselves for- ward, and fancy all round us different ; fancy our- selves in a new place ; fancy those faces which are about us gone and changed, and new ones in their places ; fancy ourselves what old age must make us, and those who are now children grown up to be their own masters. But yet we know that this settled, fixed appearance of things is only our own mistake, our own want of knowledge and of the power of foreseeing things, which, we are sure, must after all come to pass. Whether we feel it or not, our life too is but that of strangers and pilgrims, and, like the old patriarchs, we have no " continuing city." Whether we, like them, " seek one to come " is another matter ; but certain it is that, like them, we too are but on the road ; we too are passing through things temporal on our way to things eternal.

It is of the greatest importance to us to feel this ; first, because it is true, and what is true is the best thing in the end to know and believe, though perhaps it is not always at the time the most pleasant ; and next, because not to feel it is to be without faith and hope, to be without any reason for looking forward.

It was the great proof of the faith of the old saints that they did really believe in God and the world to come, and that " He is a rewarder of those who diligently seek Him," and " a consuming fire " to those who disobey Him. I say, it was the proof of this belief and conviction in the old saints that they did feel their life to be but a journey.

And if we live and think and feel as if we had already got home for good, and were settled here in this world, it is difficult for us to be thinking much of the city and home which are to come, or to be " seeing afar off" God's promises, and welcoming and saluting them as visitors from a better country, whose greatness we shall one day see and be glad of.

It is difficult to feel it. For God has appointed us all our duties and work in life ; and how can we do these unless we throw ourselves heartily into them ; unless we feel settled and at home in them ; unless we feel as if we were bound to them for good ; unless we feel interest in them, and love and attachment to the place and the things among which we carry on our work ? How can we feel as "strangers and pilgrims," when in reality we seem to be the most fixed and settled of mankind ? How can we feel like "dwellers in tabernacles" when we know that our life is spent in the same house for years ? How can we look forward to change when our happiness, our success, nay, our duty, require us not to be restless, but to give our best attention to that which our hand finds to do ? How are we to feel that all we do is but a shadow soon to pass away and be forgotten, when we know that to do our work well at all we must feel about it as if it were the most important thing in the world, and worth all the pains that we can take about it ? How can we get to feel as "strangers and pilgrims" without losing our interest, and becoming slack about doing our part to keep the work of the world going on ? How can we throw ourselves heartily into our work, as God has made it our duty to do, and work as if we were working in our settled and appointed home, without losing the real, ever-present feeling that we are travellers passing through life very quickly, and without forgetting the place to which we are really bound ?

The two things are not so contrary, if we think a
moment.   For, consider the life of such a one as the
Patriarch Abraham.   As the Bible tells us, he lived
all his days confessing himself a stranger and a
pilgrim on the earth.   His thoughts were ever on
that end of his travelling, the home where his God
would receive him, the " city . . . whose builder and
maker is God."   Yet, do you suppose that he did
nothing but dream of that ?   Do not you suppose
that his days actually passed as yours do ?   Do you
suppose that he did not, like men now, rise in the
morning and go forth to his work and to his labour
until the evening ?   Do you suppose that he, who
was rich in cattle, and in men-servants and maid-
servants, had not as busy a day in looking after his
possessions as men have who have great works to
look after now, and that his thoughts were not full
of them ?   Do you suppose that when he happened
to be fixed in a spot—the mountain by Bethel, the
plain of Mamre, the wells in the desert—he did not
feel himself for the time settled and at home, and
go about his daily business with a quiet heart, free
from restlessness and anxiety ?   Surely, with the
great promises beckoning him onwards from his
country and his father's house, and making him feel
that even the land of promise was no true and abid-
ing home for him, yet the days, as they came and
went, passed over him as they do to us, each bringing its business, its task, its duty, its unexpected joy,
its bitterness and grief ;—and to each he gave what
was its due.

The way to think of him is as of a man who
leaves his own country and emigrates into a distant

land, meaning to carry on a business there, to make
a livelihood, to make provision for his family, and
then to return and die at home. While he is in the
foreign land, that *seems* his home ; and yet he feels
with all his heart that it is not. He is taken up
with his work there, and is busy early and late with
the things of that foreign land, as if it were all in all
to him ; and yet his object and aim, that which is
at the end of all, that for which all else is done, is
far away in the land to which his thoughts go—the
land to which he means to go back. He may not
talk much about it in the foreign land ; he may
even feel that to think too much of it, and dwell on
the hope of seeing it again, may weaken his activity
and hinder the very thing which he wants and is
working for. He speaks, perhaps, the foreign language ; he has his home and settled abode there ;
he goes on as if he was a citizen of that country ;
yet all the time there is the thought of his true
country in his heart,—he knows that he is but a
" stranger and pilgrim " where he is. He knows it
is no use to hurry, but that the years are passing
fast ; and yet the mainspring of all he does is something out of sight, something which does not come to
the surface every day,—the hope of ending in a home
very different from his present one,—one which
seems so fixed and settled, yet is, with regard to his
thoughts and wishes, no more than a traveller's tent.

Whether we will or no, we are " strangers and
pilgrims " ; we cannot alter or unmake that. Our
life is passing away. We are travelling onward to
something very different from our present state.
While we are travelling,—while we are, as it were,

C.   T

banished and in exile from the land we hope for, we
have many things to employ us, many important
works to do, many great duties to fulfil, much good
to sow the seed of,—at any rate, the ordinary tasks
of the day to discharge.   These we must do ; and
done they cannot be unless we throw our hearts
and powers into them.   But besides this, we have to
remember that we are but travellers, doing the work
of sojourners, who cannot expect always to be where
they are now, and to see the fruit of all that engages
them now.

Oh then, in the midst of our work, let us let in
the remembrance of that heavenly country which is
so much better.   There are times and seasons when
it has the right to come in, and asks to come in.
In the hurry and hot haste of seed-time and harvest,
or of some anxious and difficult work, it is hard to
think that this is but the work of travellers and
pilgrims, that perhaps the end and finish of it is not
to come for us at all.   But all our times are not
times of hurry and effort.   And then let faith have
its entrance ; then let us look forward to the end
whither we are going ; then let us allow the feeling
that we are travellers to come over us with its full
force ;   then let us place ourselves in fancy at the
end of our journey, and consider what we shall see
and whom we shall meet when we are dead.

Surely, whatever thoughts filled Abraham's mind
in the heat and hurry of the midday, these were the
high hopes, this the solemn faith, which came to him
as the morning brightened, and when the evening
fell over the fields.   Then he lifted up his soul, and
saw the time when morning and evening would

cease to be.   Then he saw far off, yet seeming near, the home of the everlasting city.   Then he knew that he was nearer to it than he was yesterday. Then his eyes were opened, and he knew that *God is*, and that to those who seek Him He is their shield and crown, and their exceeding great reward.

Then, thinking of all these things, he confessed with joy that he was "a stranger and pilgrim" on the earth, and turned with fresh hope and strength to the work of the day before him, or with fresh peace and confidence to his rest when it was over. Then, in the sacred silence of prayer and meditation, there came to him, to sanctify and influence the life of every day, those thoughts which arrest us and bring tears into our eyes on Sundays, but which too often fade away and vanish as the week goes on.

THE CHRISTIAN LIFE NO TRIFLING MATTER

"Not as fools, but as wise."—EPHESIANS v. 15.

ST. PAUL throughout this passage is urgently pressing the rules of Christian living from the facts of
Christian truth. Live as Christians, he says, because
you know what you are, and what has been done
for you as Christians. Christ descended, Christ
ascended, Christ gives gifts to men; *therefore*, I ad-
jure you, walk not as other Gentiles walk in the
vanity of their mind. They, knowing no better, pass
their lives in uncleanness and vanity: ye have not
so learned Christ and His truth. The " new man "
from heaven is your Lord and your example; therefore put off the old man and his deeds of shame and
darkness. Ye are sealed with the Spirit of God;
therefore grieve Him not with corrupt communication, with bitterness and clamour and evil-speaking.
" God, for Christ's sake, hath forgiven you; " therefore
be ye kind one to another, tender-hearted, forgiving
as ye have been forgiven; " be ye therefore followers
of God," who has forgiven you. Christ has loved us,
and given Himself a sacrifice to God for us; do
you therefore walk in love as He did. You know
that the kingdom of God and of Christ is the kingdom

of the truth, the kingdom of holiness and goodness; therefore let no impure deed or word be even so much as named among *you*, who hope to inherit that kingdom. " Ye were sometimes darkness, but now are ye light in the Lord : walk as children of light . . . and have no fellowship with the unfruitful works of darkness, but rather reprove them." There is no hiding from the light ; it makes all things plain and manifest. Light is come to us, and has shown us what we are, and where we are going ; the light calls to us, at once in its certainty and in its gladdening comfort. " Awake thou that sleepest, and arise from the dead, and Christ shall give thee light."

With this light then shining on us, let us think what we are about. Let us not go on at random, as if having the light made no difference to us as to how we must feel and how we must live.

And St. Paul seems to draw up all that he has been saying in a short earnest appeal to every one who has sense to understand his words : " See then that ye walk circumspectly," as men who know what they are about ; "not as fools, but as wise ; . . . understanding what the will of the Lord is." The will of the Lord, whom you know to be your Saviour and your Judge ; and who wills you to live holily, righteously, and soberly in this present world.

" Not as fools, but as wise." St. Paul, as I said, appeals to us as reasonable creatures ; he appeals to our common sense, to what must be clear to our own mind and judgment, as soon as we give the subject any serious thought. I am but asking you, he seems to say, to look at

matters round you, and concerning you, as they
really are, and to judge for yourselves accordingly.
Let your rule of living and acting and feeling be
according to the real state of things amid which you
know you live, which you believe and acknowledge
and profess.

If you have any common sense, the things which
you know and believe of yourself and the world
about you must make a difference to your way of
going on. A fool is he who will take no count of
his circumstances ; who will have his own way in
the teeth of all the certain facts of the world around
him ; who insists on living just as if they were different, or as if he could make them different by
choosing. Consider your real circumstances, St.
Paul says : think what you know about your condition, and your place and outlook in this life : think
of what, without any manner of doubt, you have
learnt to believe all day long of what this life is,
what it was given you for, and what is to come after
it : think of the part which God has taken in it to
help and save you ; what Christ has done and given
and promised ; and then consider how " wise men "
and not " fools," men of common sense and plain
straightforward understanding, ought to shape their
lives amid circumstances such as these :—knowing
all they know, living in such a world, and dealing
with such certain facts, as we have to do with.

Suppose it had been different. Suppose for a
moment that all that we know and believe had never
been,—were wiped out of thought and knowledge.
Suppose that we had never heard of a God ; that we
found ourselves alone on earth, not knowing in the

slightest degree how we came here, why we were living; whether God had made us or not, or what He meant us for. Suppose that all we knew of our life were that *there it was*, with its beginning, about which we could know nothing—with its end, after which we could know nothing more. Suppose that the thoughts and language of men had been as silent about God, our Maker and Ruler, as are the winds and the stars; that no one had ever heard of Him; that we were to Him as the brute creatures, which live and die without knowing Him.

Or suppose that we had only heard of Him by dim and uncertain report, as the heathen may, but that He had never had any dealings with us, and we knew not where to find Him, or what He was.

Imagine this to be our state, passing through life without the faintest notion of what life is, where it comes from, and whither it goes; having no light to guide us but what we could get for ourselves; having no help out of this world, no comfort, no refuge, no prospects: nothing but the dark unknown hopeless grave. Suppose this was the condition of things in which we were living. There would be no prayer, for there would be no God to pray to, or to hope in. There would be no faith, no love of God, no obedience. I do not say that there would be no sense of right and wrong: it is hard even to imagine man without that, and conscience; but there would be nothing to support right and to condemn wrong: there would be nothing which we could guess at to show us what was right and what was wrong: there might be hope and a sense of peace in doing right rather than wrong, but there would be no all-seeing

and holy Eye to watch, no good and loving Father
to please, no great Judge and Rewarder to accept
at last.   We should be in the world as those whom
no one cared for ; forlorn outcasts, knowing their
own bitterness, knowing pain and sickness, and heart-
ache and death,—knowing all the evils of the world,
and, too surely, the evil of their own hearts ; knowing that, somehow, they were *wrong* and in ruin, but
without any one above to look up to and to think of
them, without redemption, without remedy, without
hope.

Then, when you have taken in what it would be
thus to know life, thus to pass through it, then turn
and consider what is, in fact, the case with us.   We
cannot, without difficulty, imagine what I have been
supposing.   We cannot, without an effort and strain,
fancy a world, fancy our human existence, without
God, and the knowledge of God.   Not we only,
but the whole world, knows God.   Even the very
heathen, in one way or another, with the grossest
and foulest errors about Him, yet dimly see His
awful Power and Godhead amid the darkness of their
idolatries.   The thought of God is the first and
easiest of thoughts to us.   His Name is everywhere ;
good and evil alike own and fear Him.   His mercy
is our first refuge in distress ; we pray to Him, and
are sure He listens to us, and believe in His loving-
kindness.   We know where we come from — even
from His will and His hand.   We know why we are
here—even to grow up, through gifts and through
trials, to a fitness for something higher and greater
than this life.   We know what we are meant for,—
whither we are going ; we are born, we die, for the

life of the world to come, for the life that has no end. We know something of the strange and awful mystery of our sin, of the terrible struggle within us, between good and evil, between light and darkness ; we know that we are fallen, but we know that we have the power of recovery, and are meant to be restored.

We know that we need not yield to sin, that we may triumph over it, and cast it out of our hearts. We know too, not merely that there is a difference between right and wrong, but what it is that the Eternal Judge of the world thinks right and thinks wrong ; what is like Him and what is unlike Him ; what it is His will that we should follow, and what it is His will that we should depart from.

But this is little. Heathens knew something of this ; forgetful Jews knew more. But we Christians have a knowledge of the mighty works of God which leaves all this behind. We know that God has been with men, has spoken to them, has made them know by their own knowledge something of His mind, His thoughts, His goodness, His wrath, His love. We believe in Jesus Christ, the everlasting Son of the Father, the Maker, and Light and Life of men. We believe that when He took upon Him to deliver man, He did not abhor the Virgin's womb. We believe even more than this : we believe that He died for our sins, and that when He had overcome the sharpness of death, He did open the kingdom of Heaven to all believers. We believe that He sitteth at the right hand of God, in the glory of the Father. We believe that He shall come to be our Judge. We believe that in this world of sin and trouble and death we have in Him one who hears all prayers, and heals all wrongs, and can bind up every broken heart. There men may appeal to a love which has made even God's world look new ; " We pray Thee, *therefore*, help Thy servants, whom Thou hast redeemed with Thy precious blood." Go where we may, look where we will, we are met, in manifold shapes, with the memorial of one state of salvation. Turn our eyes where we will, they encounter something which reminds us of the cross of Christ.

I go back to the text, " Walk . . . not as fools, but as wise." Put these two pictures side by side : life as we supposed it just now, without knowing whether God is, or anything about Him, without knowing what we are living for, or who made us, or what is to become of us ; and on the other side life in which man throws himself on the love of God, as His servant, redeemed by the precious blood of Christ.

As men of common sense, St. Paul appeals to us : is it possible that the manner of feeling and thinking and acting, which might be natural under the first set of circumstances, can suit the other ? Would any man of sense, who knew and believed that this last was the fact, think of living as if all that we knew of were the first ? Would it not be one of those things which would seem past belief if it were not that it is one of the common sights of our ex- perience that men can actually, in a certain manner, know and believe what St. Paul teaches us about our state here, and yet live a life which they might live just as well if they were absolutely without God in the world ? And are not St. Paul's words but the words of plain truth and soberness, when he calls upon us,—" not as fools, but as wise," as men who wish to have some sense and consistency in what they do,—when, I say, he calls on us, and warns us, knowing and believing what we do, not to live as if we did not know it.

It was lowering man and his soul, with its great gifts of reason and conscience and knowledge, of love and sympathy and brotherhood, of justice and truth, and courage which could face death,—it was lowering man so endowed below the beasts that perish, when men, even in their ignorance and un-certainty about God, said, " Let us eat and drink, for to-morrow we die." But only think, quietly and seriously, of the distance which we are from that uncertainty and ignorance. Think of what to us is certain, of what to us is clear and plain. Think what we look back to. Think what, past the grave, and past the judgment, lies before us. Think that it is our lot to live in the customary and continual belief of a Divine Saviour, who cared so much for us as to come down among us ; and who gave His life for our sins, that we might be forgiven, and might live. Is it wisdom or is it folly to shape our lives by the truth of which we are convinced, by the facts of which we are certain ? Is it wisdom or is it folly, knowing all this, to live as we might live if we knew nothing, and had nothing but this life and this world before us ; or to live as St. Paul, in these chapters of the Epistle to the Ephesians, teaches Christian men and women to live, doing the will and fulfilling the purposes of the God with whom they have so much to do ?

XXX

THE FIRST AND GREAT COMMANDMENT

"This is the first and great commandment."—St. Matthew xxii. 38.

Speaking to a Christian congregation, I need not say *what* this commandment is. You all know, as far as head knowledge goes,—at least you all might and ought to answer, without any one telling you, what commandment Christ was speaking of. There can be but one which to us is the first and great commandment. The Jewish lawyer might come to Jesus to ask Him which is the great commandment of the law, but even he knew it quite well. He did not ask because he did not know, he asked "tempting" Christ,—as people ask when they want to get something from another's mouth to puzzle or condemn him. But we, at any rate, have this answer of our Master Christ to teach us, even if the light of our own reason was not enough,—that to us there can be only one "first and great commandment" to be thought of, and that one, *the love of God*. "Thou shalt love the Lord thy God with all thy heart, and with all thy soul, and with all thy mind."

The love of God is the chief and principal part of the religion which we are taught in the New Testament, and Christians were meant to be different

from the rest of the world in this one thing above all
others, that they knew and loved God.   This is so
plain that there is no need to say a word to prove
it.   Open what part of the New Testament you
please, and you find it, in one way or another, speaking of the love of God.   The great things which
Christ has done for us are told us, and dwelt upon,
to make us love the God who so loved us.   The
greatest hope and promise which it gives us for the
time to come is the fuller knowledge and love of
God.   St. Paul and St. John and the Evangelists
say a great deal in their writings about the love of
God, but it is plain that beyond what they *say*, their
whole hearts and minds and lives were full of it : in
their smallest and lightest actions it is there ; it is
plainly the only thing which was the reason and
motive of all they propose to themselves, or attempt,
or wish for.   Why should they labour as they did,
but from their love of God ?   Why should they be so
patient and happy in their afflictions, but that they
loved God, and gladly suffered for His sake ?   Why
should they have been so full of zeal, but out of love
of God ?   What made them write so much, write
with such tenderness, such wisdom, such firmness
and seriousness in exhorting and rebuking, such
deep insight into the mind of man and the counsels
of God, but that they loved Him above all things ?
The love of God was in all they did and thought
and spoke and felt ; it filled and ruled their lives, it
made them die for Him cheerfully and gladly.   So
that, as I said, the New Testament makes the love
of God the one great mark of the Gospel, and
shows us also how truly it was the great mark

of the Gospel in those whom Christ first sent to preach it.

But now the question is, What is meant by the love of God? because it must mean something. It cannot be a mere form of words, to signify merely that men are to be well-behaved and respectable and honest and just to one another, and brave and careful of their families, and hard-working and sober. You will not suppose that I mean that these are matters of little consequence, or that any one can be a good Christian, a true follower of Jesus Christ, who wants these qualities. What I mean is, that though he who loves God must have all these qualities, yet this cannot be all that is meant by what the Gospel is always speaking about, the love of God.

For the Bible does not use words at random. When it uses a word it means by it what that word stands for and is used for among men. When it speaks of love, it means what is meant by the word love. We know what love means when we speak of loving our friends, or loving our father or mother or family, or loving our home. It does not mean merely being just and honest to them, and behaving respectably to them. It means all this indeed, but it means a great deal more too. It means that we feel in our hearts drawn to them; that we feel pleasure in doing them good and making them happy; that we like to be with them, and miss them when they are away; that we rejoice with them when they are glad, and grieve when they are sorrowful. It means that we care for them, and think about them, and delight in them for themselves,— for nothing else but themselves.

Well then, when the Bible speaks of our being able to love Almighty God, of our duty and blessedness as Christians consisting in the love of God, it means something by love which we can form an idea of by knowing what love means when spoken of among men.   It means that it is not outward conduct only, but the feelings and affections of our hearts, which God expects us to give Him.   The Bible wishes to raise us to feel towards Almighty God in our hearts the same sort of affection which we all of us understand when we speak of loving our friends on earth.   It seeks to make us not merely believe in God, not merely obey the words of God, but love Him.

To believe in God is necessary, and to obey Him is necessary, but it is imperfect Gospel religion till the heart has learnt to love Him,—to delight in Him, to lean on Him, to trust in Him, to be glad to think of Him and praise Him, to pour out its fears and sorrows before Him, to hope for Him as its everlasting good, and to think of His presence and the communion with Him in heaven as its great and satisfying reward.   This is what the Gospel calls Christians to reach after, and what it offers them. It is indeed a wonderful thing that mortal and sinful men can love the Almighty and Invisible God.   But that is the promise and the call of Jesus Christ, and till we have begun to learn what it is to love our heavenly Father in our hearts, we have not yet learnt what the Gospel has to give us.

But now, I can imagine a good many persons saying in their heart, How can this be meant for us ? How is it possible that what seem such high and great things can be meant for us? How can we be expected to think much about God, we who have so little time to ourselves, we who had so little opportunity of learning when we were young ; who can understand but a small part of the prayers, or the sermons, or the Bible itself, even when it is read to us? These things seem above us. They are for those who have had time to read and learn, and can understand difficult matters. God cannot have called us to such things.

Now, the first thing I will say to this is, Was not the Gospel first preached to the poor? and do you suppose that the poor, among whom Christ lived, out of whom He chose His Apostles, and to whom He sent them preaching, were so different from poor, hard-working men and women now? Surely they were not. I am sure, on the other hand, that the poor people of our own time and country, wherever Christ's Word is preached, have a great deal more preparation for learning to know and love God than the poor Jews to whom Christ ministered when He was on earth. And most of those to whom St. Paul and St. John and St. Peter wrote their Epistles were not the rich and the learned, but the poor.

Yet the Apostles could speak to them freely of the love of God, and the poor men and women to whom they wrote could understand them ; because they had learned that " first and great command-ment " ; they had learned truly to love God, to feel real love and trust and hope and thankfulness to Him in their very hearts, just as they felt love to their friends and families.

If then any should think in their heart that it is no use for them to think of loving Almighty God, because they are so hard-worked, and only understand things that concern their families and their labour, I ask them this question, How can you tell till you have tried? And have you ever tried to put yourself in the way of coming at last to know and love Almighty God? Have you really ever taken any trouble about it?

You must not expect God in a moment to turn your heart away from the love of the world, and give you in a moment the comfort and blessing of loving Him. Only God's Holy Spirit can teach you to love God; only He can change your heart and give you the new heart and the new spirit, without which no man can love God. But He will not come and do His great work in you, the work that He only can do, if He sees that you do not care whether He comes or not.

So I ask, Have you ever really thought to yourself, Do I love God, and shall I ever come to love Him as the holy men we read of in the Bible loved Him? If you have not cared at all about the matter, of course it is not wonderful that you feel no love for Him now. But you must not talk about its being your condition in life, or your want of learning, or your hard work, which makes it impossible that you should ever be able to reach so far as the love of God. You have not tried, you have not given yourself the least trouble about the matter. Can you judge from this careless way of living what God might, of His goodness, help you to do, if you really wished that you might learn before you die the

C.   U

unspeakable comfort of loving Him with a true and holy love? You have not used heartily any of God's means of grace, you have foolishly thought that everything was quite well with you; how can you expect God to give you more grace, when you have not used what He has already given you? What business have you to say that the blessing of setting their hearts and their love upon God is not meant for poor and unlearned persons,—to give up the thought and wish and hope of coming yourselves to love Him,—when you will not put yourselves in the way of His salvation?

It would be a real denial of all the words of grace and mercy in the New Testament to suppose that a man's being rich or poor, learned or unlearned, in high station or in low, made the least difference as to his being able, by God's grace, to know and love his heavenly Father and his Redeemer with all the love of his heart; to love Him, as Christ says, with all his heart and mind and strength. All you who hear me now might, if you would, come to know that a Christian life is not merely a quiet, orderly, sober, respectable life,—a life of outward respect to God's law and word,—but a life of love to Almighty God, a life in which you could feel as much comfort and joy and peace in loving God as you can feel in loving your children or your parents or your friends.

But how should you get to it? My brethren, most assuredly the love of God is God's own gift, and His most precious one. He must give it to you; all that you can do is to seek and wish and ask for it, and to take care not to do that which may prevent Him from giving it you; to prepare your hearts for the time when it may please Him to visit you with His consolation.   But remember you must begin by fearing Him, if you are ever to love Him.

And what I am going to say now is what lies in the power of all to try and remember.   If you wish to come in time to know by experience what a blessed thing it is to love God in your real inward heart, keep in mind these few simple points :—

1. You must not have idols in your hearts, or set the stumbling-block of your iniquity before your face, if you ever hope to love God.   Sin is like a poison, which kills the love of God and heavenly things.   When a man begins in earnest, by God's help, to cast out his sins and evil desires, then he is beginning to be in a way in which he may come at last to know God with the love of his soul, and to rejoice in that blessed comfort.

2. The way to fight against and by degrees to overcome our sins, is in every one's power, if they would but use it.   A man does not need to be book-learned, or to be clever, to resist his sins, and to receive God's cleansing and pardoning grace. His sins are the wrong evil deeds which he does one by one.   He need not have done them.   He knows that he had the power to say *no*, or to keep back his eyes, or his hand, or his tongue, when he was tempted.   He need not do them any more, if he will only manfully call God to help him to try. Well then, the next time you are tempted, *go and try* ; make a beginning.   Perhaps something may happen to provoke you very much ; if you were to open your mouth you could not help, you say, bursting out into passionate and bitter words ; well then,

make a strong effort, shut your mouth, think of God, and resolve not to answer a word for the time ; turn away, and do not speak till your anger has cooled down. Is there any one among us who can say that he cannot do this ? Of course not—a child can do this, if only he will. Then surely there is not one among us who may not, if he only will, make a beginning of resisting his temptations and overcoming his sins. He will not succeed perfectly at first ; no one can do a difficult thing well for the first time. But if he will only make a beginning, and go on doing what all of us can do if we only choose, God will help him, and watch over him, and give him daily more and more strength, till he is able, with Christ at his side, to overcome and put to flight the wicked one and his fiery darts.

3. We cannot hope to love God without knowing Him ; we cannot hope to know Him without communing with Him in the only way in which we can do so,—in prayer. As long as we do not pray, or try to pray, it is certainly quite hopeless that we should ever come to love God, for we cannot keep Him in mind without praying to Him, and we cannot expect His grace will come to us unless we ask for it.

Most of us, I know, have not time to pray much, but I am afraid that many make that a reason for not praying at all. I will mention two things which any one in this congregation, any family in this parish, could do, as a beginning, if only they would. There is no one, man, woman, or child, but might, if they pleased, say their prayers to God in the morning ;—surely in the evening too, if they had but a heart to it ; but I speak now of the morning. There is no one, I am quite sure, who could not spare five minutes,— and many could spare more,—to kneel down at their bedside and say two or three short prayers from the Prayer-book, with the Lord's Prayer, keeping their thoughts fixed and attentive on what they are saying. Next, there is not a household in which on the Sunday evening the father and mother could not gather the whole family together for a little while, while some one read a chapter, or a few verses from the Bible, or a Psalm, and afterwards the head of the family prayed for God's blessing on them all for the week to come, and gave Him thanks for His past goodness. I do not believe that any one who did even so much regularly for one or two years, with a humble and sincere wish to please Christ, would be in any doubt at the end whether a poor man, be he ever so unlearned or hard-worked, could come to feel and understand something of the goodness of God,—something of what it is to love Him with the true love of his heart.

4. There is, lastly, one great means of blessing which is open to the poorest, and where the poorest may learn, if only he will come with a true heart, to love and adore and rejoice in the great God who has made and redeemed him, and has promised to be his everlasting reward—the Holy Communion. Oh! my brethren, if instead of avoiding that Holy Sacrament, making up your minds that it cannot be meant for such as you, and passing your lives without ever coming near it, you would trust your Saviour, who calls you there; you would trust Christ who loved you, and gave the Holy Sacrament for your comfort

and salvation ; if only you would come and taste and
see that the Lord is gracious, you would not talk of
poor men not being able to feel love to God as the
Bible says that Christians ought to love Him.

"This is the first and great commandment," said
our Master Christ, not to a few, but to all of us.
All of us are called to fulfil it, all of us may find our
blessedness in fulfilling it. Would that we could
believe that to love God is indeed to be perfectly
happy. If we loved God with all our heart, how
little would this world be to us. If we loved God,
how little should we be tempted by the sins which
ruin men's souls, and make them miserable. If we
loved God, and felt how He loved us, how light
would the sufferings of this present time seem, how
ready should we be to endure affliction for His sake,
how comforted should we be in sickness or sorrow to
know that God would give to us all this exceeding
and unspeakable comfort,—the comfort and the consolation and the joy, which passeth all understanding,
of really loving Him above all things, trusting Him,
hoping for Him, as our unfailing and everlasting
portion ; a Father and Friend who can never
change, a Rewarder who can make the loss of all
things sweet to us, a Saviour who in the hour and
bitterness of death can give us peace.

This was what St. Paul found in loving God and
being loved by Him. "Who shall separate us from
the love of Christ?" he cries out in the midst of his
fiery persecutions. "Shall tribulation, or distress, or
persecution, or famine, or nakedness, or peril, or
sword? . . . Nay, in all these things we are more than
conquerors through Him that loved us. For I am

persuaded, that neither death, nor life, nor angels, nor principalities, nor powers, nor things present, nor things to come, nor height, nor depth, nor any other creature, shall be able to separate us from the love of God, which is in Christ Jesus our Lord." May God give us all to know the comfort of this love, for we all, rich and poor, teachers and taught, high and low, can never be happy without it.

XXXI

THE PERFECT LIGHT OF GOD

" This then is the message which we have heard of Him, and declare
    unto you, that God is Light, and in Him is no darkness at all."—
    1 ST. JOHN i. 5.

THIS, that is, is the message which we, the
Apostles, have heard from Him, who was the Word
of Life, who came down from heaven to make men
have a more certain and more perfect knowledge of
Almighty God ; who came to reveal to us the truth
by which we might believe on Him and live. This
is the message brought by Him who was from the
beginning, whom living men on earth had seen with
their eyes, and listened to, and looked upon, and
handled with their hands. This is the message
brought by the only-begotten Son about His Father;
the message brought by Him who alone of all beings
was with the Father, and knew the Father, and could
reveal the Father to men. This was what Jesus
Christ had taught His Apostles, and made them
understand and believe : "that God is Light, and in
Him is no darkness at all." In Him is no shade, or
speck, or stain. In Him is no fault or shortcoming,
In Him is no error, or mistake, or uncertainty. In
Him is no deceit or falsehood. In Him is nothing
to cloud the brightness of perfection. All in Him is

righteous : all in Him is truth : all in Him is wise :
all in Him is holy.

It seems a very simple thing to say that "God is
light, and in Him is no darkness at all." We almost
wonder at the Bible taking so much trouble to say
it. For, we might think, how could God be otherwise? How could we imagine God to be imperfect,
wanting in goodness, and holiness, and wisdom, and
truth? How could God *be* God unless He were all
Perfect,—Light without a shade of darkness?—And
this is true.

But how is it that we have come to have these
thoughts of God? How is it that it seems to us so
plain and unquestionable a thing that God should be
all Light, without any spot or imperfection? It is
that we have got our thoughts of God from Jesus
Christ His Son, and from those who have declared
His message to us in the Bible. It is that the
Gospel has become so much a matter of course
to us, that its truth has come to seem to us our own
thoughts. It *does*, indeed, seem to us the plainest
thing in the world that we should think it impossible
to believe of God that He is anything but most Holy
and Good and Perfect ; but it is not our own wisdom
and understanding which has impressed this upon us.
We owe it to the Gospel, and to the deep root which
the Gospel teaching has struck in the thoughts of
men.

But it was by no means so plain and simple a
truth to the world when St. John wrote his Epistle.
He wrote when the world believed in idols and false
gods without number. And those false gods were
not thought of as we think of God. They were

not thought of as being all Light, and having in them
no darkness at all. They were believed to be not more
perfect, not more holy, not more pure and good, than
the men who worshipped them. All the evil things
which men find in themselves, and in one another,
they were ready to find in the gods whom they
prayed to and trusted in. It was indeed a *new*
message when Christ's Apostles came and told the
heathen that " God is Light, and in Him is no darkness at all." A new message ; and in those days, a
strange and hard one. For men liked to believe
that God was no holier and better than themselves.
They liked to believe that the sins and works of
darkness in which they took pleasure were also
found above in the God who ruled the world. It
was, they thought, an excuse for their sin, that in
those to whom they prayed the same sin was found.
It was not to any one either a welcome or a likely
message that " God is Light, and in Him is no
darkness at all."

But those days of idolatry and ignorance are
past ; and perhaps we think that we do not need
to be reminded that God is Light—perfectly Pure
and Holy and True and Good. We do not want
to be taught this truth in words, for in words we
know it and acknowledge it. But we do still want
to be taught it in its meaning and truth. We do
want to be reminded that there are those still who
do not in their hearts believe that God is Light ;
who do not feel and inwardly acknowledge that
in Him there is no darkness of sin and folly and
weakness at all.

For is it not so that, instead of really believing

that God is Light, without stain or shade of sin, we often make Him out in our thoughts to be what we like and wish Him to be? What does the sinner *wish* God to be? He wishes God to be kind and indulgent to his sin. He wishes God to be of that nature that He will not take notice or care, if the sinner follows his own way, and breaks the commandments. He wishes God to shut His eyes to the thing, when a man goes against his own conscience, and does what he knows is wrong. He wishes God to be a God who always rewards and never punishes; who will do good to us whether we obey Him or not; who will be equally ready to receive and accept us, whether we come to Him in truth or in pretence, whether we serve Him or serve ourselves. A God who is blind, and can be taken in, and imposed upon; a God who will put up with any excuses, and bear any hypocrisy; a God who does not care enough about goodness and truth to punish those who will have none of goodness and truth,—this is the God whom the sinner wishes to have; this is the God whom he would like to believe in. And, I am afraid, this is the God whom he too often fashions to himself in his own thoughts, and persuades himself is the God who made the world, and who sent His only-begotten Son to die, that He might redeem and save it.

And do we never fall into such thoughts of God? Do we never sin, hoping that, after all, God will not think so severely of our sin as the Bible seems to make out that He will? Do we never comfort and flatter ourselves with such general excuses as that God is merciful, and will not be hard upon us, and

is very long-suffering, and will not require of us to
be so very strict, or so very good, or so very holy, or
so very self-denying ?   Do we not, instead of taking
the Bible, and reading there the true character of
the God whom we worship, make an image according to our own imperfections and sins, and call it
God ?   We sneer at the superstitions of the heathen.
But what is it when we do wrong, and think to
satisfy and make friends with God by setting against
the sin which we have done, or the duty we have
neglected, something else which we think we have
done right, and which will please Him ?   What is
this but thinking that God is one who can be bought
over, and bribed, and bargained with, as we are ?   Is
this the God who " is Light, and in Him is no darkness " ?   Can we be said really to believe in Him, when
we treat Him as if He were foolish, and could not see
through our cunning devices, and could be flattered
into good humour with us, and be prevailed upon to
treat us as favourites ?

We should shudder to say in so many words that
God is a respecter of persons ; but do not we too often
treat Him as if He were, and think of Him as if He
might be, if He were only so to us ?   Do we not do
so when we make no doubt that He will let *us* off
easier than He lets off others ?   Do we not do so
when we think of Him as just and true and holy
when He has to deal with the sins and offences of
the world in general ; but as laying aside His justice
and holiness when He comes to deal with our sins in
particular ?

Again : what a sad show of our real thoughts
about God is to be found in the manner of our

worship and in our prayers. Who that really believed in the perfection of God could worship Him
as I am afraid our conscience must tell us that we so
often worship Him, — that so many worship Him
every Sunday? If He "is Light, and in Him is no
darkness at all," what must He think of worship
which only pretends to worship and honour Him?
of prayer which does not really ask in spirit for the
thing it speaks about? If I kneel down and say
over a number of words which are in sound full of
repentance for sin, and honour to God's law, and the
desire to do better, and requests to be strengthened
and taught and guided ; and yet all the time mean
nothing real by all this,—what thought can I have
of the God, whom I can suppose likely to endure all
this, and leave it unpunished? And from carelessness,
and want of being serious, and taking pains about our
prayers, does not this happen to most of us, much
oftener than we should like to confess to others?
Are there not some who must be aware that their
prayers are said in this way only, and never in any
other ; never with any truth and reality, never with
any trying in earnest to pray? Can it be said
of us that, in such a case, we have right and true
thoughts about God? Can it be said that we
really believe the great message brought by Jesus
Christ, that "God is Light, and in Him is no darkness at all?"

So that it is no unnecessary thing to remind
people of this, though they know it, that God is
not like weak and imperfect men ; but that far
above all that we can imagine of perfect purity, and
goodness, and holiness, and truth, and love and

justice, "God is Light, and in Him is no darkness
at all." We cannot strive too earnestly to get this
belief stamped and graven in our hearts ; for we are
certainly under the temptation to be setting up in
our hearts a fancy and an image of God which is
not the true one, which is made simply after our
own likeness, and to suit our convenience and our
sins.

God is what He is, whatever we may think. And
earnestly ought we to strive and pray that we may
know Him as He is, and always think of Him as He
is. He changes not ; and what He has declared
Himself to be by His Son, and in His Holy Book,
that He will remain. Our foolish thoughts of Him
cannot prevail on Him to leave His perfection, and
become like what we may, in our folly, imagine Him.
If He hates sin, He will not be prevailed on *not* to
care about it, that we may escape harmless. If He
is truth, He will not give up His truth that our
feigned excuses may succeed. Merciful and gracious,
ready to pardon, to purify, to strengthen,—that we
know He is. Let us not make a mocking resem-
blance of all this, to favour our sins and our hypocrisy,
and deceive ourselves into calling it the God of
Love.

Let us keep before our minds this message of St.
John, and try to understand and believe its great and
solemn meaning. When we kneel down to pray, let
us set before our thoughts that we are going to speak
to, and to hold communion with, Him in whom is no
darkness at all ; who is pure and perfect Light, Light
which no sin can bear, Light which pierces through
and makes manifest all secrets and devices. Let us

keep it before us, in all our doings, that God is Light; that He is one who is not to be deceived about sin; that He is one whom it is impossible to reconcile to sin ; one to whom it is vain to make excuses for doing what is wrong.   Let us pray Him to give us true and right thoughts about Himself.   For as a man's God is, so is the man himself.   According to what we believe of God, such will be our hearts and our thoughts about what is right and wrong, about what is good and what is sin.

"God is Light : " and "if we say that we have fellowship with Him, and walk in darkness, we lie, and do not the truth : but if we walk in the light, as He is in the light, we have fellowship" with the Father and the Son.   We have fellowship, a fellowship not of this world, but of the kingdom of heaven, one with another ; "and the blood of Jesus Christ His Son cleanseth us from all sin."

For, as St. John is well aware, walking in the light, and earnestly trying to serve God and follow Christ, does not mean being altogether without sin. But it does mean earnestly striving against it,— earnestly and honestly repenting of it.   "If we say that we have no sin, we deceive ourselves, and the truth is not in us."   "If we say we have not sinned, we make Him a liar ; " we contradict the revelation which He has made of His goodness and perfect holiness,—"and the truth is not in us."   But if we are honest and true to our consciences and to God, "If we confess our sins, He is faithful and just to forgive us our sins, and to cleanse us from all unrighteousness."

May we so walk through the darkness to the
Perfect Light : and so find each day the darkness
growing less thick and heavy, and the dawn of the
everlasting morning brightening more and more
to us.

XXXII

FAREWELL SERMON

" But this I say, brethren, the time is short : it remaineth, that both
    they that have wives be as though they had none ; and they that
    weep, as though they wept not ; and they that rejoice, as though
    they rejoiced not ; and they that buy, as though they possessed
    not ; and they that use this world, as not abusing it : for the fashion
    of this world passeth away."—1 CORINTHIANS vii. 29-31.

IT is one of the secrets of the power which the
Bible has over us, that it throws itself with such
sympathy into all our interests and all our feelings,
simply as men. Its divine teaching and wisdom
comes to us under human forms, and in the language
of human experience. Coming from heaven, and
telling of God and eternity, it clothes itself in human
shape, and speaks the words of human life, of human
gladness, of human anxiety and sorrow and fear. It
is a history of men, of families, of friendships, of the
ups and downs of agitated lives, of the affection of
fathers and children, of husbands and wives, of
brethren and companions, of those who have joyed
together and mourned together. It is a record of
what men have actually found in these few short
years of their sojourn on earth,—of their love, of
their grief, of their quarrels and enmities—of their
wisdom and goodness and enjoyment of life,—of
the mistakes and follies and sins and sufferings

C.   X

which are so familiar to us. It fears not to speak
as we speak, when our feelings are strong. The
prophet of immortality, it yet echoes in the Psalms
all our awe and downheartedness and dread at the
prospect of death. The messenger to us of the most
assured and loftiest hope, it is not ashamed to speak
with us the language of our bitterest agony and
distress ; at times it seems not to refuse even the
fellowship of our despair. And on the other hand,
man's heart cannôt rejoice and pour forth the over-
flow of its joy, in gladness more abounding and more
rapturous than that of the songs of the Bible.
Whatever chances and changes we meet with,
whatever touches and moves and stirs our souls,
however life comes to us, blessing us with happiness,
or charged with duties, or dark with pain and change,
in the Bible we may find our likeness, in the Bible
we shall find our thoughts anticipated, in the Bible
we shall find the words of those who saw what we
see, who found what we find, who felt what we feel.
And so it repeats our common feelings and words
about the passing away of time and life. What comes
home to us from time to time with such piercing
truth, as to the way in which the years slip away
from us, altering all that we are accustomed to rest
upon, and bringing us so much nearer to the end,—all
this we find faithfully and most feelingly written in
a hundred places in our Bible. We cannot express
what we think and feel half as forcibly and impressively as it is written there. And our Bible is
to us as our friend. We feel that it understands us.
We feel that it knows what we are, that it throws
itself even into our weakness and our heart-aches, that

it takes up our load with us, and claims a right to
comfort us because it knows what weighs us down.
In our sadness it is sad ; in our affliction it is
afflicted ; that it may win us on to trust its promise,
to be strengthened with its courage, to drink in its
hope. "Oh ! remember how short my time is, wherefore hast Thou made all men for nought." "Mine
age is even as nothing in respect of Thee ; and verily
every man at his best state is but vanity." "I am a
stranger with Thee, and a sojourner, as all my fathers
were. O spare me a little, that I may recover my
strength, before I go hence and be no more seen."
What words of more hopeless anguish ever burst
from human lips, than these which are written in
the Book which is our witness that man was *not*
made for nought, which God has given us as our
counter-charm to death, as our guide to everlasting
life.

We may then, unblamed, indulge our natural
feelings, when the truth is brought home to us per-
sonally, that indeed the "time is short": that "the
fashion of this world passeth away." To-day is such
a day for you and for me. To-day is a day when
those who have long lived together, and worked
together, and learned to know one another, come to
the parting of the roads. We can no longer travel
together : we must go, you to one path, I to the
other. To-day is a day which finishes and winds up
a large piece in all our lives who have been together
so long ; finishes all that I have been to you and
you to me. It is not indeed that we shall not see
one another's faces again ; it is not that, I hope.
But this is the last time that I shall speak to you

as your clergyman ; the last time that you meet
to worship with me as my parishioners. A great
gap is going to open between you and me for
evermore in this world. And we are come to its
edge.

We have been together a long time, as we count
time here—nearly nineteen years. Those who were
the old people when I came are mostly gone.
Those who were the middle-aged are become old.
The children whom I first baptized, and taught in
school, and prepared for confirmation, are now men
and women, dispersed, many of them, from the
homes where they were born to new ones ; some
to the ends of the earth. We have lived together
through eventful times ; the most eventful times
which this century has yet seen, even though it
began with the great French war, which closed with
Waterloo. Here, in our deep tranquillity and peace,
while we were from year to year ploughing and
sowing, mowing the fields and reaping the harvests,
passing from winter to summer and from summer to
winter, we heard at a distance the rumours of great
wars and the strife and downfall of nations. We
remember the winter nights when we thought of our
soldiers in the Crimean war, and waited for the
news, not knowing what the morning might bring.
We were together, and felt the horror, the shock, the
agony of the Indian mutiny,—the pity, the shame,
the wild thoughts of vengeance which we now
hardly like to call back to our recollection. We were
living together and working together, as we were
last month, when new kingdoms were fought for and
founded on the continent of Europe, in Italy, in

Germany, changing its face and its destiny. We
looked on with amazement, with perplexity, with
divided feelings, but with the deepest interest, at the
fiercest and strongest and most obstinate struggle the
world ever saw, the four years' civil war in the great
state across the ocean, which sprung from our blood,
and speaks our language. And now last year you
have seen the catastrophe which exceeds all ; you
have seen what ambition can still do in this world
which thought itself so much wiser and more reasonable than of old ; you have seen the madness which
threw away an empire, and the cruel strength which
gained one ; you have seen how war is carried on in
modern days, with what calm precision and science,
with what recklessness of human misery ; you have
seen what two years ago seemed the proudest and
strongest of nations, in the course of a few months
beaten down into ruin and shameful anarchy. And
you have not only looked on : labouring men gave of
their narrow means to help the sick and wounded in
this terrible war; labouring men gave of their weekly
wages, not once for all, but regularly week by week,
for four months, to help their countrymen in Lan-
cashire in the great distress caused by the American
War.

These are the times we have lived through together, these are the things we look back to, since
we first knew one another.

But these are not the things which are in our
remembrance now. In our perfect quiet we yet
have had our own changes. We have had much to
interest us, to stir and touch our hearts. And in the
eyes of Him who counts the hairs of our head, our

interests, and our changes, are of weight ; they have
been marked and recorded.   My thoughts, and I am
sure yours also, go back to many solemn and many
joyful days ; to festivals and weddings and christen-
ings and funerals ; to many a happy Christmas, and
Christmas Eves, with the lighted church, and the holly
leaves, in the dark winter night ; to many a glad
and peaceful Easter ; to many a summer school-feast ;
to many a blessed Communion together.   I think of
all the changes in the houses of the parish ; who
lived in them once, and who fill their places now.
I see again the faces which used to be so familiar to
me, which have now passed away.   I cannot go
along a road, through the woods, or across a field,
I cannot look out on a prospect, I cannot enter a
house, but it brings back something—some bright
day, some happy meeting, some fear, some deliverance, some heavy tidings, some summons to me to
hasten, in the dark chill morning, or the late night,
or the warm summer day,—to some deathbed, to
take the last leave before it was too late.   How it
all comes back, through all these years, as if it was
only yesterday, and as if I and you had not so
deeply changed !   The Sunday services, and the
school, and the visits, and the kindly greetings,
and the anxieties and the hopes,—yes, and the
worries too, and disappointments,—the things I
hoped for and could not see.

    And now all is over.   It is finished and done.
Never more in this world will it be as it has been.
Other things are before all of us now.   For what is
past, as far as we are concerned in it, there only
remains the judgment.

And yet not only that.   There *is* something more.   There is, to me at least, the call, the obligation to the deepest and most earnest thankfulness for the choicest and most abounding blessings which God has to give ; thankfulness for unbroken peace and happiness ; thankfulness that death has not once crossed my threshold , thankfulness for the kindest and most unchanging of friends whom I have met with here ; thankfulness that with the poor as well as the rich of my people, and my neighbours, I have been allowed to be on the footing of an equal and a friend, to feel with them, to speak to them, as man with man.

And I have one particular reason just now to feel thankful.   I have been here long enough to see, through your goodwill and help, through the munificence and liberality of some of our friends, our church put in order.   Three years ago I could not have left it to a successor without feelings of shame. Now, I hope it is not quite unsuitable for the great and holy use for which a church is meant.

But there is something, too, besides thankfulness.   In nineteen years, with a people so willing, so ready to listen to me, with such kind hearts, so quickly touched and moved, what might not have been done ?   And what has been done ?   What use for our improvement in all good things have we each of us made of the time that we have lived together, almost as one family ?   These are serious and heart-searching questions , questions, too, which one day we must answer.   This is not the time nor the place.   But they are not questions to be forgotten in our secret souls, either by you or by me.

Wishes that the time might come over again, hopes
that if it were we should make better use of it, are
but idle, though they are so natural.   But they point
to the truth.   They are our own witnesses that we
have not done as well as we might have done ; that
we have much to wish otherwise ; much undone or
done poorly; strength and time wasted ; opportunities
missed and misused, much to repent of, much to be
ashamed of and sorry for.   I believe indeed I have
cared for you.   I have tried, at least I have wished,
to seek your good.   But yet, with all my regrets at
a time like this, mingles very painfully the remembrance of much which it is now too late to attempt
to do.   If when we have done all we are but unprofitable servants, what must we be when there is
so much that we have not done?

And now, for the last time, may I speak as your
adviser, and speak plainly.   New things are beginning with you in a measure.   And I think, too, that
your hearts are tender, and that you are feeling that
kindliness and sympathy which open, if you will, an
entrance to yet higher things.   Do not miss this time.
It is the time when God is inclining you, is helping
you, to be more serious, more impressed with the
realities of life, more ready to think of what is past,
and of what is to come.   Settle with yourselves that
with this change you will try to do something more
in the way of earnest religious living.

If you have not said your prayers, or have left
them off, begin saying them again.   If your church-
going has been irregular, make it steady and fixed.
If, able to come twice, you have come but once, do
what is right, and begin to come twice.   If you have

been indifferent to what the Bible tells you of your Saviour, ask Him now to help and guide you. I say nothing of other things of which you know I have often spoken. But I leave this word with you —a new time is beginning with you. Make a fresh start.

Next, will you suffer me to give you a practical warning? You have been long accustomed to me, to my ways; no doubt, too, to my faults and short-comings. And being accustomed to things blinds our judgment, and makes us unfair to other things which are different. Will you try and take care not to be so unfair? I need not say how greatly I value your regard, your affection, of which I have had so many proofs. But do not let yourselves make com-parisons between the old and the new, at least against the new. Probably you would be wrong. At any rate, there are more right ways than one, and a thing is not right merely because you are accustomed to it. Never forget the temptation which at first may cross you, that if you are not careful and fair you may do injustice to the greatest and most self-devoted earnestness, the deepest love of souls, the purest sense of duty, the warmest love to yourselves, only because they come in a form which is new to you.

I know I have been long to-day, but you will pardon me, for it is my last time, and perhaps I shall never speak to you more—certainly not as your clergyman. And while I can yet speak to you, I have something to ask of you. First, about myself. In so long a time it cannot be but that I must have made mistakes, misunderstood others, judged harshly, spoken hastily, and, what still more weighs on my conscience, sometimes not spoken when I ought to have spoken, or not earnestly enough. If any of you remember aught of this kind—if I have ever, by fault or unknowingly, hurt any, done them injustice, caused them offence, vexed or troubled them, or in any way done them wrong, I humbly and earnestly beg them to forgive, as if I begged them on my death-bed—and it is not less solemn a parting. And so too, if by any fault of mine I have neglected them; if, when they were wrong, I have not sufficiently warned them; if I have not given them the care I ought to have done, —I pray you to forgive me, and to ask that I may be forgiven,—forgiven for what I know, and, much more, for what I do not know.

And next, about yourselves. In any place, even the smallest, there must be differences and misunderstandings. Wherever there may be such, wherever they have not been healed, and keep neighbours apart, grant me, I pray you, this last favour. Grant me this last request that I have to make to you. Let bygones be bygones. Give me the great consolation of believing that my going away has softened and drawn your hearts one to another; that you feel that we have really been all one together, and that, in this, harsher feelings are lost. You will not be sorry for it when you come to die. To me it will make up for much if I can but hope that I leave behind me kinder thoughts and willingness to forget past differences in those whom I equally care for, and who, for the sake of all, for the sake of Christ their Redeemer, ought to be at one.

And now the end is come. We shall go home to our firesides, never more to meet as we have met this afternoon, as we have met wellnigh every Sunday afternoon for nearly nineteen years. And is not the time short? Have we indeed brought " our years to an end as it were a tale that is told "? It has passed as the days will again pass between this and our last day in this life. " Man goeth forth to his work and to his labour until the evening." And the evening, the last evening, is here.

O kind and loving friends, O warm-hearted and attached neighbours, O loyal affectionate hearts, we must be together no more. You have been to me what no other people have ever been to me, what I cannot hope that any others ever will be. There is but one place where again we can be together, and that is not on this side the grave. Here we part for good. O my dear friends, let us look on to that other meeting and being together. Let us wait, and help one another, and remember one another till that meeting comes ; it will not be long coming.

How shall I bid you farewell? May we not take the words in which the great Apostle bade farewell to those whom he loved? Can I wish you better than he wished in to-day's Epistle : " For this cause we . . . do not cease to pray for you, and to desire that ye might be filled with the knowledge of His will in all wisdom and spiritual understanding ; that ye might walk worthy of the Lord unto all pleasing, being fruitful in every good work, and increasing in the knowledge of God ? "

May I not end with his earnest adjuration? " Finally, brethren, farewell. Be perfect, be of good comfort, be of one mind, live in peace ; and the God of love and peace shall be with you." " And now, brethren, I commend you to God, and to the word of His grace, which is able to build you up, and to give you an inheritance among all them which are sanctified."

THE END

Printed by R. & R. CLARK, LIMITED, *Edinburgh.*

WORKS BY R. W. CHURCH

LATE DEAN OF ST. PAUL'S; HONORARY FELLOW OF
ORIEL COLLEGE, OXFORD

HUMAN LIFE AND ITS CONDITIONS. Sermons preached before the University of Oxford in 1876-1878, with Three Ordination Sermons. Crown 8vo. 6s.

ACADEMY.—"They never aim at oratorical display, nor attain any high flight of passionate utterance, yet we are sensible throughout of an earnest though controlled enthusiasm."

THE GIFTS OF CIVILIZATION, and other Sermons and Lectures delivered at Oxford and in St. Paul's Cathedral. Second Edition. Crown 8vo. 7s. 6d.

GUARDIAN.—"A suggestive and fascinating volume, which, if we mistake not, will make its way in quarters where ordinary sermons are but little read, and tell upon the world by its singular adaptation to the more serious tones of modern thought."

DISCIPLINE OF THE CHRISTIAN CHARACTER. And other Sermons. Second Edition. Crown 8vo. 4s. 6d.

SPECTATOR.—"One of the noblest series of Sermons which it has ever been our privilege to read; surely it ought to be one of the most popular books of the day."
GUARDIAN.—"A remarkable series of sermons."

ADVENT SERMONS. 1885. Crown 8vo. 4s. 6d.

GUARDIAN.—"They are worthy of the preacher, and therefore worthy to rank among the great sermons of our Church; and not only so, but they will be found full of strengthening and consoling power for simple and devout Christians, whose minds are cast down and oppressed by the thought of the unknown future that lies before them."

VILLAGE SERMONS. Preached at Whatley. Crown 8vo. 6s.

SCOTSMAN.—"The thinking is clear as crystal, and the language simplicity itself. . . . The discourses are of a very practical kind, and enforce duty with a mingled fidelity and kindliness which is altogether admirable."

VILLAGE SERMONS. Second Series. Crown 8vo. 6s.

VILLAGE SERMONS. Third Series. Crown 8vo. 6s.

TIMES.—"In these sermons we see how a singularly gifted and cultivated mind was able to communicate its thoughts on the highest subjects to those with whom it might be supposed to have little in common. . . . His village sermons are not the by-work of one whose interests were elsewhere in higher matters. They are the outcome of his deepest interests and of the life of his choice. . . . These sermons are worth perusal, if only to show what preaching, even to the humble and unlearned hearers, may be made in really competent hands."

PASCAL, and other Sermons. Crown 8vo. 6s.

CATHEDRAL AND UNIVERSITY SERMONS. Crown 8vo. 6s.

MACMILLAN AND CO., LTD., LONDON.

THE COLLECTED EDITION OF

DEAN CHURCH'S MISCELLANEOUS WRITINGS.

In Ten Volumes. Globe 8vo. 5s. each.

RECORD.—" In the whole literature of the Oxford Movement there is no one work likely to exercise a greater charm over its readers, or to become more commonly appealed to in future."

TIMES.—" Will quickly take its place among the most interesting of the many extant accounts of what is called ' The Oxford Movement.' "

GLOBE.—" Will certainly rank next in interest to Newman's autobiography itself."

Of the collected edition the *SCOTSMAN* says—" Dean Church has written well, thoughtfully, and with the literary grace which good scholarship gives to style, on many other subjects than the topics of religion. The collected editions of his miscellaneous writings will be heartily welcomed by all lovers of literature. . . . Learning, earnest thought, discriminating judgment, and a cultivated power of expression give these essays substantial value, which shows to more advantage in their present form than in the pages of old magazines. The volumes are printed elegantly and are handy in shape."

MANCHESTER GUARDIAN.—" His style has the scholarly finish of the best educated English in all ages. . . . It is hardly a hyperbole to say that if the question ' What do you mean by scholarship in the general sense?' were asked, no better answer could be given than ' Read Dean Church and you will see.' "

BACON. (*English Men of Letters Series.*) Crown 8vo. 1s. 6d.; sewed, 1s

TIMES.—" By a happy choice, Dean Church has been invited to contribute a little volume on Bacon to the series of *English Men of Letters.* We doubt if any one could have done the work better. . . . It is a vivid and comprehensive sketch of an extraordinary career."

SPENSER. (*English Men of Letters Series.*) Crown 8vo. 1s. 6d.; sewed, 1s.

SATURDAY REVIEW.—" This volume which contains the most mature work of a really eminent writer. . . . Without any display of critical apparatus, it is by far the most complete study we yet possess of the second founder of our poetry."

MACMILLAN AND CO., LTD., LONDON.

5.1.99

A Catalogue

of

Theological Works

published by

Macmillan & Co., Ltd.

St. Martin's Street
London, W.C.

CONTENTS

THEOLOGICAL CATALOGUE

The Bible

HISTORY OF THE BIBLE

THE BIBLE IN THE CHURCH. By Right Rev. Bishop WEST-COTT. 10th Edition. Pott 8vo. 4s. 6d.

BIBLICAL HISTORY

THE HOLY BIBLE. (Eversley Edition.) Arranged in Paragraphs, with an Introduction. By J. W. MACKAIL, M.A. 8 vols. Globe 8vo. 5s. each.

    Vol. I. Genesis—Numbers. II. Deuteronomy—2 Samuel. III. 1 Kings—Esther. IV. Job—Song of Solomon. V. Isaiah—Lamentations. VI. Ezekiel—Malachi. VII. Matthew—John. VIII. Acts—Revelation.

THE MODERN READER'S BIBLE. A Series of Books from the Sacred Scriptures presented in Modern Literary Form. The Text is that of the Revised Version. It is used by special permission of the University Presses of Oxford and Cambridge. Edited by R. G. MOULTON, M.A. Pott 8vo. 2s. 6d. each volume.

    THE PROVERBS. ECCLESIASTICUS. ECCLESIASTES—WISDOM OF SOLOMON. THE BOOK OF JOB.

    DEUTERONOMY. GENESIS. THE EXODUS. THE JUDGES. BIBLICAL IDYLLS—SOLOMON'S SONG, RUTH, ESTHER, TOBIT. THE KINGS. THE CHRONICLES.

    ISAIAH. JEREMIAH. EZEKIEL. DANIEL. SELECT MASTERPIECES OF BIBLICAL LITERATURE. THE PSALMS AND LAMENTATIONS. 2 Vols.

    ST. MATTHEW AND ST. MARK, AND THE GENERAL EPISTLES.

    ST. LUKE AND ST. PAUL. 2 Vols.

    THE GOSPEL, EPISTLES, AND REVELATION OF ST. JOHN. BIBLE STORIES (Old Testament). BIBLE STORIES (New Testament).

ST. JAMES'S GAZETTE.—"While the sacred text has in no way been tampered with, the books are presented in modern literary form and are furnished with an introduction and notes by Professor Richard G. Moulton. The notes are scholarly, and of real help to the student.'

BIBLE LESSONS. By Rev. E. A. ABBOTT, D.D. Crown 8vo. 4s. 6d.

SIDE-LIGHTS UPON BIBLE HISTORY. By Mrs. SYDNEY BUXTON. Illustrated. Crown 8vo. 5s.

THE STUDENT'S LIFE OF JESUS. By G. H. GILBERT, Ph.D. Crown 8vo. 5s. net.

THE STUDENT'S LIFE OF PAUL. By G. H. GILBERT, Ph.D. Crown 8vo. 5s. net.

THE REVELATION OF JESUS: A Study of the Primary Sources of Christianity. By G. H. GILBERT, Ph.D. Crown 8vo. 5s. net.

Biblical History—*continued.*

STORIES FROM THE BIBLE. By Rev. A. J. CHURCH. Illustrated. Two Series. Crown 8vo. 3s. 6d. each.

BIBLICAL QUOTATIONS IN OLD ENGLISH PROSE WRITERS. By ALBERT S. COOK, Ph.D., Rutgers Professor of the English Language and Literature in Yale University. 8vo. 17s. net.

BIBLE READINGS SELECTED FROM THE PENTATEUCH AND THE BOOK OF JOSHUA. By Rev. J. A. CROSS. 2nd Edition. Globe 8vo. 2s. 6d.

CHILDREN'S TREASURY OF BIBLE STORIES. By Mrs. H. GASKOIN. Pott 8vo. 1s. each. Part I. Old Testament ; II. New Testament ; III. Three Apostles.

THE NATIONS AROUND ISRAEL. By A. KEARY. Cr. 8vo. 3s. 6d.

VILLAGE SERMONS. By Rev. F. J. A. HORT, D.D. 8vo. 6s.
    This Volume contains a Series of Sermons dealing in a popular way with the successive Books of which the Bible is made up. They form an admirable introduction to the subject.

HISTORY, PROPHECY, AND THE MONUMENTS, OR, ISRAEL AND THE NATIONS. By Prof. J. F. M'CURDY. 8vo. 14s. net each. Vol. I. To the Downfall of Samaria. Vol. II. To the Fall of Nineveh.   [*Vol. III. in the Press.*

AMERICAN HISTORICAL REVIEW.—"His method is to interweave the histories of the connected peoples in each period, to point out the historical presuppositions and moral principles in the prophetic writings, and to treat the social constitution in separate sections. This method has obvious advantages in the hands of a competent scholar and good writer, and is employed by Mr. M'Curdy with excellent effect. His presentation of the material is admirable in arrangement ; his style, though somewhat formal and Gibbonesque, is clear and picturesque."

TIMES.—"A learned treatise on the ancient history of the Semitic peoples as interpreted by the new light obtained from the modern study of their monuments."

EXPOSITORY TIMES.—"The work is very able and very welcome. . . . It will take the place of all existing histories of these nations."

A CLASS-BOOK OF OLD TESTAMENT HISTORY. By Rev. Canon MACLEAR. With Four Maps. Pott 8vo. 4s. 6d.

A CLASS-BOOK OF NEW TESTAMENT HISTORY. Including the connection of the Old and New Testament. By the same. Pott 8vo. 5s. 6d.

A SHILLING BOOK OF OLD TESTAMENT HISTORY. By the same. Pott 8vo. 1s.

A SHILLING BOOK OF NEW TESTAMENT HISTORY. By the same. Pott 8vo. 1s.

THE BIBLE FOR HOME READING. Edited, with Comments and Reflections for the use of Jewish Parents and Children, by C. G. MONTEFIORE. Part I. TO THE SECOND VISIT OF NEHEMIAH TO JERUSALEM. 2nd Edition. Extra Crown 8vo. 4s. 6d. net. Part II. Containing Selections from the Wisdom Literature, the Prophets, and the Psalter, together with extracts from the Apocrypha. Extra Crown 8vo. 5s. 6d. net.

JEWISH CHRONICLE.—"By this remarkable work Mr. Claude Montefiore has put the seal on his reputation. He has placed himself securely in the front rank of contemporary teachers of religion. He has produced at once a most original, a most instructive, and almost spiritual treatise, which will long leave its ennobling mark on

Jewish religious thought in England. . . . Though the term 'epoch-making' is often misapplied, we do not hesitate to apply it on this occasion. We cannot but believe that a new era may dawn in the interest shown by Jews in the Bible."

THE OLD TESTAMENT

SCRIPTURE READINGS FOR SCHOOLS AND FAMILIES. By C. M. YONGE. Globe 8vo. 1s. 6d. each ; also with comments. 3s. 6d. each.—First Series : GENESIS TO DEUTERONOMY.—Second Series : JOSHUA TO SOLOMON.—Third Series: KINGS AND THE PROPHETS.—Fourth Series : THE GOSPEL TIMES.—Fifth Series : APOSTOLIC TIMES.

THE DIVINE LIBRARY OF THE OLD TESTAMENT. Its Origin, Preservation, Inspiration, and Permanent Value. By Rev. A. F. KIRKPATRICK, B.D. Crown 8vo. 3s. net.

TIMES.—"An eloquent and temperate plea for the critical study of the Scriptures."

MANCHESTER GUARDIAN.—"An excellent introduction to the modern view of the Old Testament. . . . The learned author is a genuine critic. . . . He expounds clearly what has been recently called the 'Analytic' treatment of the books of the Old Testament, and generally adopts its results. . . . The volume is admirably suited to fulfil its purpose of familiarising the minds of earnest Bible readers with the work which Biblical criticism is now doing."

THE DOCTRINE OF THE PROPHETS. Warburtonian Lectures 1886-1890. By Rev. A. F. KIRKPATRICK, B.D. 2nd Edition. Crown 8vo. 6s.

SCOTSMAN.—"This volume gives us the result of ripe scholarship and competent learning in a very attractive form. It is written simply, clearly, and eloquently ; and it invests the subject of which it treats with a vivid and vital interest which will commend it to the reader of general intelligence, as well as to those who are more especially occupied with such studies."

GLASGOW HERALD.—"Professor Kirkpatrick's book will be found of great value for purposes of study."

BOOKMAN.—"As a summary of the main results of recent investigation, and as a thoughtful appreciation of both the human and divine sides of the prophets' work and message, it is worth the attention of all Bible students."

THE PATRIARCHS AND LAWGIVERS OF THE OLD TESTAMENT. By FREDERICK DENISON MAURICE. New Edition. Crown 8vo. 3s. 6d.

THE PROPHETS AND KINGS OF THE OLD TESTAMENT. By the same. New Edition. Crown 8vo. 3s. 6d.

THE CANON OF THE OLD TESTAMENT. An Essay on the Growth and Formation of the Hebrew Canon of Scripture. By Rev. Prof. H. E. RYLE. 2nd Edition. Crown 8vo. 6s.

This edition has been carefully revised throughout, but only two substantial changes have been found necessary. An Appendix has been added to Chapter IV., dealing with the subject of the Samaritan version of the Pentateuch ; and Excursus C (dealing with the Hebrew Scriptures) has been completely re-written on the strength of valuable material kindly supplied to the author by Dr. Ginsburg.

EXPOSITOR.—"Scholars are indebted to Professor Ryle for having given them for the first time a complete and trustworthy history of the Old Testament Canon."

EXPOSITORY TIMES.—"He rightly claims that his book possesses that most English of virtues—it may be read throughout. . . . An extensive and minute research lies concealed under a most fresh and flexible English style."

The Old Testament—*continued*.

THE MYTHS OF ISRAEL. THE ANCIENT BOOK OF GENESIS. WITH ANALYSIS AND EXPLANATION OF ITS COMPOSITION. By AMOS KIDDER FISKE, Author of "The Jewish Scriptures," etc. Crown 8vo. 6s.

THE EARLY NARRATIVES OF GENESIS. By Rev. Prof. H. E. RYLE. Cr. 8vo. 3s. net.

PHILO AND HOLY SCRIPTURE, OR THE QUOTATIONS OF PHILO FROM THE BOOKS OF THE OLD TESTAMENT. With Introd. and Notes by Prof. H. E. RYLE. Cr. 8vo. 10s. net.

In the present work the attempt has been made to collect, arrange in order, and for the first time print in full all the actual quotations from the books of the Old Testament to be found in Philo's writings, and a few of his paraphrases. For the purpose of giving general assistance to students Dr. Ryle has added footnotes, dealing principally with the text of Philo's quotations compared with that of the Septuagint; and in the introduction he has endeavoured to explain Philo's attitude towards Holy Scripture, and the character of the variations of his text from that of the Septuagint.

The Pentateuch—

AN HISTORICO-CRITICAL INQUIRY INTO THE ORIGIN AND COMPOSITION OF THE HEXATEUCH (PENTATEUCH AND BOOK OF JOSHUA). By Prof. A. KUENEN. Translated by PHILIP H. WICKSTEED, M.A. 8vo. 14s.

The Psalms—

THE PSALMS CHRONOLOGICALLY ARRANGED. An Amended Version, with Historical Introductions and Explanatory Notes. By Four Friends. New Edition. Crown 8vo. 5s. net.

GOLDEN TREASURY PSALTER. The Student's Edition. Being an Edition with briefer Notes of "The Psalms Chronologically Arranged by Four Friends." Pott 8vo. 2s. 6d. net.

THE PSALMS. With Introductions and Critical Notes. By A. C. JENNINGS, M.A., and W. H. LOWE, M.A. In 2 vols. 2nd Edition. Crown 8vo. 10s. 6d. each.

Isaiah—

ISAIAH XL.—LXVI. With the Shorter Prophecies allied to it. By MATTHEW ARNOLD. With Notes. Crown 8vo. 5s.

A BIBLE-READING FOR SCHOOLS. The Great Prophecy of Israel's Restoration (Isaiah xl.-lxvi.) Arranged and Edited for Young Learners. By the same. 4th Edition. Pott 8vo. 1s.

Zechariah—

THE HEBREW STUDENT'S COMMENTARY ON ZECH-ARIAH, Hebrew and LXX. By W. H. LOWE, M.A. 8vo. 10s. 6d.

THE NEW TESTAMENT

THE AKHMIM FRAGMENT OF THE APOCRYPHAL GOSPEL OF ST. PETER. By H. B. SWETE, D.D. 8vo. 5s. net.

GUARDIAN.—"Cambridge may claim the honour not only of having communicated without delay the new discovery to the general public, but also of having furnished scholars with the most complete and sober account of the contents, character, and date of the Gospel of Peter that has yet appeared."

THE SOTERIOLOGY OF THE NEW TESTAMENT. By W. P. DU BOSE, M.A. Crown 8vo. 7s. 6d.

THE MESSAGES OF THE BOOKS. Being Discourses and Notes on the Books of the New Testament. By Dean FARRAR. 8vo. 14s.

ON A FRESH REVISION OF THE ENGLISH NEW TESTA-MENT. With an Appendix on the last Petition of the Lord's Prayer. By Bishop LIGHTFOOT. Crown 8vo. 7s. 6d.

DISSERTATIONS ON THE APOSTOLIC AGE. By Bishop LIGHTFOOT. 8vo. 14s.

BIBLICAL ESSAYS. By Bishop LIGHTFOOT. 8vo. 12s.

THE UNITY OF THE NEW TESTAMENT. By F. D. MAURICE. 2nd Edition. 2 vols. Crown 8vo. 12s.

A GENERAL SURVEY OF THE HISTORY OF THE CANON OF THE NEW TESTAMENT DURING THE FIRST FOUR CENTURIES. By Right Rev. Bishop WESTCOTT. 7th Edition. Crown 8vo. 10s. 6d.

NEW TESTAMENT HANDBOOKS. Edited by SHAILER MATHEWS, Professor of New Testament History at the University of Chicago.

A HISTORY OF NEW TESTAMENT TIMES IN PALES-TINE (175 B.C.–70 A.D.). By SHAILER MATHEWS, A.M. Crown 8vo. 3s. 6d.

A HISTORY OF THE TEXTUAL CRITICISM OF THE NEW TESTAMENT. By MARVIN R. VINCENT, D.D. Crown 8vo. 3s. 6d.

THE NEW TESTAMENT IN THE ORIGINAL GREEK. The Text revised by Bishop WESTCOTT, D.D., and Prof. F. J. A. HORT, D.D. 2 vols. Crown 8vo. 10s. 6d. each.—Vol. I. Text; II. Introduction and Appendix.

Library Edition. 8vo. 10s. net. [*Text in Macmillan Greek Type.*

School Edition. 12mo, cloth, 4s. 6d.; roan, 5s. 6d.; morocco, 6s. 6d. ; India Paper Edition, limp calf, 7s. 6d. net.

The New Testament—*continued.*

GREEK-ENGLISH LEXICON TO THE NEW TESTAMENT. By W. J. HICKIE, M.A. Pott 8vo. 3s.

ACADEMY.—"We can cordially recommend this as a very handy little volume compiled on sound principles."

GRAMMAR OF NEW TESTAMENT GREEK. By Prof. F. BLASS, University of Halle. Authorised English Translation. 8vo. 14s. net.

TIMES.—"Will probably become the standard book of reference for those students who enter upon minute grammatical study of the language of the New Testament."

THE GOSPELS—

PHILOLOGY OF THE GOSPELS. By Prof. F. BLASS. Crown 8vo. 4s. 6d. net.

GUARDIAN.—"On the whole, Professor Blass's new book seems to us an important contribution to criticism. . . . It will stimulate inquiry, and will open up fresh lines of thought to any serious student."

THE SYRO-LATIN TEXT OF THE GOSPELS. By the Rev. FREDERIC HENRY CHASE, D.D. 8vo. 7s. 6d. net.

The sequel of an essay by Dr. Chase on the old Syriac element in the text of Codex Bezae.

TIMES.—"An important and scholarly contribution to New Testament criticism."

THE COMMON TRADITION OF THE SYNOPTIC GOSPELS, in the Text of the Revised Version. By Rev. E. A. ABBOTT and W. G. RUSHBROOKE. Crown 8vo. 3s. 6d.

SYNOPTICON: An Exposition of the Common Matter of the Synoptic Gospels. By W. G. RUSHBROOKE. Printed in Colours. 4to. 35s. net. Indispensable to a Theological Student.

A SYNOPSIS OF THE GOSPELS IN GREEK AFTER THE WESTCOTT AND HORT TEXT. By Rev. ARTHUR WRIGHT, M.A. Demy 4to. 6s. net.

"Every such effort calls attention to facts which must not be overlooked, but yet to the scholar they are but as dust in the balance when weighed against such solid contributions as Rushbrooke's *Synopticon* or Wright's *Synopsis*, which provide instruments for investigation apart from theories."—Professor Armitage Robinson at Church Congress, Bradford, 1898.

THE COMPOSITION OF THE FOUR GOSPELS. By Rev. ARTHUR WRIGHT. Crown 8vo. 5s.

CAMBRIDGE REVIEW.—"The wonderful force and freshness which we find on every page of the book. There is no sign of hastiness. All seems to be the outcome of years of reverent thought, now brought to light in the clearest, most telling way. . . . The book will hardly go unchallenged by the different schools of thought, but all will agree in gratitude at least for its vigour and reality."

INTRODUCTION TO THE STUDY OF THE FOUR GOSPELS. By Right Rev. Bishop WESTCOTT. 8th Ed. Cr. 8vo. 10s. 6d.

FOUR LECTURES ON THE EARLY HISTORY OF THE GOSPELS. By the Rev. J. H. WILKINSON, M.A., Rector of Stock Gaylard, Dorset. Crown 8vo. 3s. net.

THE LEADING IDEAS OF THE GOSPELS. By W. ALEXANDER, D.D. Oxon., LL.D. Dublin, D.C.L. Oxon., Archbishop of

The Gospels—*continued.*

Armagh, and Lord Primate of All Ireland. New Edition, Revised and Enlarged. Crown 8vo. 6s.

GUARDIAN.—"The originality of the general conception, the ingenious and poetical manner in which it is worked out, and the smallness of its size, give this volume special claims on the attention of non-theological readers."

BRITISH WEEKLY.—"Really a new book. It sets before the reader with delicacy of thought and felicity of language the distinguishing characteristics of the several gospels. It is delightful reading. . . . Religious literature does not often furnish a book which may so confidently be recommended."

Gospel of St. Matthew—

THE GOSPEL ACCORDING TO ST. MATTHEW. Greek Text as Revised by Bishop WESTCOTT and Dr. HORT. With Introduction and Notes by Rev. A. SLOMAN, M.A. Fcap. 8vo. 2s. 6d.

MANCHESTER GUARDIAN.—"It is sound and helpful, and the brief introduction on Hellenistic Greek is particularly good."

Gospel of St. Mark—

THE GREEK TEXT. With Introduction, Notes, and Indices. By Rev. H. B. SWETE, D.D., Regius Professor of Divinity in the University of Cambridge. 8vo. 15s.

TIMES.—"A learned and scholarly performance, up to date with the most recent advances in New Testament criticism."

SCHOOL READINGS IN THE GREEK TESTAMENT. Being the Outlines of the Life of our Lord as given by St. Mark, with additions from the Text of the other Evangelists. Edited, with Notes and Vocabulary, by Rev. A. CALVERT, M.A. Fcap. 8vo. 2s. 6d.

Gospel of St. Luke—

THE GOSPEL ACCORDING TO ST. LUKE. The Greek Text as Revised by Bishop WESTCOTT and Dr. HORT. With Introduction and Notes by Rev. J. BOND, M.A. Fcap. 8vo. 2s. 6d.

GLASGOW HERALD.—"The notes are short and crisp—suggestive rather than exhaustive."

THE GOSPEL OF THE KINGDOM OF HEAVEN. A Course of Lectures on the Gospel of St. Luke. By F. D. MAURICE. Crown 8vo. 3s. 6d.

THE GOSPEL ACCORDING TO ST. LUKE IN GREEK, AFTER THE WESTCOTT AND HORT TEXT. Edited, with Parallels, Illustrations, Various Readings, and Notes, by the Rev. ARTHUR WRIGHT, M.A. Demy 4to. 7s. 6d. net.

Gospel of St. John—

THE CENTRAL TEACHING OF CHRIST. Being a Study and Exposition of St. John, Chapters XIII. to XVII. By Rev. CANON BERNARD, M.A. Crown 8vo. 7s. 6d.

EXPOSITORY TIMES.—"Quite recently we have had an exposition by him whom many call the greatest expositor living. But Canon Bernard's work is still the work that will help the preacher most."

THE GOSPEL OF ST. JOHN. By F. D. MAURICE. Cr. 8vo. 3s. 6d.

THE ACTS OF THE APOSTLES.

ADDRESSES ON THE ACTS OF THE APOSTLES. By the late ARCHBISHOP BENSON. 8vo.   [*In the Press.*

The Acts of the Apostles—*continued.*

THE OLD SYRIAC ELEMENT IN THE TEXT OF THE
   CODEX BEZAE. By F. H. CHASE, B.D.   8vo.   7s. 6d. net.

THE ACTS OF THE APOSTLES IN GREEK AND ENGLISH.
   With Notes by Rev. F. RENDALL, M.A.   Cr. 8vo.   9s.

SATURDAY REVIEW.—"Mr. Rendall has given us a very useful as well as a
very scholarly book."

BRITISH WEEKLY.—"On the whole the book is a valuable addition to New
Testament literature, being thoroughly up-to-date both in its scholarship and in its
general information and critical judgment."

MANCHESTER GUARDIAN.—"Mr. Rendall is a careful scholar and a thoughtful writer, and the student may learn a good deal from his commentary."

THE ACTS OF THE APOSTLES.   By F. D. MAURICE.   Cr.
   8vo.   3s. 6d.

THE ACTS OF THE APOSTLES.   Being the Greek Text as
   Revised by Bishop WESTCOTT and Dr. HORT.   With Explanatory
   Notes by T. E. PAGE, M.A.   Fcap. 8vo.   3s. 6d.

ACTS OF THE APOSTLES.   The Authorised Version, with Introduction and Notes, by T. E. PAGE, M.A., and Rev. A. S.
   WALPOLE, M.A.   Fcap. 8vo.   2s. 6d.

BRITISH WEEKLY.—"Mr. Page's Notes on the Greek Text of the Acts are very
well known, and are decidedly scholarly and individual. . . . Mr. Page has written an
introduction which is brief, scholarly, and suggestive."

SCOTSMAN.—"It is a much more scholarly edition than is usually found prepared
for use in schools, and yet keeps its learning well within the limits of the needs and the
capacities of young students of the Bible."

THE CHURCH OF THE FIRST DAYS.   THE CHURCH OF
   JERUSALEM.   THE CHURCH OF THE GENTILES.   THE CHURCH
   OF THE WORLD.   Lectures on the Acts of the Apostles.   By
   Very Rev. C. J. VAUGHAN.   Crown 8vo.   10s. 6d.

THE EPISTLES of St. Paul—

ST. PAUL'S EPISTLE TO THE ROMANS.   The Greek Text,
   with English Notes.   By Very Rev. C. J. VAUGHAN.   7th Edition.
   Crown 8vo.   7s. 6d.

ST. PAUL'S EPISTLE TO THE ROMANS.   A New Translation by Rev. W. G. RUTHERFORD.   [*In the Press.*

PROLEGOMENA TO ST. PAUL'S EPISTLES TO THE
   ROMANS AND THE EPHESIANS.   By Rev. F. J. A. HORT.
   Crown 8vo.   6s.

Dr. MARCUS DODS in the *Bookman.*—"Anything from the pen of Dr. Hort is sure to
be informative and suggestive, and the present publication bears his mark. . . . There
is an air of originality about the whole discussion ; the difficulties are candidly faced, and
the explanations offered appeal to our sense of what is reasonable."

TIMES.—"Will be welcomed by all theologians as 'an invaluable contribution to the
study of those Epistles' as the editor of the volume justly calls it."

DAILY CHRONICLE.—"The lectures are an important contribution to the study
of the famous Epistles of which they treat."

THE EPISTLE TO THE GALATIANS.   An Essay on its
   Destination and Date.   By E. H. ASKWITH, M.A.   Crown 8vo.
   3s. 6d. net.

ST. PAUL'S EPISTLE TO THE GALATIANS.   A Revised
   Text, with Introduction, Notes, and Dissertations.   By Bishop
   LIGHTFOOT.   10th Edition.   8vo.   12s.

The Epistles of St. Paul—*continued*.

ST. PAUL'S EPISTLE TO THE EPHESIANS. Greek Text, with Introduction and Notes. By Canon J. ARMITAGE ROBINSON. 8vo. [*In the Press.*

ST. PAUL'S EPISTLE TO THE PHILIPPIANS. A Revised Text, with Introduction, Notes, and Dissertations. By Bishop LIGHTFOOT. 9th Edition. 8vo. 12s.

ST. PAUL'S EPISTLE TO THE PHILIPPIANS. With translation, Paraphrase, and Notes for English Readers. By Very Rev. C. J. VAUGHAN. Crown 8vo. 5s.

ST. PAUL'S EPISTLES TO THE COLOSSIANS AND TO PHILEMON. A Revised Text, with Introductions, etc. By Bishop LIGHTFOOT. 9th Edition. 8vo. 12s.

THE EPISTLE TO THE COLOSSIANS. Analysis and Examination Notes. By Rev. G. W. GARROD. Crown 8vo. 3s. net.

THE FIRST EPISTLE TO THE THESSALONIANS. With Analysis and Notes by the Rev. G. W. GARROD, B.A. Crown 8vo. 2s. 6d. net.

THE EPISTLES OF ST. PAUL TO THE EPHESIANS, THE COLOSSIANS, AND PHILEMON. With Introductions and Notes. By Rev. J. LL. DAVIES. 2nd Edition. 8vo. 7s. 6d.

THE EPISTLES OF ST. PAUL. For English Readers. Part I. containing the First Epistle to the Thessalonians. By Very Rev. C. J. VAUGHAN. 2nd Edition. 8vo. Sewed. 1s. 6d.

NOTES ON EPISTLES OF ST. PAUL FROM UNPUBLISHED COMMENTARIES. By the late J. B. LIGHTFOOT, D.D., D.C.L., LL.D., Lord Bishop of Durham. 8vo. 12s.

GUARDIAN.—" It scarcely needs to be said, after the experience of former volumes, that the editor has done his part of the work excellently. . . . It also certainly needs not to be said that we have in the commentary much valuable contribution to the study of St. Paul, and that the whole is marked by the Bishop's well-known characteristics of sound scholarship, width of learning, and clear sobriety of judgment."

THE FIRST EPISTLE OF ST PETER, I. 1 to II. 17. The Greek Text, with Introductory Lecture, Commentary, and additional Notes. By the late F. J. A. HORT, D.D., D.C.L., LL.D. 8vo. 6s.

The Epistle of St. James—

THE EPISTLE OF ST. JAMES. The Greek Text, with Introduction and Notes. By Rev. JOSEPH B. MAYOR, M.A. 2nd Edition. 8vo. 14s. net.

EXPOSITORY TIMES.—" The most complete edition of St. James in the English language, and the most serviceable for the student of Greek."

BOOKMAN.—" Professor Mayor's volume in every part of it gives proof that no time or labour has been grudged in mastering this mass of literature, and that in appraising it he has exercised the sound judgment of a thoroughly trained scholar and critic. . . . The notes are uniformly characterised by thorough scholarship and unfailing sense. The notes resemble rather those of Lightfoot than those of Ellicott. . . . It is a pleasure to welcome a book which does credit to English learning, and which will take, and keep, a foremost place in Biblical literature."

The Epistles of St. John—

SCOTSMAN.—"It is a work which sums up many others, and to any one who wishes to make a thorough study of the Epistle of St. James, it will prove indispensable."

EXPOSITOR (Dr. MARCUS DODS).—"Will long remain the commentary on St. James, a storehouse to which all subsequent students of the epistle must be indebted."

THE EPISTLES OF ST. JOHN. By F. D. MAURICE. Crown 8vo. 3s. 6d.

THE EPISTLES OF ST. JOHN. The Greek Text, with Notes. By Right Rev. Bishop WESTCOTT. 3rd Edition. 8vo. 12s. 6d.

GUARDIAN.—"It contains a new or rather revised text, with careful critical remarks and helps; very copious footnotes on the text; and after each of the chapters, longer and more elaborate notes in treatment of leading or difficult questions, whether in respect of reading or theology. . . . Dr. Westcott has accumulated round them so much matter that, if not new, was forgotten, or generally unobserved, and has thrown so much light upon their language, theology, and characteristics. . . . The notes, critical, illustrative, and exegetical, which are given beneath the text, are extraordinarily full and careful. . . . They exhibit the same minute analysis of every phrase and word, the same scrupulous weighing of every inflection and variation that characterised Dr. Westcott's commentary on the Gospel. . . . There is scarcely a syllable throughout the Epistles which is dismissed without having undergone the most anxious interrogation."

SATURDAY REVIEW.—"The more we examine this precious volume the more its exceeding richness in spiritual as well as in literary material grows upon the mind."

The Epistle to the Hebrews—

THE EPISTLE TO THE HEBREWS IN GREEK AND ENGLISH. With Notes. By Rev. F. RENDALL. Cr. 8vo. 6s.

THE EPISTLE TO THE HEBREWS. English Text, with Commentary. By the same. Crown 8vo. 7s. 6d.

THE EPISTLE TO THE HEBREWS. With Notes. By Very Rev. C. J. VAUGHAN. Crown 8vo. 7s. 6d.

TIMES.—"The name and reputation of the Dean of Llandaff are a better recommendation than we can give of the *Epistle to the Hebrews*, the Greek text, with notes; an edition which represents the results of more than thirty years' experience in the training of students for ordination."

THE EPISTLE TO THE HEBREWS. The Greek Text, with Notes and Essays. By Right Rev. Bishop WESTCOTT. 8vo. 14s.

GUARDIAN.—"In form this is a companion volume to that upon the Epistles of St. John. The type is excellent, the printing careful, the index thorough; and the volume contains a full introduction, followed by the Greek text, with a running commentary, and a number of additional notes on verbal and doctrinal points which needed fuller discussion. . . . His conception of inspiration is further illustrated by the treatment of the Old Testament in the Epistle, and the additional notes that bear on this point deserve very careful study. The spirit in which the student should approach the perplexing questions of Old Testament criticism could not be better described than it is in the last essay."

The Book of Revelations—

THE APOCALYPSE. A Study. By the late ARCHBISHOP BENSON. 8vo. 8s. 6d. net.

LECTURES ON THE APOCALYPSE. By Rev. Prof. W. MILLIGAN. Crown 8vo. 5s.

DISCUSSIONS ON THE APOCALYPSE. By the same. Cr. 8vo. 5s.

SCOTSMAN.—"These discussions give an interesting and valuable account and criticism of the present state of theological opinion and research in connection with their subject."

SCOTTISH GUARDIAN.—"The great merit of the book is the patient and skilful way in which it has brought the whole discussion down to the present day. . . . The result is a volume which many will value highly, and which will not, we think, soon be superseded."

LECTURES ON THE REVELATION OF ST. JOHN. By Very
Rev. C. J. VAUGHAN. 5th Edition. Crown 8vo. 10s. 6d.

THE BIBLE WORD-BOOK. By W. ALDIS WRIGHT, Litt.D.,
LL.D. 2nd Edition. Crown 8vo. 7s. 6d.

Christian Church, History of the

Cheetham (Archdeacon).—A HISTORY OF THE CHRISTIAN
CHURCH DURING THE FIRST SIX CENTURIES. Cr.
8vo. 10s. 6d.

> *TIMES.*—"A brief but authoritative summary of early ecclesiastical history."
> *GLASGOW HERALD.*—"Particularly clear in its exposition, systematic in its dis-
> position and development, and as light and attractive in style as could reasonably be
> expected from the nature of the subject."

Gwatkin (H. M.)—SELECTIONS FROM EARLY WRITERS
Illustrative of Church History to the Time of Constantine. 2nd
Edition. Revised and Enlarged. Cr. 8vo. 4s. 6d. net.
To this edition have been prefixed short accounts of the writers
from whom the passages are selected.

Hardwick (Archdeacon).—A HISTORY OF THE CHRISTIAN
CHURCH. Middle Age. Ed. by Bishop STUBBS. Cr. 8vo. 10s. 6d.

A HISTORY OF THE CHRISTIAN CHURCH DURING THE
REFORMATION. Revised by Bishop STUBBS. Cr. 8vo. 10s. 6d.

Hort (Dr. F. J. A.)—TWO DISSERTATIONS. I. On
MONOΓENHΣ ΘEOΣ in Scripture and Tradition. II. On the
"Constantinopolitan" Creed and other Eastern Creeds of the
Fourth Century. 8vo. 7s. 6d.

JUDAISTIC CHRISTIANITY. Crown 8vo. 6s.

THE CHRISTIAN ECCLESIA. A Course of Lectures on the
Early History and Early Conceptions of the Ecclesia, and Four
Sermons. Crown 8vo. 6s.

Krüger (Dr. G.)—HISTORY OF EARLY CHRISTIAN
LITERATURE IN THE FIRST THREE CENTURIES. Cr.
8vo. 8s. 6d. net.

Simpson (W.)—AN EPITOME OF THE HISTORY OF THE
CHRISTIAN CHURCH. Fcap. 8vo. 3s. 6d.

Sohm (Prof.) — OUTLINES OF CHURCH HISTORY.
Translated by Miss MAY SINCLAIR. With a Preface by Prof. H.
M. GWATKIN, M.A. Crown 8vo. 3s. 6d.

> *MANCHESTER GUARDIAN.*—"It fully deserves the praise given to it by Pro-
> fessor Gwatkin (who contributes a preface to this translation) of being 'neither a meagre
> sketch nor a confused mass of facts, but a masterly outline,' and it really 'supplies a
> want,' as affording to the intelligent reader who has no time or interest in details, a con-
> nected general view of the whole vast field of ecclesiastical history."

Vaughan (Very Rev. C. J., Dean of Llandaff).—THE CHURCH
OF THE FIRST DAYS. THE CHURCH OF JERUSALEM. THE
CHURCH OF THE GENTILES. THE CHURCH OF THE WORLD.
Crown 8vo.   10s. 6d.

The Church of England

Catechism of—

CATECHISM AND CONFIRMATION. By Rev. J. C. P.
ALDOUS. Pott 8vo.   1s. net.

THOSE HOLY MYSTERIES. By Rev. J. C. P. ALDOUS. Pott
8vo.   1s. net.

A CLASS-BOOK OF THE CATECHISM OF THE CHURCH
OF ENGLAND. By Rev. Canon MACLEAR. Pott 8vo.   1s. 6d.

A FIRST CLASS-BOOK OF THE CATECHISM OF THE
CHURCH OF ENGLAND, with Scripture Proofs for Junior
Classes and Schools. By the same. Pott 8vo.   6d.

THE ORDER OF CONFIRMATION, with Prayers and Devotions. By the Rev. Canon MACLEAR. 32mo.   6d.

NOTES FOR LECTURES ON CONFIRMATION. By the
Rev. C. J. VAUGHAN, D.D. Pott 8vo.   1s. 6d.

Disestablishment—

DISESTABLISHMENT AND DISENDOWMENT. What are
they? By Prof. E. A. FREEMAN. 4th Edition. Crown 8vo.   1s.

A DEFENCE OF THE CHURCH OF ENGLAND AGAINST
DISESTABLISHMENT. By ROUNDELL, EARL OF SELBORNE.
Crown 8vo.   2s. 6d.

ANCIENT FACTS & FICTIONS CONCERNING CHURCHES
AND TITHES. By the same. 2nd Edition. Crown 8vo.   7s. 6d.

A HANDBOOK ON WELSH CHURCH DEFENCE. By the
Bishop of ST. ASAPH. 3rd Edition. Fcap. 8vo. Sewed, 6d.

CHURCH TIMES.—"It should be in the hands of all who are actively engaged in
defence of the Church in Wales."

Dissent in its Relation to—

DISSENT IN ITS RELATION TO THE CHURCH OF ENG-
LAND. By Rev. G. H. CURTEIS. Bampton Lectures for 1871.
Crown 8vo.   7s. 6d.

History of—

HISTORY OF THE CHURCH OF ENGLAND. Edited by
the DEAN OF WINCHESTER. In Seven Volumes.

Vol. I.   HISTORY OF THE CHURCH OF ENGLAND
PRIOR TO THE NORMAN CONQUEST. By the Rev. W.
HUNT, M.A. Cr. 8vo.   7s. 6d.
Other Volumes to follow.

THE STATE AND THE CHURCH. By the Hon. ARTHUR
ELLIOT. New Edition. Crown 8vo.   2s. 6d.

DOCUMENTS ILLUSTRATIVE OF ENGLISH CHURCH
HISTORY. Compiled from Original Sources by HENRY GEE,
B.D., F.S.A., and W. J. HARDY, F.S.A. Cr. 8vo.   10s. 6d.

History of—*continued.*

ENGLISH HISTORICAL REVIEW.—"Will be welcomed alike by students and by a much wider circle of readers interested in the history of the Church of England. For the benefit of the latter all the Latin pieces have been translated into English. . . . It fully deserves the hearty imprimatur of the Bishop of Oxford prefixed to it."

ACADEMY.—"The assurance of the Bishop of Oxford, that 'this is a book which will, and indeed must, be received as a great boon by English Churchmen,' is scarcely needed. A glance at the list of the documents printed and a little testing of the accuracy of their editing will convince us that the volume will be found indispensable by students. The book opens with the British Signatories at the Council at Arles, 314 A.D., and finishes with the Act of Settlement, 1700. Between these dates 124 documents are given, carefully dated, with a running analysis of their contents in the margin, and a short historical note prefixed to each. Latin and French documents are translated, and the spelling of the English ones is modernised. The translation is executed with admirable scholarship, and the editing is in every way satisfactory.'

DAILY CHRONICLE.—"Students of the English Constitution as well as students of Church History will find this volume a valuable aid to their researches."

SCOTTISH GUARDIAN.—"There is no book in existence that contains so much original material likely to prove valuable to those who wish to investigate ritual or historical questions affecting the English Church."

Holy Communion—

THE COMMUNION SERVICE FROM THE BOOK OF COMMON PRAYER, with Select Readings from the Writings of the Rev. F. D. MAURICE. Edited by Bishop COLENSO. 6th Edition. 16mo. 2s. 6d.

FIRST COMMUNION, with Prayers and Devotions for the newly Confirmed. By Rev. Canon MACLEAR. 32mo. 6d.

A MANUAL OF INSTRUCTION FOR CONFIRMATION AND FIRST COMMUNION, with Prayers and Devotions. By the same. 32mo. 2s.

Liturgy—

A COMPANION TO THE LECTIONARY. By Rev. W. BENHAM, B.D. Crown 8vo. 4s. 6d.

AN INTRODUCTION TO THE CREEDS. By Rev. Canon MACLEAR. Pott 8vo. 3s. 6d.

CHURCH QUARTERLY REVIEW.—"Mr. Maclear's text-books of Bible history are so well known that to praise them is unnecessary. He has now added to them *An Introduction to the Creeds*, which we do not hesitate to call admirable. The book consists, first, of an historical introduction, occupying 53 pages, then an exposition of the twelve articles of the Creed extending to page 299, an appendix containing the texts of a considerable number of Creeds, and lastly, three indices which, as far as we have tested them, we must pronounce very good. . . . We may add that we know already that the book has been used with great advantage in ordinary parochial work."

AN INTRODUCTION TO THE ARTICLES OF THE CHURCH OF ENGLAND. By Rev. G. F. MACLEAR, D.D., and Rev. W. W. WILLIAMS. Crown 8vo. 10s. 6d.

The BISHOP OF SALISBURY at the Church Congress, spoke of this as "a book which will doubtless have, as it deserves, large circulation."

ST. JAMES'S GAZETTE.—"Theological students and others will find this comprehensive yet concise volume most valuable."

GLASGOW HERALD.—"A valuable addition to the well-known series of Theological Manuals published by Messrs. Macmillan."

CHURCH TIMES.—"Those who are in any way responsible for the training of candidates for Holy Orders must often have felt the want of such a book as Dr. Maclear, with the assistance of his colleague, Mr. Williams, has just published."

Liturgy—*continued.*

A HISTORY OF THE BOOK OF COMMON PRAYER. By Rev. F. PROCTER. 18th Edition. Crown 8vo. 10s. 6d.

CHURCH QUARTERLY REVIEW.—"We are glad to see that Mr. Procter's *History of the Book of Common Prayer* still retains its hold on public favour, and more especially we may presume on that of candidates for theological examinations. That it too has been carefully revised and added to by its venerable and highly respected author, may be inferred from the fact that the present edition numbers 483 pages (exclusive of the Appendix), as against the 453 pages of the 13th edition (1876)."

AN ELEMENTARY INTRODUCTION TO THE BOOK OF COMMON PRAYER. By Rev. F. PROCTER and Rev. Canon MACLEAR. Pott 8vo. 2s. 6d.

TWELVE DISCOURSES ON SUBJECTS CONNECTED WITH THE LITURGY AND WORSHIP OF THE CHURCH OF ENGLAND. By Very Rev. C. J. VAUGHAN. 4th Edition. Fcap. 8vo. 6s.

Historical and Biographical—

THE ECCLESIASTICAL EXPANSION OF ENGLAND IN THE GROWTH OF THE ANGLICAN COMMUNION. Hulsean Lectures, 1894-95. By ALFRED BARRY, D.D., D.C.L., formerly Bishop of Sydney and Primate of Australia and Tasmania. Crown 8vo. 6s.

The author's preface says : " The one object of these lectures—delivered on the Hulsean Foundation in 1894-95—is to make some slight contribution to that awakening of interest in the extraordinary religious mission of England which seems happily characteristic of the present time."

DAILY NEWS.—"These lectures are particularly interesting as containing the case for the Christian missions at a time when there is a disposition to attack them in some quarters."

LIVES OF THE ARCHBISHOPS OF CANTERBURY. From St. Augustine to Juxon. By the Very Rev. WALTER FARQUHAR HOOK, D.D., Dean of Chichester. Demy 8vo. The volumes sold separately as follows :—Vol. I., 15s. ; Vol. II., 15s. ; Vol. V., 15s. ; Vols. VI. and VII., 30s. ; Vol. VIII., 15s. ; Vol. X., 15s. ; Vol. XI., 15s. ; Vol. XII., 15s.

ATHENÆUM.—"The most impartial, the most instructive, and the most interesting of histories."

THE LIFE AND LETTERS OF THE VERY REV. WALTER FARQUHAR HOOK, D.D. By the Very Rev. W. R. W. STEPHENS, F.S.A., Dean of Winchester. Crown 8vo. 7th Edition. With Portrait. 6s.

LIFE AND LETTERS OF ARCHBISHOP BENSON. By his SON. Two Vols. 8vo. 36s. net.

LIFE AND LETTERS OF AMBROSE PHILLIPPS DE LISLE. By E. S. PURCELL. Two Vols. 8vo. 25s. net.

THE OXFORD MOVEMENT. Twelve Years, 1833-45. By DEAN CHURCH. Globe 8vo. 5s.

Historical and Biographical—*continued.*

THE LIFE AND LETTERS OF R. W. CHURCH, late Dean of St. Paul's. Globe 8vo. 5s.

JAMES FRASER, SECOND BISHOP OF MANCHESTER. A Memoir. 1818-1885. By THOMAS HUGHES, Q.C. 2nd Edition. Crown 8vo. 6s.

LIFE AND LETTERS OF FENTON JOHN ANTHONY HORT, D.D., D.C.L., LL.D., sometime Hulsean Professor and Lady Margaret's Reader in Divinity in the University of Cambridge. By his Son, ARTHUR FENTON HORT, late Fellow of Trinity College, Cambridge. In two Vols. With Portrait. Ex. Cr. 8vo. 17s. net.

EXPOSITOR.—"It is only just to publish the life of a scholar at once so well known and so little known as Dr. Hort. . . . But all who appreciate his work wish to know more, and the two fascinating volumes edited by his son give us the information we seek. They reveal to us a man the very antipodes of a dry-as-dust pedant, a man with many interests and enthusiasms, a lover of the arts and of nature, an athlete and one of the founders of the Alpine Club, a man of restless mind but always at leisure for the demands of friendship, and finding his truest joy in his own home and family."

THE LIFE OF FREDERICK DENISON MAURICE. Chiefly told in his own letters. Edited by his Son, FREDERICK MAURICE. With Portraits. Two Vols. Crown 8vo. 16s.

MEMORIALS (PART I.) FAMILY AND PERSONAL, 1766-1865. By ROUNDELL, EARL OF SELBORNE. With Portraits and Illustrations. Two Vols. 8vo. 25s. net. (PART II.) PERSONAL AND POLITICAL, 1865-1895. Two Vols. 25s. net.

LIFE OF ARCHIBALD CAMPBELL TAIT, ARCHBISHOP OF CANTERBURY. By RANDALL THOMAS, Bishop of Rochester, and WILLIAM BENHAM, B.D., Hon. Canon of Canterbury. With Portraits. 3rd Edition. Two Vols. Crown 8vo. 10s. net.

LIFE AND LETTERS OF WILLIAM JOHN BUTLER, late Dean of Lincoln, sometime Vicar of Wantage. 8vo. 12s. 6d. net.

TIMES.—"We have a graphic picture of a strong personality, and the example of a useful and laborious life. . . . Well put together and exceedingly interesting to Churchmen."

IN THE COURT OF THE ARCHBISHOP OF CANTERBURY. Read and others *v.* The Lord Bishop of Lincoln. Judgment, Nov. 21, 1890. 2nd Edition. 8vo. 2s. net.

JOURNAL OF THEOLOGICAL STUDIES. Quarterly. 3s. net. (No. 1, October 1899).

CANTERBURY DIOCESAN GAZETTE. Monthly. 8vo. 2d.

JEWISH QUARTERLY REVIEW. Edited by I. ABRAHAMS and C. G. MONTEFIORE. Demy 8vo. 3s. 6d. Vols. 1-7, 12s. 6d. each. Vol. 8 onwards, 15s. each. (Annual Subscription, 11s.)

Devotional Books

Cornish (J. F.)—WEEK BY WEEK. Fcap. 8vo. 3s. 6d.

SPECTATOR.—"They are very terse and excellent verses, generally on the subject of either the Epistle or Gospel for the day, and are put with the kind of practical vigour which arrests attention and compels the conscience to face boldly some leading thought in the passage selected."

SATURDAY REVIEW.—"The studied simplicity of Mr. Cornish's verse is altogether opposed to what most hymn-writers consider to be poetry. Nor is this the only merit of his unpretentious volume. There is a tonic character in the exhortation and admonition that characterise the hymns, and the prevailing sentiment is thoroughly manly and rousing."

Eastlake (Lady).—FELLOWSHIP: LETTERS ADDRESSED TO MY SISTER-MOURNERS. Crown 8vo. 2s. 6d.

ATHENÆUM.—"Tender and unobtrusive, and the author thoroughly realises the sorrow of those she addresses ; it may soothe mourning readers, and can by no means aggravate or jar upon their feelings."
CONTEMPORARY REVIEW.—"A very touching and at the same time a very sensible book. It breathes throughout the truest Christian spirit."
NONCONFORMIST.—"A beautiful little volume, written with genuine feeling, good taste, and a right appreciation of the teaching of Scripture relative to sorrow and suffering."

IMITATIO CHRISTI, LIBRI IV. Printed in Borders after Holbein, Dürer, and other old Masters, containing Dances of Death, Acts of Mercy, Emblems, etc. Crown 8vo. 7s. 6d.

Keble (J.)—THE CHRISTIAN YEAR. Edited by C. M. YONGE. Pott 8vo. 2s. 6d. net.

Kingsley (Charles). — OUT OF THE DEEP: WORDS FOR THE SORROWFUL. From the writings of CHARLES KINGSLEY. Extra fcap. 8vo. 3s. 6d.

DAILY THOUGHTS. Selected from the Writings of CHARLES KINGSLEY. By his Wife. Crown 8vo. 6s.

FROM DEATH TO LIFE. Fragments of Teaching to a Village Congregation. With Letters on the "Life after Death." Edited by his Wife. Fcap. 8vo. 2s. 6d.

Maclear (Rev. Canon).—A MANUAL OF INSTRUCTION FOR CONFIRMATION AND FIRST COMMUNION, WITH PRAYERS AND DEVOTIONS. 32mo. 2s.

THE HOUR OF SORROW ; OR, THE OFFICE FOR THE BURIAL OF THE DEAD. 32mo. 2s.

Maurice (Frederick Denison).—LESSONS OF HOPE. Readings from the Works of F. D. MAURICE. Selected by Rev. J. LL. DAVIES, M.A. Crown 8vo. 5s.

THE COMMUNION SERVICE. From the Book of Common Prayer, with select readings from the writings of the Rev. F. D. MAURICE, M.A. Edited by the Rev. JOHN WILLIAM COLENSO, D.D., Lord Bishop of Natal. 16mo. 2s. 6d.

THE WORSHIP OF GOD, AND FELLOWSHIP AMONG MEN. By FREDERICK DENISON MAURICE and others. Fcap. 8vo. 3s. 6d.

RAYS OF SUNLIGHT FOR DARK DAYS. With a Preface by Very Rev. C. J. VAUGHAN, D.D. New Edition. Pott 8vo. 3s. 6d.

Welby-Gregory (The Hon. Lady).—LINKS AND CLUES. 2nd Edition. Crown 8vo. 6s.

Westcott (Rt. Rev. B. F., Bishop of Durham).—THOUGHTS ON REVELATION AND LIFE. Selections from the Writings of Bishop WESTCOTT. Edited by Rev. S. PHILLIPS. Crown 8vo. 6s.

The Fathers

INDEX OF NOTEWORTHY WORDS AND PHRASES FOUND IN THE CLEMENTINE WRITINGS, COMMONLY CALLED THE HOMILIES OF CLEMENT. 8vo. 5s.

Benson (Archbishop).—CYPRIAN : HIS LIFE, HIS TIMES, HIS WORK. By the late EDWARD WHITE BENSON, Archbishop of Canterbury. 8vo. 21s. net.

TIMES.—" In all essential respects, in sobriety of judgment and temper, in sympathetic insight into character, in firm grasp of historical and ecclesiastical issues, in scholarship and erudition, the finished work is worthy of its subject and worthy of its author. . . . In its main outlines full of dramatic insight and force, and in its details full of the fruits of ripe learning, sound judgment, a lofty Christian temper, and a mature ecclesiastical wisdom."

SATURDAY REVIEW.—" On the whole, and with all reservations which can possibly be made, this weighty volume is a contribution to criticism and learning on which we can but congratulate the Anglican Church. We wish more of her bishops were capable or desirous of descending into that arena of pure intellect from which Dr. Benson returns with these posthumous laurels."

Gwatkin (H. M.) SELECTIONS FROM EARLY WRITERS ILLUSTRATIVE OF CHURCH HISTORY TO THE TIME OF CONSTANTINE. 2nd Edition. Crown 8vo. 4s. 6d. net.

Hort (F. J. A.) SIX LECTURES ON THE ANTE-NICENE FATHERS. Crown 8vo. 3s. 6d.

TIMES.—" Though certainly popular in form and treatment they are so in the best sense of the words, and they bear throughout the impress of the ripe scholarship the rare critical acumen, and the lofty ethical temper which marked all Dr. Hort's work.

Krüger.—HISTORY OF EARLY CHRISTIAN LITERATURE IN THE FIRST THREE CENTURIES. Crown 8vo. 8s. 6d. net.

Lightfoot (Bishop).—THE APOSTOLIC FATHERS. Part I. ST. CLEMENT OF ROME. Revised Texts, with Introductions, Notes, Dissertations, and Translations. 2 vols. 8vo. 32s.

THE APOSTOLIC FATHERS. Part II. ST. IGNATIUS to ST. POLYCARP. Revised Texts, with Introductions, Notes, Dissertations, and Translations. 3 vols. 2nd Edition. Demy 8vo. 48s.

THE APOSTOLIC FATHERS. Abridged Edition. With Short Introductions, Greek Text, and English Translation. 8vo. 16s.

MANCHESTER GUARDIAN.—" A conspectus of these early and intensely interesting Christian 'Documents' such as had not hitherto been attainable, and thereby renders a priceless service to all serious students of Christian theology, and even of Roman history."

NATIONAL OBSERVER.—" From the account of its contents, the student may appreciate the value of this last work of a great scholar, and its helpfulness as an aid to an intelligent examination of the earliest post-Apostolic writers. The texts are constructed on the most careful collation of all the existing sources. The introductions are brief, lucid, and thoroughly explanatory of the historical and critical questions related to the texts. The introduction to the *Didache*, and the translation of the 'Church Manual of Early Christianity,' are peculiarly interesting, as giving at once an admirable version of it, and the opinion of the first of English biblical critics on the latest discovery in patristic literature."

Hymnology

Bernard (T. D.)—THE SONGS OF THE HOLY NATIVITY. Being Studies of the Benedictus, Magnificat, Gloria in Excelsis, and Nunc Dimittis. Crown 8vo. 5s.

Brooke (S. A.)—CHRISTIAN HYMNS.   Edited and arranged.
Fcap. 8vo.   2s. 6d. net.

Selborne (Roundell, Earl of)—
THE BOOK OF PRAISE.   From the best English Hymn Writers.
Pott 8vo.   2s. 6d. net.
A HYMNAL.   Chiefly from *The Book of Praise*.   In various sizes.
B. Pott 8vo, larger type.   1s.—C. Same Edition, fine paper.   1s. 6d.—
An Edition with Music, Selected, Harmonised, and Composed by
JOHN HULLAH.   Pott 8vo.   3s. 6d.

Woods (M. A.) — HYMNS FOR SCHOOL WORSHIP.
Compiled by M. A. WOODS.   Pott 8vo.   1s. 6d.

Religious Teaching

Bell (Rev. G. C.)—RELIGIOUS TEACHING IN SECOND-
ARY SCHOOLS.   For Teachers and Parents.   Suggestions as
to Lessons on the Bible, Early Church History, Christian Evidences,
etc.   By the Rev. G. C. BELL, M.A., Master of Marlborough
College.   2nd Edition.   With new chapter on Christian Ethic.
Crown 8vo.   3s. 6d.

GUARDIAN.—"The hints and suggestions given are admirable, and, as far as Bible
teaching or instruction in 'Christian Evidences' is concerned, leave nothing to be desired.
Much time and thought has evidently been devoted by the writer to the difficulties which
confront the teacher of the Old Testament, and a large portion of the volume is taken up
with the consideration of this branch of his subject."

EDUCATIONAL REVIEW.—"For those teachers who are dissatisfied with the
existing state of things, and who are striving after something better, this little handbook
is invaluable.   Its aim is 'to map out a course of instruction on practical lines, and to
suggest methods and books which may point the way to a higher standpoint and a wider
horizon.'   For the carrying out of this, and also for his criticism of prevailing methods,
all teachers owe Mr. Bell a debt of gratitude; and if any are roused to a due sense of
their responsibility in this matter, he will feel that his book has not been written in vain."

Palmer (Florence U.)—ONE YEAR OF SUNDAY SCHOOL
LESSONS FOR YOUNG CHILDREN.   Adapted for use in
the Youngest Classes.   Pott 4to.   4s. 6d.

Sermons, Lectures, Addresses, and Theological Essays

(See also 'Bible,' 'Church of England,' 'Fathers')

Abbot (Francis)—
THE WAY OUT OF AGNOSTICISM : or, The Philosophy of
Free Religion.   Crown 8vo.   4s. 6d.

Abbott (Rev. E. A.)—
CAMBRIDGE SERMONS.   8vo.   6s.
OXFORD SERMONS.   8vo.   7s. 6d.
PHILOMYTHUS.   An Antidote against Credulity.   A discussion
of Cardinal Newman's Essay on Ecclesiastical Miracles.   2nd
Edition.   Crown 8vo.   3s. 6d.
THE SPIRIT ON THE WATERS, OR DIVINE EVOLU-
TION AS THE BASIS OF CHRISTIAN BELIEF.   8vo.
12s. 6d. net.

Abrahams (I.)—**Montefiore** (C. G.)—ASPECTS OF JUDAISM. Being Sixteen Sermons.   2nd Edition.   Fcap. 8vo.   3s. 6d. net.

TIMES.—"There is a great deal in them that does not appeal to Jews alone, for, especially in Mr. Montefiore's addresses, the doctrines advocated, with much charm of style, are often not by any means exclusively Jewish, but such as are shared and honoured by all who care for religion and morality as those terms are commonly understood in the western world."

GLASGOW HERALD.—"Both from the homiletic and what may be called the big-world point of view, this little volume is one of considerable interest."

Ainger (Rev. Alfred, Master of the Temple). — SERMONS PREACHED IN THE TEMPLE CHURCH.   Extra fcap. 8vo.   6s.

Askwith (E. H.).—THE CHRISTIAN CONCEPTION OF HOLINESS.   [*In the Press.*

Bather (Archdeacon).—ON SOME MINISTERIAL DUTIES, CATECHISING, PREACHING, ETC.   Edited, with a Preface, by Very Rev. C. J. VAUGHAN, D.D.   Fcap. 8vo.   4s. 6d.

Benson (Archbishop)—

BOY-LIFE : its Trial, its Strength, its Fulness.   Sundays in Wellington College, 1859-73.   4th Edition.   Crown 8vo.   6s.

CHRIST AND HIS TIMES.   Addressed to the Diocese of Canterbury in his Second Visitation.   Crown 8vo.   6s.

FISHERS OF MEN.   Addressed to the Diocese of Canterbury in his Third Visitation.   Crown 8vo.   6s.

GUARDIAN.—"There is plenty of plain speaking in the addresses before us, and they contain many wise and thoughtful counsels on subjects of the day."

TIMES.—"With keen insight and sagacious counsel, the Archbishop surveys the condition and prospects of the church."

ARCHBISHOP BENSON IN IRELAND.   A record of his Irish Sermons and Addresses.   Edited by J. H. BERNARD.   Crown 8vo.   3s. 6d.

PALL MALL GAZETTE.—"No words of mine could appreciate, or do justice to, the stately language and lofty thoughts of the late Primate ; they will appeal to every Churchman."

ADDRESSES ON THE ACTS OF THE APOSTLES.   8vo.
[*In the Press.*

Bernard (Canon).—THE SONGS OF THE HOLY NATIVITY CONSIDERED (1) AS RECORDED IN SCRIPTURE, (2) AS IN USE IN THE CHURCH.   Crown 8vo.   5s.

To use the words of its author, this book is offered "to readers of Scripture as expository of a distinct portion of the Holy Word ; to worshippers in the congregation as a devotional commentary on the hymns which they use ; to those keeping Christmas, as a contribution to the ever-welcome thoughts of that blessed season ; to all Christian people who, in the midst of the historical elaboration of Christianity, find it good to re-enter from time to time the clear atmosphere of its origin, and are fain in the heat of the day to recover some feeling of the freshness of dawn."

C

GLASGOW HERALD.—"He conveys much useful information in a scholarly way."

SCOTSMAN.—" Their meaning and their relationships, the reasons why the Church has adopted them, and many other kindred points, are touched upon in the book with so well-explained a learning and with so much insight that the book will be highly valued by those interested in its subject."

Brooke (Rev. Stopford A.)—SHORT SERMONS. Cr. 8vo. 6s.

Brooks (Phillips, late Bishop of Massachusetts)—

THE CANDLE OF THE LORD, and other Sermons. Crown 8vo. 6s.

SERMONS PREACHED IN ENGLISH CHURCHES. Crown 8vo. 6s.

TWENTY SERMONS. Crown 8vo. 6s.

THE LIGHT OF THE WORLD. Crown 8vo. 3s. 6d.

THE MYSTERY OF INIQUITY. Crown 8vo. 6s.

ESSAYS AND ADDRESSES, RELIGIOUS, LITERARY, AND SOCIAL. Edited by the Rev. JOHN COTTON BROOKS. Crown 8vo. 8s. 6d. net.

NEW STARTS IN LIFE, AND OTHER SERMONS. Crown 8vo. 6s.

WESTMINSTER GAZETTE.—"All characterised by that fervent piety, catholicity of spirit, and fine command of language for which the Bishop was famous.

Brunton (T. Lauder). — THE BIBLE AND SCIENCE. With Illustrations. Crown 8vo. 10s. 6d.

Campbell (Dr. John M'Leod)—

THE NATURE OF THE ATONEMENT. 6th Ed. Cr. 8vo. 6s.

REMINISCENCES AND REFLECTIONS. Edited with an Introductory Narrative, by his Son, DONALD CAMPBELL, M.A. Crown 8vo. 7s. 6d.

THOUGHTS ON REVELATION. 2nd Edition. Crown 8vo. 5s.

RESPONSIBILITY FOR THE GIFT OF ETERNAL LIFE. Compiled from Sermons preached at Row, in the years 1829-31. Crown 8vo. 5s.

Canterbury (Frederick, Archbishop of)—

SERMONS PREACHED IN THE CHAPEL OF RUGBY SCHOOL. Extra Fcap. 8vo. 4s. 6d.

SECOND SERIES. 3rd Ed. 6s.

THIRD SERIES. 4th Edition. 6s.

THE RELATIONS BETWEEN RELIGION AND SCIENCE. Bampton Lectures, 1884. 7th and Cheaper Ed. Cr. 8vo. 6s.

CHARGE DELIVERED AT HIS FIRST VISITATION. 8vo. Sewed. 1s. net.

(1) The Doctrine of the Eucharist ; (2) The Practice of Confession ; (3) Uniformity in Ceremonial ; (4) The Power of the Bishops.

Carpenter (W. Boyd, Bishop of Ripon)—

TRUTH IN TALE. Addresses, chiefly to Children. Crown 8vo.
4s. 6d.

THE PERMANENT ELEMENTS OF RELIGION : Bampton
Lectures, 1887. 2nd Edition. Crown 8vo. 6s.

TWILIGHT DREAMS. Crown 8vo. 4s. 6d.

LECTURES ON PREACHING. Crown 8vo. 3s. 6d. net.

TIMES.—" These *Lectures on Preaching*, delivered a year ago in the Divinity
School at Cambridge, are an admirable analysis of the intellectual, ethical, spiritual,
and rhetorical characteristics of the art of preaching. In six lectures the Bishop deals
successfully with the preacher and his training, with the sermon and its structure, with
the preacher and his age, and with the aim of the preacher. In each case he is practical,
suggestive, eminently stimulating, and often eloquent, not with the mere splendour of
rhetoric, but with the happy faculty of saying the right thing in well-chosen words."

SOME THOUGHTS ON CHRISTIAN REUNION. Being a
Charge to the Clergy. Crown 8vo. 3s. 6d. net.

TIMES.—" Dr. Boyd Carpenter treats this very difficult subject with moderation
and good sense, and with a clear-headed perception of the limits which inexorably cir-
cumscribe the natural aspirations of Christians of different churches and nationalities for
a more intimate communion and fellowship."
LEEDS MERCURY.—" He discusses with characteristic vigour and felicity the
claims which hinder reunion, and the true idea and scope of catholicity."

Cheetham (Archdeacon). — MYSTERIES, PAGAN AND
CHRISTIAN. Being the Hulsean Lectures for 1896. Crown
8vo. 5s.

Church (Dean)—

HUMAN LIFE AND ITS CONDITIONS. Crown 8vo. 6s.

THE GIFTS OF CIVILISATION, and other Sermons and Lectures.
2nd Edition. Crown 8vo. 7s. 6d.

DISCIPLINE OF THE CHRISTIAN CHARACTER, and other
Sermons. Crown 8vo. 4s. 6d.

ADVENT SERMONS. 1885. Crown 8vo. 4s. 6d.

VILLAGE SERMONS. Crown 8vo. 6s.

VILLAGE SERMONS. Second Series. Crown 8vo. 6s.

VILLAGE SERMONS. Third Series. Crown 8vo. 6s.

TIMES.—" In these sermons we see how a singularly gifted and cultivated mind was
able to communicate its thoughts on the highest subjects to those with whom it might
be supposed to have little in common. . . . His village sermons are not the by-work of
one whose interests were elsewhere in higher matters. They are the outcome of his
deepest interests and of the life of his choice. . . . These sermons are worth perusal, if
only to show what preaching, even to the humble and unlearned hearers, may be made
in really competent hands."

CATHEDRAL AND UNIVERSITY SERMONS. Crown 8vo. 6s.

PASCAL AND OTHER SERMONS. Crown 8vo. 6s.

TIMES.—" They are all eminently characteristic of one of the most saintly of modern
divines, and one of the most scholarly of modern men of letters."
SPECTATOR.—" Dean Church's seem to us the finest sermons published since
Newman's, even Dr. Liddon's rich and eloquent discourses not excepted,—and they
breathe more of the spirit of perfect peace than even Newman's. They cannot be called
High Church or Broad Church, much less Low Church sermons ; they are simply the
sermons of a good scholar, a great thinker, and a firm and serene Christian."

CLERGYMAN'S SELF - EXAMINATION CONCERNING THE APOSTLES' CREED. Extra fcap. 8vo. 1s. 6d.

A CONFESSION OF FAITH. By an UNORTHODOX BELIEVER. Fcap. 8vo. 3s. 6d.

GRAPHIC.—"The book not only abounds with spiritual charm and metaphysical insight, but it is an excellent specimen of good hard thinking and close reasoning, in which the reader will find plenty of capital exercise for the intellectual muscles."

Congreve (Rev. John).—HIGH HOPES AND PLEADINGS FOR A REASONABLE FAITH, NOBLER THOUGHTS, LARGER CHARITY. Crown 8vo. 5s.

Cooke (Josiah P.)—
THE CREDENTIALS OF SCIENCE, THE WARRANT OF FAITH. 8vo. 8s. 6d. net.

Curteis (Rev. G. H.)—THE SCIENTIFIC OBSTACLES TO CHRISTIAN BELIEF. The Boyle Lectures, 1884. Cr. 8vo. 6s.

Davidson (R. T., Bishop of Winchester)—A CHARGE DELIVERED TO THE CLERGY OF THE DIOCESE OF ROCHESTER, October 29, 30, 31, 1894. 8vo. Sewed. 2s. net.

A CHARGE DELIVERED TO THE CLERGY OF THE DIOCESE OF WINCHESTER, Sept. 28, 30, Oct. 2, 3, 4, and 5, 1899. 8vo. Sewed. 2s. 6d. net.

Davies (Rev. J. Llewelyn)—
THE GOSPEL AND MODERN LIFE. 2nd Edition, to which is added Morality according to the Sacrament of the Lord's Supper. Extra fcap. 8vo. 6s.

SOCIAL QUESTIONS FROM THE POINT OF VIEW OF CHRISTIAN THEOLOGY. 2nd Edition. Crown 8vo. 6s.

WARNINGS AGAINST SUPERSTITION. Extra fcap. 8vo. 2s. 6d.

THE CHRISTIAN CALLING. Extra fcap. 8vo. 6s.

BAPTISM, CONFIRMATION, AND THE LORD'S SUPPER, as interpreted by their Outward Signs. Three Addresses. New Edition. Pott 8vo. 1s.

ORDER AND GROWTH AS INVOLVED IN THE SPIRITUAL CONSTITUTION OF HUMAN SOCIETY. Crown 8vo. 3s. 6d.

GLASGOW HERALD.—"This is a wise and suggestive book, touching upon many of the more interesting questions of the present day. . . . A book as full of hope as it is of ability."

MANCHESTER GUARDIAN.—"He says what he means, but never more than he means ; and hence his words carry weight with many to whom the ordinary sermon would appeal in vain. . . . The whole book is well worth study."

ABERDEEN DAILY FREE PRESS.—"An able discussion of the true basis and aim of social progress."

SCOTSMAN.—"Thoughtful and suggestive."

SPIRITUAL APPREHENSION : Sermons and Papers. Crown 8vo. 6s.

Davies (W.)—THE PILGRIM OF THE INFINITE. A Discourse addressed to Advanced Religious Thinkers on Christian Lines. By WM. DAVIES. Fcap. 8vo. 3s. 6d.

CHRISTIAN WORLD.—"We hail this work as one which in an age of much mental unrest sounds a note of faith which appeals confidently to the highest intellect, inasmuch as it springs out of the clearest intuitions of the human spirit."

MANCHESTER GUARDIAN.—"The little volume contains much that is attractive, much that is wise as well as impressive."

Ellerton (Rev. John).—THE HOLIEST MANHOOD, AND ITS LESSONS FOR BUSY LIVES. Crown 8vo. 6s.

English Theological Library. Edited by Rev. FREDERIC RELTON. With General Introduction by the late LORD BISHOP OF LONDON. A Series of Texts Annotated for the Use of Students, Candidates for Ordination, etc. 8vo.

    I. HOOKER'S ECCLESIASTICAL POLITY, Book V., Edited by Rev. Ronald E. Bayne.   [*In the Press.*

    II. LAW'S SERIOUS CALL, Edited by Rev. Canon J. H. Overton. 8s. 6d. net.

DAILY NEWS.—"A well-executed reprint. . . . Canon Overton's notes are not numerous, and are as a rule very interesting and useful."

CAMBRIDGE REVIEW.—"A welcome reprint. . . . All that it should be in paper and appearance, and the reputation of the editor is a guarantee for the accuracy and fairness of the notes."

    III. WILSON'S MAXIMS, Edited by Rev. F. Relton. 5s. 6d. net.

GUARDIAN.—"Many readers will feel grateful to Mr. Relton for this edition of Bishop Wilson's 'Maxims.' . . . Mr. Relton's edition will be found well worth possessing : it is pleasant to the eye, and bears legible marks of industry and study."

EXPOSITORY TIMES.—"In an introduction of some twenty pages, he tells us all we need to know of Bishop Wilson and of his maxims. Then he gives us the maxims themselves in most perfect form, and schools himself to add at the bottom of the page such notes as are absolutely necessary to their understanding, and nothing more."

[*Other volumes are in preparation.*

EVIL AND EVOLUTION. An attempt to turn the Light of Modern Science on to the Ancient Mystery of Evil. By the author of *The Social Horizon.* Crown 8vo. 3s. 6d. net.

EXPOSITORY TIMES.—"The book is well worth the interest it is almost certain to excite."

CHURCH TIMES.—"There can be no question about the courage or the keen logic and the lucid style of this fascinating treatment of a problem which is of pathetic interest to all of us. . . . It deserves to be studied by all, and no one who reads it can fail to be struck by it."

FAITH AND CONDUCT : An Essay on Verifiable Religion. Crown 8vo. 7s. 6d.

Farrar (Very Rev. F. W., Dean of Canterbury)—

    THE HISTORY OF INTERPRETATION. Being the Bampton Lectures, 1885. 8vo. 16s.

    Collected Edition of the Sermons, etc. Crown 8vo. 3s. 6d. each.

    SEEKERS AFTER GOD.

    ETERNAL HOPE. Sermons Preached in Westminster Abbey.

    THE FALL OF MAN, and other Sermons.

    THE WITNESS OF HISTORY TO CHRIST. Hulsean Lectures.

    THE SILENCE AND VOICES OF GOD.

    IN THE DAYS OF THY YOUTH. Sermons on Practical Subjects.

Farrar (Very Rev. F. W., Dean of Canterbury)—*continued*.
  SAINTLY WORKERS. Five Lenten Lectures.
  EPHPHATHA : or, The Amelioration of the World.
  MERCY AND JUDGMENT. A few words on Christian Eschatology.
  SERMONS AND ADDRESSES delivered in America.

Fiske (John).—MAN'S DESTINY VIEWED IN THE LIGHT
  OF HIS ORIGIN. Crown 8vo. 3s. 6d.

Foxell (W. J.)—GOD'S GARDEN : Sunday Talks with Boys.
  With an Introduction by Dean FARRAR. Globe 8vo. 3s. 6d.

  SPEAKER.—"Deals with obvious problems of faith and conduct in a strain of
  vigorous simplicity, and with an evident knowledge of the needs, the moods, the difficulties of boy-life. It is the kind of book which instils lessons of courage, trust, patience,
  and forbearance ; and does so quite as much by example as by precept."

  IN A PLAIN PATH. Addresses to Boys. Globe 8vo. 3s. 6d.

  SPEAKER.—"He handles with admirable vigour, and real discernment of a boy's
  difficulties, such high themes as the use of time, noble revenge, the true gentleman, the
  noblest victory, and progress through failure. There is nothing childish in the method of
  treatment, and yet we feel sure that a man who spoke to a congregation of lads in this
  fashion would not talk over the head of the youngest, and yet find his way to the hearts
  of those who are just passing from the restraints of school to the responsibilities of life."

Fraser (Bishop). — UNIVERSITY SERMONS. Edited by
  Rev. JOHN W. DIGGLE. Crown 8vo. 6s.

Furse (Archdeacon).—A NATIONAL CHURCH. 8vo. 6d.

Grane (W. L.)—THE WORD AND THE WAY : or, The
  Light of the Ages on the Path of To-Day. Crown 8vo. 6s.

  HARD SAYINGS OF JESUS CHRIST. A Study in the Mind
  and Method of the Master. Cr. 8vo. 5s.

Green (S. G.)—THE CHRISTIAN CREED AND THE
  CREEDS OF CHRISTENDOM. Seven Lectures delivered
  in 1898 at Regent's Park College. Crown 8vo. 6s.

Harcourt (Sir W. V.).—LAWLESSNESS IN THE NATIONAL
  CHURCH. 8vo. Sewed. 1s. net.

Hardwick (Archdeacon). — CHRIST AND OTHER MAS-
  TERS. 6th Edition. Crown 8vo. 10s. 6d.

Hare (Julius Charles)—
  THE MISSION OF THE COMFORTER. New Edition. Edited
  by Dean PLUMPTRE. Crown 8vo. 7s. 6d.

Harris (Rev. G. C.) — SERMONS. With a Memoir by
  CHARLOTTE M. YONGE, and Portrait. Extra fcap. 8vo. 6s.

Hort (F. J. A.)—THE WAY, THE TRUTH, THE LIFE.
  Hulsean Lectures, 1871. Crown 8vo. 6s.

  CAMBRIDGE REVIEW.—"Only to few is it given to scan the wide fields of truth
  with clear vision of near and far alike. To what an extraordinary degree the late Dr.
  Hort possessed this power is shown by the Hulsean Lectures just published. They carry
  us in the most wonderful way to the very centre of the Christian system ; no aspect of
  truth, no part of the world, seems to be left out of view ; while in every page we recognise the gathered fruits of a rare scholarship in the service of an unwearying thought."

JUDAISTIC CHRISTIANITY. Crown 8vo. 6s.

SCOTSMAN.—"The great merit of Dr. Hort's lectures is that succinctly and yet fully, and in a clear and interesting and suggestive manner, they give us not only his own opinions, but whatever of worth has been advanced on the subject."

GLASGOW HERALD.—"Will receive a respectful welcome at the hands of all biblical scholars. . . . A model of exact and patient scholarship, controlled by robust English sagacity, and it is safe to say that it will take a high place in the literature of the subject."

VILLAGE SERMONS. Crown 8vo. 6s.

Selected from the Sermons preached by Professor HORT to his village congregation at St. Ippolyt's, and including a series of Sermons dealing in a broad and suggestive way with the successive books of the Bible, from Genesis to Revelations.

CAMBRIDGE AND OTHER SERMONS. Crown 8vo. 6s.

Hughes (T.)—THE MANLINESS OF CHRIST. 2nd Ed. Fcap. 8vo. 3s. 6d.

GLOBE.—"*The Manliness of Christ* is a species of lay sermon such as Judge Hughes is well qualified to deliver, seeing that manliness of thought and feeling has been the prevailing characteristic of all his literary products."
BRITISH WEEKLY.—"A new edition of a strong book."

Hutton (R. H.)—

ESSAYS ON SOME OF THE MODERN GUIDES OF ENG- LISH THOUGHT IN MATTERS OF FAITH. Globe 8vo. 5s.

THEOLOGICAL ESSAYS. Globe 8vo. 5s.

ASPECTS OF RELIGIOUS AND SCIENTIFIC THOUGHT. Selected from the *Spectator*, and edited by E. M. ROSCOE. Globe 8vo. 5s.

Hyde (W. DE W.)—OUTLINES OF SOCIAL THEOLOGY. Crown 8vo. 6s.

Dr. Hyde thus describes the object of his book : "This little book aims to point out the logical relations in which the doctrines of theology will stand to each other when the time shall come again for seeing Christian truth in the light of reason and Christian life as the embodiment of love."

PRACTICAL IDEALISM. Globe 8vo. 5s. net.

Illingworth (Rev. J. R.)—SERMONS PREACHED IN A COLLEGE CHAPEL. Crown 8vo. 5s.

UNIVERSITY AND CATHEDRAL SERMONS. Crown 8vo. 5s.

PERSONALITY, DIVINE AND HUMAN. Bampton Lectures, 1894. Crown 8vo. 6s.

TIMES.—"Will take high rank among the rare theological masterpieces produced by that celebrated foundation."
EXPOSITOR.—"It is difficult to convey an adequate impression of the freshness and strength of the whole argument. . . . It is a book which no one can be satisfied with reading once ; it is to be studied."

DIVINE IMMANENCE. An Essay on the Spiritual Significance of Matter. New Edition. Cr. 8vo. 6s.

GUARDIAN.—"Altogether, we have rarely read a book of such philosophical earnestness in construing the Christian view of existence in terms of the thought and knowledge of these days, nor one more likely to bring home the knowledge of a Saviour to the modern man."

Jacob (Rev. J. A.) — BUILDING IN SILENCE, and other Sermons. Extra fcap. 8vo. 6s.

James (Rev. Herbert).—THE COUNTRY CLERGYMAN AND HIS WORK. Crown 8vo. 6s.

RECORD.—"The volume is one which should be in the hands of every candidate for Holy Orders and of every clergyman who is wishing to learn."

Jayne (F. J., Bishop of Chester).—THE VISITATION OF THE KINGDOM OF GOD. A Charge delivered to the Clergy of the Diocese at his third Visitation, October 29, 1896. 6d.

Jellett (Rev. Dr.)—

THE ELDER SON, and other Sermons. Crown 8vo. 6s.

Joceline (E.)—THE MOTHER'S LEGACIE TO HER UN-BORN CHILD. Cr. 16mo. 4s. 6d.

Jones (Jenkin Lloyd).—JESS: BITS OF WAYSIDE GOSPEL. Cr. 8vo. 6s.

Kellogg (Rev. S. H.)—THE LIGHT OF ASIA AND THE LIGHT OF THE WORLD. Crown 8vo. 7s. 6d.

THE GENESIS AND GROWTH OF RELIGION. Cr. 8vo. 6s.

SCOTSMAN.—"Full of matter of an important kind, set forth with praiseworthy conciseness, and at the same time with admirable lucidity. . . . Dr. Kellogg has done the work allotted to him with great ability, and everywhere manifests a competent acquaintance with the subject with which he deals."

Kingsley (Charles)—

VILLAGE AND TOWN AND COUNTRY SERMONS. Crown 8vo. 3s. 6d.

THE WATER OF LIFE, and other Sermons. Crown 8vo. 3s. 6d.

SERMONS ON NATIONAL SUBJECTS, AND THE KING OF THE EARTH. Crown 8vo. 3s. 6d.

SERMONS FOR THE TIMES. Crown 8vo. 3s. 6d.

GOOD NEWS OF GOD. Crown 8vo. 3s. 6d.

THE GOSPEL OF THE PENTATEUCH, AND DAVID. Crown 8vo. 3s. 6d.

DISCIPLINE, and other Sermons. Crown 8vo. 3s. 6d.

WESTMINSTER SERMONS. Crown 8vo. 3s. 6d.

ALL SAINTS' DAY, and other Sermons. Crown 8vo. 3s. 6d.

ACADEMY.—"We can imagine nothing more appropriate than this edition for a public, a school, or even a village library."

Kirkpatrick (Prof. A. F.)—THE DIVINE LIBRARY OF THE OLD TESTAMENT. Its Origin, Preservation, Inspiration, and Permanent Value. Crown 8vo. 3s. net.

THE DOCTRINE OF THE PROPHETS. Warburtonian Lectures 1886-1890. 2nd Edition. Crown 8vo. 6s.

Knight (W. A.)—ASPECTS OF THEISM.   8vo.   8s. 6d.

LETTERS FROM HELL.   Newly translated from the Danish.   With an Introduction by Dr. GEORGE MACDONALD.   Twenty-eighth Thousand.   Crown 8vo.   2s. 6d.

Lightfoot (Bishop)—

LEADERS IN THE NORTHERN CHURCH : Sermons Preached in the Diocese of Durham.   2nd Edition.   Crown 8vo.   6s.

ORDINATION ADDRESSES AND COUNSELS TO CLERGY.   Crown 8vo.   6s.

CAMBRIDGE SERMONS.   Crown 8vo.   6s.

SERMONS PREACHED IN ST. PAUL'S CATHEDRAL.   Crown 8vo.   6s.

SERMONS PREACHED ON SPECIAL OCCASIONS.   Crown 8vo.   6s.

A CHARGE DELIVERED TO THE CLERGY OF THE DIOCESE OF DURHAM, 25th Nov. 1886.   Demy 8vo.   2s.

ESSAYS ON THE WORK ENTITLED "Supernatural Religion."   8vo.   10s. 6d.

DISSERTATIONS ON THE APOSTOLIC AGE.   8vo.   14s.

BIBLICAL ESSAYS.   8vo.   12s.

TIMES.—"As representing all that is now available of the Bishop's profound learning and consummate scholarship for the illustration of his great subject, the present volume and its successor will be warmly welcomed by all students of theology."

Macmillan (Rev. Hugh)—

BIBLE TEACHINGS IN NATURE.   15th Ed.   Globe 8vo.   6s.

THE TRUE VINE ; OR, THE ANALOGIES OF OUR LORD'S ALLEGORY.   5th Edition.   Globe 8vo.   6s.

THE MINISTRY OF NATURE.   8th Edition.   Globe 8vo.   6s.

THE SABBATH OF THE FIELDS.   6th Edition.   Globe 8vo.   6s.

THE MARRIAGE IN CANA.   Globe 8vo.   6s.

TWO WORLDS ARE OURS.   3rd Edition.   Globe 8vo.   6s.

THE OLIVE LEAF.   Globe 8vo.   6s.

THE GATE BEAUTIFUL AND OTHER BIBLE TEACHINGS FOR THE YOUNG.   Crown 8vo.   3s. 6d.

SPEAKER.—"These addresses are, in fact, models of their kind—wise, reverent, and not less imaginative than practical ; they abound in choice and apposite anecdotes and illustrations, and possess distinct literary merit."

DAILY CHRONICLE.—"The poetic touch that beautifies all Dr. Macmillan's writing is fresh in every one of these charming addresses.   The volume is sure to meet with cordial appreciation far beyond the sphere of its origin."

GLEANINGS IN HOLY FIELDS.   Crown 8vo.   3s. 6d.

Mahaffy (Rev. Prof.)—THE DECAY OF MODERN PREACHING : AN ESSAY.   Crown 8vo.   3s. 6d.

Marshall (H. Rutgers)—INSTINCT AND REASON: An Essay with some Special Study of the Nature of Religion. 8vo. 12s. 6d. net.

Mathews (S.).—THE SOCIAL TEACHING OF JESUS. AN ESSAY IN CHRISTIAN SOCIOLOGY. Crown 8vo. 6s.

Maurice (Frederick Denison)—

THE KINGDOM OF CHRIST. 3rd Ed. 2 Vols. Cr. 8vo. 12s.

THE CONSCIENCE. Lectures on Casuistry. 3rd Ed. Cr. 8vo. 4s. 6d.

DIALOGUES ON FAMILY WORSHIP. Crown 8vo. 4s. 6d.

THE DOCTRINE OF SACRIFICE DEDUCED FROM THE SCRIPTURES. 2nd Edition. Crown 8vo. 6s.

THE RELIGIONS OF THE WORLD. 6th Edition. Cr. 8vo. 4s. 6d.

ON THE SABBATH DAY; THE CHARACTER OF THE WARRIOR; AND ON THE INTERPRETATION OF HISTORY. Fcap. 8vo. 2s. 6d.

LEARNING AND WORKING. Crown 8vo. 4s. 6d.

THE LORD'S PRAYER, THE CREED, AND THE COMMANDMENTS. Pott 8vo. 1s.

Collected Works. Crown 8vo. 3s. 6d. each.

SERMONS PREACHED IN LINCOLN'S INN CHAPEL. In Six Volumes. 3s. 6d. each.

CHRISTMAS DAY AND OTHER SERMONS.

THEOLOGICAL ESSAYS.

PROPHETS AND KINGS.

PATRIARCHS AND LAWGIVERS.

THE GOSPEL OF THE KINGDOM OF HEAVEN.

GOSPEL OF ST. JOHN.

EPISTLE OF ST. JOHN.

FRIENDSHIP OF BOOKS.

PRAYER BOOK AND LORD'S PRAYER.

THE DOCTRINE OF SACRIFICE.

THE ACTS OF THE APOSTLES.

CHURCH TIMES.—"There is probably no writer of the present century to whom the English Church owes a deeper debt of gratitude. . . . Probably he did more to stop the stream of converts to Romanism which followed the secession of Newman than any other individual, by teaching English Churchmen to think out the reasonableness of their position."

SPEAKER.—"These sermons are marked in a conspicuous degree by high thinking and plain statement."

TIMES.—"A volume of sermons for which the memory of Maurice's unique personal influence ought to secure a cordial reception."

SCOTSMAN.—"They appear in a volume uniform with the recent collective edition of Maurice's works, and will be welcome to the many readers to whom that edition has brought home the teaching of the most popular among modern English divines."

Milligan (Rev. Prof. W.)—THE RESURRECTION OF OUR LORD. Fourth Edition. Crown 8vo. 5s.

SPECTATOR.—"The argument is put with brevity and force by Dr. Milligan, and every page bears witness that he has mastered the literature of the subject, and has made a special study of the more recent discussions on this aspect of the question. . . . The remaining lectures are more theological. They abound in striking views, in fresh and vigorous exegesis, and manifest a keen apprehension of the bearing of the fact of the Resurrection on many important questions of theology. The notes are able and scholarly, and elucidate the teaching of the text."

THE ASCENSION AND HEAVENLY PRIESTHOOD OF OUR LORD. *Baird Lectures*, 1891. Crown 8vo. 7s. 6d.

Moorhouse (J., Bishop of Manchester)—

JACOB : Three Sermons. Extra fcap. 8vo. 3s. 6d.

THE TEACHING OF CHRIST. Its Conditions, Secret, and Results. Crown 8vo. 3s. net.

CHURCH WORK : ITS MEANS AND METHODS. Crown 8vo. 3s. net.

CHURCH TIMES.—"It may almost be said to mark an epoch, and to inaugurate a new era in the history of Episcopal visitation."
TIMES.—"A series of diocesan addresses, full of practical counsel, by one of the most active and sagacious of modern prelates."
GLOBE.—"Throughout the volume we note the presence of the wisdom that comes from long and varied experience, from sympathy, and from the possession of a fair and tolerant mind."
MANCHESTER GUARDIAN.—"Full of interest and instruction for all who take an interest in social and moral, to say nothing of ecclesiastical, reforms, and deserves to find careful students far beyond the limits of those to whom it was originally addressed."

Myers (F. W. H.)—SCIENCE AND A FUTURE LIFE. Gl. 8vo. 5s.

Nash (H. S.).—GENESIS OF THE SOCIAL CONSCIENCE. THE RELATION BETWEEN THE ESTABLISHMENT OF CHRISTIANITY IN EUROPE AND THE SOCIAL QUESTION. Crown 8vo. 6s.
SCOTSMAN.—"The book is eloquently, and at times brilliantly, written. . . . But few readers could go through it without being inspired by its clever and animated handling of philosophical ideas."
MANCHESTER GUARDIAN.—"An interesting and suggestive little book."

Pattison (Mark).—SERMONS. Crown 8vo. 6s.

PHILOCHRISTUS. Memoirs of a Disciple of the Lord. 3rd Ed. 8vo. 12s.

Pike (G. R.)—THE DIVINE DRAMA THE DIVINE MANIFESTATION OF GOD IN THE UNIVERSE. Crown 8vo. 6s.

Plumptre (Dean). — MOVEMENTS IN RELIGIOUS THOUGHT. Fcap. 8vo. 3s. 6d.

Reichel (Bishop).—SERMONS. With a Memoir. Crown 8vo. 6s.

Rendall (Rev. F.)—THE THEOLOGY OF THE HEBREW CHRISTIANS. Crown 8vo. 5s.

Ridding (George, Bishop of Southwell).—THE REVEL AND THE BATTLE. Crown 8vo. 6s.

TIMES.—"Singularly well worth reading."

MANCHESTER GUARDIAN.—"Marked by dignity and force."

Robinson (Prebendary H. G.)—MAN IN THE IMAGE OF GOD, and other Sermons. Crown 8vo. 7s. 6d.

Robinson (Canon J. Armitage)—HOLY GROUND. Three Sermons on the War in South Africa. 8vo. Sewed. 1s. net.

Seeley (Sir J. R.)—ECCE HOMO : A Survey of the Life and Work of Jesus Christ. Globe 8vo. 5s.

NATURAL RELIGION. Globe 8vo. 5s.

ATHENÆUM.—" If it be the function of a genius to interpret the age to itself, this is a work of genius. It gives articulate expression to the higher strivings of the time. It puts plainly the problem of these latter days, and so far contributes to its solution ; a positive solution it scarcely claims to supply. No such important contribution to the question of the time has been published in England since the appearance in 1866 of *Ecce Homo.* . . . The author is a teacher whose words it is well to listen to ; his words are wise but sad ; it has not been given him to fire them with faith, but only to light them with reason. His readers may at least thank him for the intellectual illumination, if they cannot owe him gratitude for any added favour. . . . A book which we assume will be read by most thinking Englishmen."

MANCHESTER GUARDIAN.—"The present issue is a compact, handy, well-printed edition of a thoughtful and remarkable book."

Selborne (Roundell, Earl of).—LETTERS TO HIS SON ON RELIGION. Globe 8vo. 3s. 6d.

THE CATHOLIC AND APOSTOLIC CHURCH. Globe 8vo. 3s. 6d.

Service (Rev. John).—SERMONS. With Portrait. Crown 8vo. 6s.

Stanley (Dean)—

THE NATIONAL THANKSGIVING. Sermons preached in Westminster Abbey. 2nd Edition. Crown 8vo. 2s. 6d.

Stewart (Prof. Balfour) and **Tait** (Prof. P. G.)—THE UNSEEN UNIVERSE; OR, PHYSICAL SPECULATIONS ON A FUTURE STATE. 15th Edition. Crown 8vo. 6s.

Stubbs (Dean)—

CHRISTUS IMPERATOR. A Series of Lecture-Sermons on the Universal Empire of Christianity. Edited by Very Rev. C. W. STUBBS, D.D., Dean of Ely. Crown 8vo. 6s.

The discourses included in this volume were delivered in 1893 in the Chapel-of-Ease to the Parish Church of Wavertree—at that time the centre of much excellent social work done by Mr. Stubbs, who had not

yet been promoted to the Deanery of Ely. The following are the subjects
and the preachers :—The Supremacy of Christ in all Realms : by the Very
Rev. Charles Stubbs, D.D., Dean of Ely.—Christ in the Realm of History :
by the Very Rev. G. W. Kitchin, D.D., Dean of Durham.—Christ in the
Realm of Philosophy : by the Rev. R. E. Bartlett, M.A., Bampton
Lecturer in 1888.—Christ in the Realm of Law : by the Rev. J. B.
Heard, M.A., Hulsean Lecturer in 1893.—Christ in the Realm of Art :
by the Rev. Canon Rawnsley, M.A., Vicar of Crosthwaite.—Christ in the
Realm of Ethics : by the Rev. J. Llewelyn Davies, D.D., Vicar of Kirkby
Lonsdale, and Chaplain to the Queen.—Christ in the Realm of Politics :
by the Rev. and Hon. W. H. Freemantle, M.A., Canon of Canterbury.—
Christ in the Realm of Science : by the Rev. Brooke Lambert, B.C.L.,
Vicar of Greenwich.—Christ in the Realm of Sociology : by the Rev. S. A.
Barnett, M.A., Warden of Toynbee Hall, and Canon of Bristol.—Christ
in the Realm of Poetry : by the Very Rev. Charles Stubbs, D.D., Dean
of Ely.

SCOTSMAN.—" Their prelections will be found stimulating and instructive in a high
degree. The volume deserves recognition as a courageous attempt to give to Christianity
its rightful place and power in the lives of its professors."

SURSUM CORDA : A DEFENCE OF IDEALISM.
Fcap. 8vo. 3s. 6d.

Talbot (Bishop).—A CHARGE DELIVERED TO THE
CLERGY OF THE DIOCESE OF ROCHESTER, October
24, 25, and 26, 1899. 8vo. Sewed. 2s. net.

Temple (Archbishop). *See* Canterbury.

Trench (Archbishop).—HULSEAN LECTURES. 8vo. 7s. 6d.

Van Dyke (Henry).—THE GOSPEL FOR AN AGE OF
DOUBT. The Yale Lectures on Preaching, 1896. Cr. 8vo.
8s. 6d.

SCOTSMAN.—" While the lectures are in no danger of being challenged as hetero-
dox, the last charge that will be made against the author will be that he fails to discern
the spirit of the age or the attitude of mind, and the outstanding reasons of that attitude,
of multitudes of thoughtful and reverent people towards the teaching of the Churches."

Vaughan (C. J., Dean of Llandaff)—

MEMORIALS OF HARROW SUNDAYS. 5th Edition. Crown
8vo. 10s. 6d.

HEROES OF FAITH. 2nd Edition. Crown 8vo. 6s.

LIFE'S WORK AND GOD'S DISCIPLINE. 3rd Edition.
Extra fcap. 8vo. 2s. 6d.

THE WHOLESOME WORDS OF JESUS CHRIST. 2nd
Edition. Fcap. 8vo. 3s. 6d.

FOES OF FAITH. 2nd Edition. Fcap. 8vo. 3s. 6d.

COUNSELS FOR YOUNG STUDENTS. Fcap. 8vo. 2s. 6d.

THE TWO GREAT TEMPTATIONS. 2nd Ed. Fcap. 8vo. 3s. 6d.

ADDRESSES FOR YOUNG CLERGYMEN. Extra fcap. 8vo.
4s. 6d.

Vaughan (C. J., Dean of Llandaff)—*continued.*

"MY SON, GIVE ME THINE HEART." Extra fcap. 8vo. 5s.

TEMPLE SERMONS. Crown 8vo. 10s. 6d.

AUTHORISED OR REVISED? Sermons on some of the Texts in which the Revised Version differs from the Authorised. Crown 8vo. 7s. 6d.

LESSONS OF THE CROSS AND PASSION. WORDS FROM THE CROSS. THE REIGN OF SIN. THE LORD'S PRAYER. Four Courses of Lent Lectures. Crown 8vo. 10s. 6d.

UNIVERSITY SERMONS. NEW AND OLD. Cr. 8vo. 10s. 6d.

NOTES FOR LECTURES ON CONFIRMATION. Fcap. 8vo. 1s. 6d.

THE PRAYERS OF JESUS CHRIST: a closing volume of Lent Lectures delivered in the Temple Church. Globe 8vo. 3s. 6d.

DONCASTER SERMONS. Lessons of Life and Godliness, and Words from the Gospels. Cr. 8vo. 10s. 6d.

RESTFUL THOUGHTS IN RESTLESS TIMES. Cr. 8vo. 5s.

LAST WORDS IN THE TEMPLE CHURCH. Globe 8vo. 5s.

SATURDAY REVIEW.—"These discourses in thought, in style, have so much that is permanent and fine about them that they will stand the ordeal of being read by any serious man, even though he never heard Dr. Vaughan speak.

UNIVERSITY AND OTHER SERMONS. Crown 8vo. 6s.

TIMES.—"As specimens of pure and rythmical English prose, rising here and there to flights of sober and chastened eloquence, yet withal breathing throughout an earnest and devotional spirit, these sermons would be hard to match."
SCOTSMAN.—"All are marked by the earnestness, scholarship, and strength of thought which invariably characterised the pulpit utterances of the preacher."

Vaughan (Rev. D. J.)—THE PRESENT TRIAL OF FAITH. Crown 8vo. 5s.

QUESTIONS OF THE DAY, SOCIAL, NATIONAL, AND RELIGIOUS. Crown 8vo. 5s.

NATIONAL OBSERVER.—"In discussing *Questions of the Day* Mr. D. J. Vaughan speaks with candour, ability, and common sense."
SCOTSMAN.—"They form an altogether admirable collection of vigorous and thoughtful pronouncements on a variety of social, national, and religious topics."
GLASGOW HERALD.—"A volume such as this is the best reply to those friends of the people who are for ever complaining that the clergy waste their time preaching antiquated dogma and personal salvation, and neglect the weightier matters of the law."
MANCHESTER GUARDIAN.—"He speaks boldly as well as thoughtfully, and what he has to say is always worthy of attention."
EXPOSITORY TIMES.—"Most of them are social, and these are the most interesting. And one feature of peculiar interest is that in those sermons which were preached twenty years ago Canon Vaughan saw the questions of to-day, and suggested the remedies we are beginning to apply."

Vaughan (Rev. E. T.)—SOME REASONS OF OUR CHRISTIAN HOPE. Hulsean Lectures for 1875. Crown 8vo. 6s. 6d.

Venn (Rev. John).—ON SOME CHARACTERISTICS OF BELIEF, SCIENTIFIC AND RELIGIOUS. 8vo. 6s. 6d.

Ward (W.)—WITNESSES TO THE UNSEEN, AND OTHER ESSAYS. 8vo. 10s. 6d.

ST. JAMES'S GAZETTE.—"Mr. Ward's reputation as a philosophical thinker at once accurate, candid, and refined, and as the master of a literary style alike vigorous, scholarly, and popular, has been amply established by his previous works. That it is well worthy of his reputation, is enough to say in commendation of his new book."

DAILY CHRONICLE.—"His whole book recalls men to those witnesses for the unseen, which laboratories cannot analyse, yet which are abundantly rational."

TIMES.—"A series of brilliant and suggestive essays. . . . This pregnant and suggestive view of the larger intellectual tendencies of our own and other ages is enforced and illustrated by Mr. Ward with much speculative insight and great literary brilliancy."

Welldon (Right Rev. J. E. C., Bishop of Calcutta).—THE SPIRITUAL LIFE, and other Sermons. Crown 8vo. 6s.

SCOTTISH LEADER.—"In a strain of quiet, persuasive eloquence, Bishop Welldon treats impressively of various aspects of the higher life. His discourses cannot fail both to enrich the heart and stimulate the mind of the earnest reader."

GLASGOW HERALD.—"They are cultured, reverent, and thoughtful productions."

Westcott (B. F., Bishop of Durham)—

ON THE RELIGIOUS OFFICE OF THE UNIVERSITIES. Sermons. Crown 8vo. 4s. 6d.

GIFTS FOR MINISTRY. Addresses to Candidates for Ordination. Crown 8vo. 1s. 6d.

THE VICTORY OF THE CROSS. Sermons preached during Holy Week, 1888, in Hereford Cathedral. Crown 8vo. 3s. 6d.

FROM STRENGTH TO STRENGTH. Three Sermons (In Memoriam J. B. D.) Crown 8vo. 2s.

THE REVELATION OF THE RISEN LORD. Cr. 8vo. 6s.

THE HISTORIC FAITH. 3rd Edition. Crown 8vo. 6s.

THE GOSPEL OF THE RESURRECTION. 6th Ed. Cr. 8vo. 6s.

THE REVELATION OF THE FATHER. Crown 8vo. 6s.

CHRISTUS CONSUMMATOR. 2nd Edition. Crown 8vo. 6s.

SOME THOUGHTS FROM THE ORDINAL. Cr. 8vo. 1s. 6d.

SOCIAL ASPECTS OF CHRISTIANITY. Crown 8vo. 6s.

ESSAYS IN THE HISTORY OF RELIGIOUS THOUGHT IN THE WEST. Globe 8vo. 5s.

THE GOSPEL OF LIFE. Cr. 8vo. 6s.

THE INCARNATION AND COMMON LIFE. Crown 8vo. 9s.

TIMES.—"A collection of sermons which possess, among other merits, the rare one of actuality, reflecting, as they frequently do, the Bishop's well-known and eager interest in social problems of the day."

CHRISTIAN ASPECTS OF LIFE. Crown 8vo. 7s. 6d.

CHURCH TIMES.—"We heartily commend this volume to the notice of our readers. . . . The Church of England is not likely to lose touch with the people of this country so long as she is guided by Bishops who show such a truly large-hearted sympathy with everything human as is here manifested by the present occupier of the see of Durham."

LITERATURE.—"A sermon of the national day of rest, and some attractive personal reminiscences of school days under James Prince Lee, are among the choicest parts of the volume, if we are to single out any portions from a work of dignified and valuable utterance."

DAILY NEWS.—"Through every page . . . runs the same enlightened sympathy with the living world. One forgets the Bishop in the Man, the Ecclesiastic in the Citizen, the Churchman in the Christian."

34   MACMILLAN & CO.'S THEOLOGICAL CATALOGUE
Westcott (Bishop)—*continued.*

THE OBLIGATIONS OF EMPIRE. Cr. 8vo. Sewed. 3d. net.

White (A. D.)—A HISTORY OF THE WARFARE OF
SCIENCE WITH THEOLOGY IN CHRISTENDOM. In
Two Vols. 8vo. 21s. net.

TIMES.—"Is certainly one of the most comprehensive, and, in our judgment, one of
the most valuable historical works that have appeared for many years. . . . He has
chosen a large subject, but it is at least one which has clear and definite limits, and he
has treated it very fully and comprehensively in two moderate volumes. . . . His book
appears to us to be based on much original research, on an enormous amount of careful,
accurate, and varied reading, and his habit of appending to each section a list of the
chief books, both ancient and modern, relating to it will be very useful to serious students.
He has decided opinions, but he always writes temperately, and with transparent truth-
fulness of intention."

DAILY CHRONICLE.—"The story of the struggle of searchers after truth with
the organised forces of ignorance, bigotry, and superstition is the most inspiring chapter
in the whole history of mankind. That story has never been better told than by the
ex-President of Cornell University in these two volumes."

Wickham (Very Rev. Dean)—WELLINGTON COLLEGE
SERMONS. Crown 8vo. 6s.

Wilkins (Prof. A. S.)—THE LIGHT OF THE WORLD : an
Essay. 2nd Edition. Crown 8vo. 3s. 6d.

Wilson (J. M., Archdeacon of Manchester)—

SERMONS PREACHED IN CLIFTON COLLEGE CHAPEL.
Second Series. 1888-90. Crown 8vo. 6s.

ESSAYS AND ADDRESSES. Crown 8vo. 2s. 6d. net.

GUARDIAN.—"We heartily welcome a new edition of Archdeacon Wilson's
Essays and Addresses."

SPEAKER.—"We are glad to welcome a new edition of the Archdeacon of
Manchester's *Essays and Addresses.* . . . These addresses are manly, straightforward,
and sagacious ; and they are, moreover, pervaded with a deep sense of responsibility and
unfailing enthusiasm."

SOME CONTRIBUTIONS TO THE RELIGIOUS THOUGHT
OF OUR TIME. Crown 8vo. 6s.

THE GOSPEL OF THE ATONEMENT. Being the Hulsean
Lectures for 1898. Crown 8vo. 3s. 6d.

SPEAKER.—"This volume deserves a cordial welcome, and will reward a careful
study. It is marked by a candour and courage, a sincerity and liberality of spirit, which
prove very attractive."

OXFORD MAGAZINE.—"They contain a good deal of strong thought and
delicate expression."

SPECTATOR.—"A notable pronouncement."

TWO SERMONS ON THE MUTUAL INFLUENCES OF
THEOLOGY AND THE NATURAL SCIENCES. 8vo.
Sewed. 6d. net.

Wood (C. J.) SURVIVALS IN CHRISTIANITY. Cr. 8vo. 6s.

MANCHESTER GUARDIAN.—"Striking, stimulating and suggestive lectures.
. . . The author writes with the boldness and conviction of a mystic ; he brings wide
reading to bear upon every branch of his subject, and his book is impressive and
interesting throughout."

Printed by R. & R. CLARK, LIMITED, *Edinburgh.*

5.3.00.